Praise for
The Life and Many Deaths of
Harry Houdini

"This extensively annotated critical analysis of Houdini's life and times rings true. A fascinating figure while he lived, Houdini remains no less fascinating nearly seventy years after he died."

—*Chicago Tribune*

"Clearly written, fair-minded and scrupulously researched . . . Brandon's book should become the definitive work."

—*The Seattle Times*

"Brandon probes for meaning—not in the jargon of a psychologist but with the persistence of someone who has to know what made Houdini tick."

—*The San Diego Union-Tribune*

"An entertaining biography of a legendary figure."

—*Kirkus Reviews*

"Brandon draws the reader inexorably into the magical, slightly crazed world of the Great Houdini."

—*Publishers Weekly*

"A compelling account of a peculiar life."

—*The Times* (London)

ABOUT THE AUTHOR

After reading French and Spanish at Cambridge, RUTH BRANDON worked for several years in current affairs television. She abandoned this for written journalism, but soon discovered that she preferred writing books. She likes to think of biography as a framework within which to look at cultural history. She also writes detective stories, and has just finished her first "literary" novel. She lives in the country with her husband and daughter and spends part of every year in France with her family.

THE LIFE
and
MANY DEATHS
of
HARRY HOUDINI

Ruth Brandon

RANDOM HOUSE TRADE PAPERBACKS
NEW YORK

Grateful acknowledgment is made to Alley Music Corp. and Trio Music Corp. for
permission to reprint excerpts from "Two Ladies" by John Kander and Fred Ebb
from *Cabaret*. Copyright © 1966 by Alley Music Corp. and Trio Music Corp.
All rights reserved. Reprinted by permisson.

Illustration nos. 1, 12, 14, 16, 20, 21, 30, 32, 33, 34, 35, 39, 47, 48 are
reproduced by permission of the Houdini Historical Center, Appleton,
Wisconsin; 2, 3, 4, 6, 17, 18, 27, 28, 37, 41, 51, the Library of Congress; 9, 11, 13, 15,
19, 29, 31, the Hoblitzelle Theater Arts Collection, Harry Ransom Humanities Research
Center, The University of Texas at Austin; 10, 49, 50, the collection of Jay Marshall; 38,
39, 40, 42, 43, 44, the Harry Price Library, University of London; 46, Morris Young.

Library of Congress Cataloging-in-Publication Data
Brandon, Ruth.
The life and many deaths of Harry Houdini/Ruth Brandon.
p.   cm.
Includes bibliographical references and index.
ISBN 0-8129-7042-X
1. Houdini, Harry, 1874–1926. 2. Magicians—United States—
Biography. I. Title.
GV1545.H8B73   1994   793.8'092—dc20   94-4080
[B]

Book design by Lilly Langotsky

For Phil,
a Houdini fan

Acknowledgments

Among the many pleasures of writing this book has been the chance to make the acquaintance of magic and theatre historians and collectors of magic and Houdiniana. They have been unfailingly charming, helpful and generous. I should especially like to thank: Patrick Culliton; Frank Dailey; Dr. E. A. Dawes; Jack Flosso; Mick Hanzlik; Ronald Hilgert; Frank Koval; Elaine and Robert Lund; Brooks Macnamara; Jay Marshall; Henry Muller; Sidney Radner; James Randi; Charles Reynolds; Dan Waldron; Dr. Morris Young.

I have also been the grateful recipient of some exceptional professional help: from librarians—Joan F. Higbee at the Rare Books and Special Collections Division, Library of Congress, Melissa Miller at the Hoblitzelle Theater Arts Collection, University of Texas at Austin, Moira Thomas at the Houdini Historical Center, Appleton, Wisconsin, and Alan Wesencraft at the Harry Price Library, University of London—and from my editors, Susan Bell, Dan Franklin and Lesley Bryce, and my agents, Caradoc King and Ellen Levine. Many, many thanks to them all.

Finally, I have as usual battened, intellectually and materially, on long-suffering friends, in particular Jan Bayer, Diana Vincent-Daviss, Caroline Humphrey, Nick Humphrey and Philip Steadman. They have as always offered help, support and suggestions, all gratefully received.

Contents

*The Life and Many Deaths of
Harry Houdini*

1

$\mathcal{T}$HE MANACLED DIVER

On 30 June 1909, it was announced that Harry Houdini would jump, manacled, into the North Sea just off Aberdeen in eastern Scotland. He would attempt, as he had done on many previous occasions, to free himself from his bonds and surface before his lungs burst. If he failed, he would of course drown.

The attempt was to be made from a point in the bay a little beyond the pierhead at one o'clock. But at midday the harbour authorities told Houdini that they could not permit it: conditions were too unsafe. No small boat could survive the seas that were coming in that squally day. By then, however, hundreds of people had already gathered to watch the jump, and more were arriving every minute.

Houdini . . . arrived at the dock gates, from which the start in the boat was to be made, and on being informed of the conditions outside the pier, drove out to see what they were like for himself. Returning he expressed his determination to make the dive, and at once got into negotiations with Captain Forbes of the tug John

McConnachie, which was lying at Poora Jetty. The captain told him
he had no fear of going out into the bay, but with the sea that was
on it would be impossible to launch a small boat from the tug for
the purpose of picking him up after he came to the surface, as they
would probably never get it alongside again. It was proposed that
the dive might then be made in the channel, but this part of the
water being under the jurisdiction of the harbour authorities, they
would not allow of that. By this time thousands of people had
arrived on the pier, and they lined the channel all the way from the
Poora Jetty to the pierhead, while on the other side of the water
there was also a vast crowd. Unwilling to disappoint the spectators
who had assembled to see a spectacle, and confident of making the
dive even in the stormy weather, Houdini determined to at least go
into the bay and see how the sea actually was from the tug.
Accordingly the tug left Poora Jetty with Houdini and his
attendants, Mr Gilbert of the Palace Theatre, and a few other
passengers. As the pierhead was reached, it was seen that it was
absolutely impossible to make the attempt there, the waves being so
strong. The seas were coming washing over the prow of the tug,
drenching those who were even standing on the bridge. The boat
was turned about, and for a time it seemed settled that the dive
would have to be completely postponed till some other time. When
just about the head of the channel, however, Houdini expressed his
determination to carry out his purpose there, if only the necessary
permission could be obtained from the harbour authorities. [They]
offered no objections. Houdini then at once prepared for action.
Having divested himself of his clothes he was manacled by one of
the attendants. A heavy chain was put round his neck, crossed on
his breast, and each end fastened to his arms above the elbows. His
hands were then carried behind his back and heavy handcuffs placed
and hooked on his wrists. A small boat having been set down—the
sea here was much calmer than out in the bay—to pick him up
when he regained the surface, he dived off the bridge, over the right
side of the vessel. A strong wind was blowing and it was cold. The
pier was crowded with thousands who were all in tense excitement
. . . The odds seemed great against the diver. After about 18
seconds he reappeared, his right hand and arm free, and the fetters
in his left hand. A lifebuoy at once thrown to him which he
clutched. He was pulled to the side of the tug and hauled on board
amid the loud cheers of the spectators on the pier and also from

those on board the tug. He went underneath to the engine and got
dried and by the time the tug had got alongside the jetty again he
was on deck in a long dressing gown apparently none the worse.

He appeared, as always, calm and businesslike. But this was not
because he was unaware of the dangers he ran. After a similar jump
six months earlier he remarked: "I expect the grim fiend is following
me up in these tricks, and he may catch me some day yet." The
reporter characterised this remark as "quaint" and "curious." But
for Houdini the consciousness of a possibly imminent death was as
much part of the day's work as the meticulous preparations that had
to be made before every show, every demonstration. Death was his
constant companion. And it was that shadowy figure behind
Houdini's compact and muscular frame that the crowd had really
come to see.

Otherwise he was alone. How alone, the first photograph shows
more poignantly than any words. This picture is actually of a different jump, in Boston: but all the essentials are the same. There is the
crowd, tense with concentration, packed into every available cranny.
And there, between the bridge and the water, is the small figure of
the manacled Houdini. His entourage—his assistants, his wife—followed him everywhere, but finally he was on his own.

Death always loomed: but not, on occasions such as this, too omi-
nously. Houdini's aim in performing these jumps was publicity, not
suicide. He had taken his precautions and he knew what he was
doing. His team, of course, played a vital part. The reporter noted
that it was "one of his attendants" who fastened the handcuffs and
chains. And both the items themselves and the way they were put on
were of the utmost importance.

Handcuffs were Houdini's stock-in-trade. He liked to carry a
good variety around with him—he listed fifteen different preferred
types, light ones which he could easily open. As for how he opened
them, the methods varied. Keys and picklocks were the most usual

methods; but some, such as the regulation English cuffs (used in most police stations) could be opened by tapping them sharply in the right place on some hard surface.

In an under water escape, the cuffs themselves presented even less of a problem than usual. Onstage, it was Houdini's habit to ask for "challenge" cuffs from the audience, into which he would be locked and from which he would escape. The escape was always done in the privacy of his curtained "cabinet," with its range of conveniently concealed picklocks. But in an under water jump there was no time to fiddle around with keys, and no need, either. In the excitement of the moment, with the craning crowds pressing in, the attendant boats filled with journalists and photographers, the sense of a momentous drama about to take place, no one was likely to insist on checking the handcuffs, especially if they looked massive enough—"heavy," as the Aberdeen reporter noticed. In fact the cuffs on these occasions were almost certainly "gaffed"—they could be opened without a key.

As for the heavy chain, that served several purposes. One was to add the weight that would pull Houdini quickly down to the bottom, so that he could make his escape in plenty of time without any danger of his methods being spied out. Another was psychological. A long, heavy chain is an impressive-looking thing. But in fact the longer the chain (or piece of rope) the harder it is to tie it so that no slack is left which will facilitate the beginning of an escape. And in Aberdeen (as on every such occasion—this was his invariable procedure), it will be noted that Houdini's hands were handcuffed behind his back *after* he was chained. The visual effect was formidable. But it meant that as soon as his hands were freed he had the use of them to detach himself from the chain.

The stripping down before he jumped, to bathing trunks or even less, was a regular feature of his appearances. He would strip not only for a dive such as this, where it was the natural thing, but under any circumstances and in any location: in a police station, a prison cell, onstage whenever the stunt permitted. Many of his publicity pictures are in the near nude. One reason for this was to reinforce the sense that he had nothing to hide: where was he to hide it? But, as so often with Houdini, the overt reason concealed and justified more powerful, covert attractions. The publicity photographs, naked in his chains, a posing pouch just to be made out behind the array of hardware, convey a powerful sexual rush—all the stronger for being completely innocent. Houdini was pre-Freudian. That was an essential element of his act. Its charge lay in his numbing lack of self-awareness.

The crowd naturally knew nothing of all this. As far as they were concerned, they were watching one man pit himself against the elements, with the odds stacked fearfully against him. In their minds they jumped with him; they agonised as, second after second, he failed to reappear; and the tumult when, eventually, he surfaced spoke as much of their own relief as of his triumph. It seemed to them that they had witnessed a miracle. So that with every successful feat, the ambiguity of Houdini's reputation increased. What he did seemed impossible. Was he really nothing more than a mere illusionist?

2

RABBITS FROM A HAT

For my sixth birthday, my parents hired a magician. They believed in doing things properly: immigrants' children know about properly. So lots of uncomfortable little gold chairs were set out for us in rows. But we were so entranced that we forgot even to wriggle as the top-hatted, tailcoated conjurer performed his ancient tricks. Eggs and coins appeared from nowhere. Silk handkerchiefs were flourished, singly, before us and placed ceremoniously in the top hat from which they were immediately extracted knotted together in a string. The same hat was turned upside down, shaken, shown to be empty. The next moment, a quivering white rabbit was lifted out and offered to us all to stroke.

We knew, of course, that these were tricks, not real magic. But they *seemed* like magic: could they not *be* magic? That was what we would have liked to believe. Harry Houdini once pointed out that "all magicians are shy of working before children," because children have no preconceived notions of what is going to happen and so are more likely to spot what *is* happening. But there was not in our particular group of polite little girls one of those sophisticates who sits poised to call after every trick: "I know how you did that, mister!" Our attention was easily beguiled. We looked obediently towards a gesturing right hand while substitutions were made with the left; we concentrated enviously upon a child called to the front to help, while the rabbit was pulled from its pocket inside the conjurer's tailcoat or behind that table whose velvet cloth so conveniently deadened sound, and upon which the top hat was so handily set. Misdirection, the fundamental technique of all illusion, had us in its thrall.

A large part of the enchantment was the very fact that we had no idea what to expect next. In a world where rabbits pop out of hats, anything may happen. We were given no indications. One of the first rules of conjuring is that you don't announce to your audience what it is you are trying to do. You may not achieve it; but if nobody knows what you were attempting, nobody knows you failed. And the more an audience remains in limbo, the more suggestible it becomes.

The parallel between the unpredictable and (to the audience) mysterious world of magic and that of the poor immigrant, set down in a strange country, is a striking one. Where he came from, he knew what to expect. The framework of his world, even if hostile, was familiar and explicable. In the new country, this is no longer the case. Everything is arbitrary. The language, the climate, the clothes, the customs—all are different. There is a more or less total disorientation: a state in which the immigrant is at the mercy of every shark or petty official who chooses to impose upon him. Luck is the only logic. My grandfather, a rabbinical student, told the authorities at Ellis Island that he was a locksmith. Perhaps he thought America was already oversupplied with rabbis. They gave him a lock to pick, and when (being no Houdini) he failed, they sent him back to Europe on the next boat.

No wonder people will put up with so much for so long in the home country. Anything—almost anything—is preferable to being cast adrift. The circumstances of emigrants at home must be extreme. Only famine, unrelenting prospectless poverty or intolerable persecution render life sufficiently unbearable to set off waves of mass migration.

"Mass migration": how the words trip off the tongue. The fleeing multitudes—jamming roads, crowding into transit camps, queuing for rations—are categorised in the mind's filing system with earthquakes, floods, hurricanes: unavoidable natural phenomena which we may try to ameliorate or choose to ignore. But all these words cloak a million individual terrors. What did Cecilia Weiss imagine when, with her five boys, including Ehrich (the future Houdini), then aged four, she left Budapest, that most European of cities, for New York?

The Weisses were on the run from anti-Semitism. According to Ehrich's younger brother Theodore, who was himself to become a magician under the stage name Hardeen:*

> Father insulted by prince Erik—challenged to dule—which was
> fought following morning and Father killing his opponent then fled
> to London and stayed there for a time after which he took sailing
> vessel to New York. After reaching New York kept going to
> Appleton Wis. where he had friends by the name of Hammel, one
> being Mayor of Appleton at that time. About 1874.
>   A short time passed and as there were no syniogues in the town,
> the Mayor wanted to send to Milwaukee for one, but up spoke Mr.
> S. M. Weiss and said "Why I am a Rabbi" and was given the job.
>   He at once sent for Mrs. W. and soon after her arrival Houdini
> was born April 6th 1874. And he was named Ehrich Prach after
> Prince Ehrich.

A likely story! The notion that any nobleman of the Austro-Hungarian Empire, let alone a prince, would sully his sword by duelling

---

*Neither Hardeen nor Houdini could spell. In all cases I have quoted from manuscript sources exactly as written.

with a lowly Jew is only slightly less implausible than that (as Weiss family legend had it) a timid student of the Torah might react to an insult by challenging the prince and then killing him. Even less likely is it that the victorious rabbi would, in his triumph, go on to name his newborn son after his victim. But the bones are there. Budapest, that centre of urbane civilisation, was not racked by pogroms in the way of wilder lands further east. But the rigidly hierarchical Hapsburg domain—the Holy Roman Empire—was staunchly and intolerantly Catholic. Jews were permitted to live there, but they had to know their place. Samuel Weiss stepped out of line. He had to get out. So he made his way to Appleton, where some compatriots were living; and his family followed him.

The adopted child who invents a romantic family history for himself is a commonplace; and in the same way every immigrant must reinvent himself, more or less drastically. The old rules by which one could place oneself within a society no longer apply. What possible connection was there between the culture of ancient Budapest and the recently established farming community of Appleton, on the Fox River in the further reaches of the American Midwest?

In this situation the facts of the old world lose all importance as facts. They become merely a background against which the reinvented immigrant chooses to set himself off. But of course the history he selects for himself tells us more about him—the reinvented man—than would the pedantic truth about a background now so completely irrelevant. This was particularly true in Houdini's case. His life, which he never ceased to invent, was a Gothick fiction, and the beginning of the story had to fit its continuation. So he portrayed his parents as he would have wished them to be: as romantic participants in the cultural and noble life of Budapest.

Nevertheless, some facts are known. It is a fact that Samuel Weiss's first wife was the cousin of a well-known opera singer, Rosa Szillag. She died giving birth to a son, Armin (Herman), in 1863, when Samuel was thirty-four. He naturally wanted to remarry; and

Houdini liked to tell how this came about. A bashful friend asked Samuel to propose on his behalf to pretty Miss Cecilia Steiner. Samuel (according to this tale) realised that it was his own feelings he was expressing, and, Miss Steiner preferring the active to the passive suitor, they were married despite the fact that he was thirteen years older than she was, had a small income and few prospects, and already had a child. Their first child died in 1865, but another, Nathan, arrived in 1868, and a third, William, in 1870. In 1874 Erik or Ehrich, the future Houdini, was born.

The family's circumstances in Budapest, like their reason for leaving the city, are obscured by webs of legend. Prince Erik, according to this myth, was not the only royal acquaintance of the Weiss family. Houdini's younger sister, Gladys, wrote to his wife Bess in 1938, twelve years after his death: "You must remember how our blessed mother would swell with pride when she displayed the worn prayer-rug, don't you? I can still hear her boast in her gentle manner, that the Kaiserin Josaphine had walked on it many times when she visited some orphan asylum directly oppisite our home. On these occasions her Royal Highness looked in on our family to pay respect to our important and intellectual dad." Maybe; then again, maybe not.

The mythologising does not stop there. According to a rumour circulating among American magicians just after Houdini's death, Samuel Weiss was Cecilia Steiner's second husband, and he was not Ehrich's father but his stepfather; Theodore was their first child together. Cecilia's first husband had killed a man in Austria and had been sent to prison.

One can see how this story may have evolved. There is the legend of the fatal duel, now transposed to the first husband; such a tale might also explain the physical dissimilarities between Ehrich and Theodore—the former was a very short man, the latter very tall and burly—and the lack of sympathy between Houdini and his father. But what, then, of William and Nathan? If Rabbi Weiss was no great catch for pretty Miss Steiner, it is hardly imaginable that any respectable man would have taken on the widow and three young sons of a convicted murderer. Houdini had little in common with Samuel Weiss, but that he was his son can hardly be doubted.

Houdini himself always gave his date of birth as 6 April 1874, and its place as Appleton. But there is no record of his having been born in Wisconsin, and in the 1880 census Erik, then aged six, is recorded as having been born in Hungary, as is Theodore, then aged four: only their youngest brother, Leopold, then ten months old, was, according to this document, born in America. Gladys, the youngest, and the only daughter, had yet to arrive. But if there is no record of Ehrich's birth in Wisconsin, there is a certificate attesting to his birth—or the birth of an Erik Weiss—in Budapest on 24 March 1874; and, although Gladys put up some story of an infant Ehrich having died in Hungary and Houdini having been named for this dead brother, we may take it that there was only one Ehrich Weiss and that he was born in Budapest.

Why *this* pretence? Could it possibly matter, in America, that land of immigrants, whether or not one was actually born stateside or arrived there at the age of four weeks, or four years? To Cecilia Weiss, apparently, it did matter—for it was she who bestowed the new birthday upon her son. "Re the Birthdays," Houdini wrote to Theodore in 1913, not long after she had died, "I shall *celebrate mine?* always APRIL 6th. It hurts me to think I cant talk it over with Darling Mother and as SHE always wrote me on April 6th, that will be my adopted birthdate."

Why should Cecilia have minded so much about such a seemingly trivial detail? Perhaps April 6 was the date Samuel Weiss arrived in Wisconsin, or at least in America; and perhaps, for her, this signalled the start of a new life, so that Ehrich's life, which was just beginning, started for all intents and purposes on that day. It began, then, as it was to continue: uneasy; opaque; defiantly American.

3

METAMORPHOSIS

The very first trick ever performed by Houdini on the professional stage was a simple but effective illusion known generally as the "Substitution Trunk," though he preferred to call it "Metamorphosis." Houdini and his partner would bring a large trunk onto the stage. It was opened and a sack or bag produced from inside it. Houdini, bound and handcuffed, would get into the sack, which was then sealed or tied around the neck. The trunk was closed over the bag and its occupant. It was locked, strapped and chained. Then a screen was drawn around it. The partner (after they married, this was always Mrs. Houdini) stepped behind the screen which, next moment, was thrown aside— by Houdini himself. The partner had meanwhile disappeared. A committee of the audience was called onstage to verify that the ties, straps, etc., around the trunk had not been tampered with. These were then laboriously loosened; the trunk was opened; and there, inside the securely fastened bag, was—Mrs. Houdini!

Metamorphosis, like invisibility, is one of the great mythic powers. These powers (or the ability to mimic them) remain at the heart of the illusionist's art. When the lady vanishes, or Dr. Jekyll turns into Mr. Hyde before our very eyes, a delightful conspiracy to believe is enacted between the sceptical brain and the luxuriant, atavistic imagination. We *know* that the substitution was not done by magic; but we remember the princess's kiss releasing the prince from his frog's body, the fairy godmother turning pumpkins into carriages, mice into white horses. The ability to change one's form at will has always been an attribute of gods and fairies. When Danae was imprisoned by her father so that she would be inaccessible to all men—literally, impregnable—Zeus turned himself into a shower of rain and fell into her lap. And if this was the way to insinuate oneself across barriers, it was also a way of escape. When the witch Baba Yaga chases the little girl she has been fattening for her supper, the girl bars her way by means of a magic comb which turns into a forest when she throws it to the ground, and a magic handkerchief which turns into a river.

But offstage, and outside the realms of mythology, escape and metamorphosis are not so easily achieved. The Weisses had moved to America, but this did not turn them into Americans. The family settled in Appleton because they had friends who were already there. This was the usual rule: amid the uncharted seas of the new country, the greenhorn made for a familiar rock, or for what is known in Yiddish as landsleit—people from the same place. Thus the ambiguous nature of the greenhorn's adventure was defined from the beginning. He would re-create, as far as possible, the old life in the new home.

Take the question of language. "Polish," wrote Eva Hoffman, now an editor of *The New York Times Book Review,* of her thirteen-year-old self, newly arrived in Canada, "is becoming a dead language, the language of the untranslatable past . . . [English] is beginning to invent another me." But it is more difficult for adults to reinvent themselves in this way. The language of the Weiss household remained German. "My mother," wrote Houdini, "was educated on the continent and proficient in five languages. When the family moved to Appleton, Wis., where I was born, she kept in retirement much of the time and did not take up English studies." Mrs. Weiss never did learn to speak or write English, and Dr. Weiss only tried to do so when he moved to New York at the age of fifty-nine—with what little success may be imagined. (The one extant recording of Houdini's voice shows that he spoke, to the very end of his life, with a distinctly central European accent, with very little of an American twang.) This meant not only that the transactions of everyday life outside the ghetto (which they thus brought with them) remained problematic, but that psychologically the elder Weisses remained Hungarian and not American.

Appleton, at the time the Weisses arrived there, had been in existence for nearly thirty years. The first white settler had built his cabin in 1846; the first ten acres of wheat were sown two years later. By 1874 it was a flourishing agricultural community. "Who that has seen Appleton rise up from the primeval forest within the last twenty years, with her railroads and bridges, her palaces, homes and stately churches, her public schools and noble college . . . can help prophesying for her a brilliant future?" mused the *Appleton Crescent* in 1874. The prophecy was not fulfilled. It is still hard to conceive of a place more totally unlike urbane, cosmopolitan Budapest than the sleepy little town of Appleton, Wisconsin.

On the whole, the Weiss family preferred it. They lived over a storefront on the main street; and, despite the differences and the difficulties in their being so adamantly foreign, they were happy there. "My parents spent the happiest days of their life in that place," Houdini told the popular novelist Edna Ferber, the second of Appleton's three most famous offspring. (The third was Senator Joe McCarthy.) ". . . It was a great pleasure to Mrs. Houdini and myself to know that the 'girl' who welcomed me in Appleton has like myself helped advertize that little berg amongs the other inhabitants of America." He signed himself "Harry Houdini (From Appleton Wisc.)."

Some months after his mother's death (she died in the summer of 1913), Houdini wrote to his brother Theodore: "I actually dreampt of Appleton Wisc a short time back and beheld Pa and Ma drinking coffee under the trees in that park. I ran for camera, as usual, and knew in my dream I had none in Appleton still I searched for it and stopped every once in a while to feats my eyes on both our Parents so calmy drinking and chatting as they did when you and I were romping kids . . . In my dream I feared they would note by my actions that I was excited, but you know how dreams are, only possibly visions of the brains efforts."

A Freudian interpretation of this dream (by Dr. Bernard Meyer) sees it as an expression of "the excitement and the fear of being detected" of a boy watching his parents engage in sex, as may well have happened in the various cramped living quarters of that numerous family: this is what the dream conveys when "stripped of its censorship." Meyer suggests that this may have been the origin of Houdini's lifelong inability to sleep, brought on by the consciousness that his parents were waiting for the children to go to sleep before they could indulge in sex. Certainly Houdini liked to recount how, as a baby, he had slept hardly at all, his "eyes roaming around," taking only "catlike naps" after which he would be as wide awake as ever. (He used this story in his publicity: it was published in numerous "souvenir programmes.") Presumably, since he cannot have been aware of this himself at the time, he had it from his mother. The habit continued. Later in his life he had to wear a black silk blindfold if he was to get any sleep at all.

But to the ordinary reader the scene conjured up is far from sinister. On the contrary, it is a peaceful and pleasant one. In Appleton Dr. and Mrs. Weiss found what they had been seeking—a haven. Their children grew up ignorant of that anti-Semitism which had propelled them on their great journey. Houdini was deeply shocked when, twenty years later, he registered its existence while he was touring Germany on the crest of his first great wave of success. "It may interest you to know that although a Jew must be a soldier, he cannot be an officer, as there is a secret feeling among the Europeans against Jews," he wrote. "In Bohemia and Austria they think as much of a nigger as a jew, and it has surprised me greatly to think that such things exist in this country." (Houdini was an ardent Germanophile.) It would not have surprised his parents.

Other conclusions may also be drawn from these letters—as indeed from all the letters this compulsive correspondent ever wrote. The most obvious is that the writer was a man of great intelligence but unhappy with words. His head seethed with thoughts which he wished desperately to communicate: but the most straightforward means of communication—language—was not satisfactorily available to him. He could only express himself in the clumsiest way. His spelling was dreadful, his syntax barely existent. His handwriting was an illiterate scrawl, which is perhaps the reason he typed his letters whenever he could ("Managed to hire a writing machine at last," he begins the letter describing his dream). In short, it is clear that he had little, if any, formal schooling.

On the face of it, this is surprising. Once they were settled in their new home, why should the Weiss children not have received an education? Appleton boasted not only schools but a college campus (Lawrence, which was progressive enough to admit women as well as men). But the sad fact was that they were *not* settled; and this was because they had failed to metamorphose into Americans.

Not only the language of the Weiss household but its entire family structure was that of Budapest rather than Appleton. In contrast to most Jewish immigrants to America, who arrived from muddy shtetls to the stony bewilderment of the big city, the Weisses moved from sophisticated Budapest to the backwoods. But in Budapest as in the shtetl, the centre of every European Jewish community, its most respected member, was the rabbi—a word which means, simply, "my teacher." Intellect was all; every man aspired to be a scholar. Even where he had to spend his working life in business, his spare time would be passed in prayer and disputation. Everything else, the altogether less lofty day-to-day business of coping, was the realm of his wife, who would labour at life's base necessities while her husband removed himself to the world of Torah or Talmud.

There is a special word in Yiddish for this breed of all-encompassing, all-competent homemaker: balabosta. A successful balabosta needs considerable drive, fortitude and organisational skills. She is the true adult of the family, the one to whom they all turn, the sheet-anchor.

But while these qualities are recognised, revered and, where possible, lavishly rewarded—as in the well-known figure of the Jewish American Princess—it is taken for granted that the balabosta will look to her husband for guidance, worldly or spiritual. She needs a strong character—but not so strong that she will not know her place. "It's not a good thing," mourned my grandfather when I went to university. "She'll get a mind of her own. It's not a good thing in a woman."

Cecilia Weiss was a balabosta. At home in Budapest she could have coped in spite of the least worldly of husbands. But what was appropriate for Budapest did not do in Wisconsin. What Rabbi Weiss had to teach was irrelevant to Wisconsin—even Jewish Wisconsin. What the Appleton community wanted was someone more like David Hammel, who had invited him there in the first place. Hammel had just the qualities necessary if one was to do well in a frontier town like this, where the Indians had not yet been wholly dispossessed of their lands. The first of these was adaptability. Hammel's name crops up constantly in the local paper, in a variety of capacities. He dealt in horses and lumber, and some years later went into wheat farming and milling. He was active in local politics and was happy to give a deserving coreligionist a hand up: in 1871 Moses Kahn, who had been a clerk in his employ and had established himself in the town, set himself up in business as a storekeeper, and by 1876, when the Weiss family arrived, was flourishing. But Rabbi Weiss was not of this ilk, and never would be. In Appleton it soon became clear that he was an anomaly. And at his age, he was hardly likely to change. The community wanted somebody more forward-looking—in a word, more American. So in 1882, when the new Temple Zion was built, he was fired.

When Samuel Weiss died in 1892 Cecilia described their marriage as "twenty-eight years of heaven." But this heaven certainly bore little relation to their earthly surroundings. Without the rabbi's stipend life could not be sustained in Appleton. So they moved to Milwaukee, a large city with more Jews who might want what Rabbi Weiss had to offer. But his success, or lack of it, may be judged by the number of times they moved from one address to another in that city. They made at least five moves between 1883 and 1887; it is more likely that these were on account of needing to find somewhere cheaper, or having to keep one step ahead of the rent collector, than because more commodious accommodation was on offer. Of this time Houdini said that "Such hardships became our lot that the less said on the matter the better." For the rest of his life, he disliked Milwaukee. In 1912, when he was thirty-eight, he returned there for a week in the course of a tour. "I did not like it at all," he told a friend. "For many reasons, some which I do not care to put in writing."

All this meant that he was deprived of any real education. The child of a family as poor as young Ehrich Weiss's had more pressing concerns than school. The fact that the son of a Jewish scholar should end up so completely untaught says something about the scale of the family's poverty, or his father's lack of control, or both. However, money had to be earned from somewhere. He recalled selling newspapers and shining shoes on Milwaukee street corners. At some point there seems to have been an interval of enforced study. A scrawled note survives which appears to have been written from some institution, presumably at the period when Ehrich was ten or eleven: "darling mother at last the time has arrived when I am allowed to write you a few lines how slowly the time passes but still my term will soon be over and we shall be united in happiness again, your loving son Ehrichovitz."

This is a fairly extraordinary outpouring for a boy to write to his mother, however homesick he may be. In fact Houdini never shrank from exposing the depths of his soul (insofar as he could make them out), often in terms of toe-curling sentimentality, compared with which this note is a model of restraint. His mother was already the only one who counted for him. She was the one who kept things together in the pitiless world of America where his father had patently failed. Rabbi Weiss was tolerated with mild affection, a more or less useless appendage, while the boy, and later, the man, was to spend his entire life yearning to be "united in happiness" with his mother. These two ever-frustrated desires—to express his soul's contents to the world, to live an ideal life with his mother—were to shape and dominate his life.

In 1885, when he was eleven, Ehrich's elder half-brother Herman died of tuberculosis in New York. Death was to be the third of Houdini's chief preoccupations. This was the first death he encountered personally. A little later, on his twelfth birthday, his father finally admitted defeat. He was never going to be able to provide satisfactorily for his family. He made Ehrich promise to take care of his mother, as long as she lived. On the brink of puberty, adult life and responsibilities had begun.

What was Ehrich to do? Clearly, Milwaukee held few prospects. He decided that the best course would be to leave home and see if he could earn some money. Not long afterwards, a postcard arrived for Mrs. C. Weiss (there is no mention of Mr. Weiss) at 517 Sixth Street, Milwaukee: "I am going to Galvaston, Texas, and will be home in about a year. My best regards to all. Did you get my picture if you didn't write to Mead Bros. Woodstock Ill. Your truant son, Ehrich Weiss." Houdini later stuck this in a scrapbook and added: "This postal card mailed by myself when I ran away from home to earn some money. I was on my way to Texas? got into wrong freight car and went to Kansas City Mo. This card was mailed in a place called Withers. I remember being in Hannibal Mo. The post mark on the card reads Hanibal and St. Joseph RR. 1886."

Ehrich did not return to Milwaukee, but worked his way over the next two years to New York. There he found his father, whom he had left in Milwaukee but who had decided to try his luck at running a Hebrew school in the city with the biggest Jewish population in America. Rabbi Weiss was living in Mrs. Leffler's boarding house at 244 East Seventy-ninth Street. He and Ehrich put their money together and found a flat on East Seventy-fifth Street. The family was summoned from Milwaukee and "We lived there, I mean starved there, several years." Later, they moved to 305 East Sixty-ninth Street, where they were to remain for many years more.

Their poverty was abject. There were certainly a lot of Jews in New York, but not many of them wanted what Samuel (and so many others) had to offer. Ehrich took odd jobs. He was working as a messenger boy one December when he heard his father pacing the floor and muttering in despairing tones, "The Lord will provide. The Lord will provide." The resourceful Ehrich lettered a card:

> Christmas is coming
> Turkeys are fat
> Please drop a quarter
> In the Messenger Boy's hat.

Before he came home that evening (or so he said: this story recalls others, and may have been yet another myth) after a successful day, he hid the coins everywhere about himself—up his sleeves, in his hair, in his jacket, behind his ears. When he got home he commanded his mother to "Shake me! I'm magic!" She obeyed, with gusto: coins sprayed everywhere. There was almost enough to pay the overdue rent.

Once again, the essence, if not the detail, is probably true. But had the Weisses come to America in order to live off what a boy could get by begging?

Back in Hungary, the Weiss family was connected to one of the great conjuring dynasties of the nineteenth century. Samuel Weiss's first wife was a cousin of the opera singer Rosa Szillag (or Czillig). She was married to Carl or (as he was usually known) Compars Herrmann, an extremely successful magician known throughout Europe and America in the mid-nineteenth century. ("Compars is the real name," Houdini was to assure a friend. "I have copies photographed of his marriage certificate and that is the name that appears and generally? when a man gets married he usually gives his right name.") Compars was the first magician ever to be invited to perform at the White House, which he did before President Lincoln on 21 November 1861. He was not, however, as famous as his younger brother Alexander, whom he introduced as his legitimate successor at his farewell performance in New York City and who, with his Mephistophelean appearance and the assistance of his clever wife Adelaide, became known throughout the world during the 1880s and 90s as Alexander "The Great." Compars meanwhile retired with a fortune to Vienna, where he died in 1887 at the age of seventy-two. This was no mere distant connection: "My dear old Dad and Compars Herrmann were great companions," Houdini told another magical friend, adding "and for business reasons have never given out the facts, because they might think that at one time I was seeking publicity." He never did use the Herrmann connection—possibly the only time in his life Houdini ever passed up the chance of publicity. Reflected glory was not for him.

Young Ehrich never met Compars Herrmann himself. But even when he was a very young child he was fascinated by magic. It spoke to him. "You know how a fresh kid is," he told an interviewer. " 'Oh, I see how he does that!' I used to exclaim. The difference between me and most youngsters was that I really did see."

The abounding tales of his childhood magical exploits carry the mythic fuzz Houdini liked to generate. But there is little doubt as to the actual performance that awoke his obsessional interest in magic. A publicity pamphlet described how "a circus coming to the town of Appleton, changed the entire world for this boy. He did not carry water to the elephants; instead, he stood amazed in front of the stand, for there he beheld the greatest, most wonderful human being he had ever seen. The man was dressed in a misfitting dress suit, had a goatee and mustache . . . and was taking rabbits out of a black-brown high hat. He cut off a man's arm, leg and head and brought him back to life. He took coins from the air.—The boy was hypnotized. Not coming home for his supper that night, a search was made and they found the boy still at the platform, but by now he was seated on it, the magician taking eggs from his mouth and cards and a spring snake from his coat . . . By accident the magician dropped or had the misfortune to expose one of the tricks and to the astonishment of the young man, the worshipper of magic, he saw that there was no occult power vested in the performance . . . He gradually solved the problems that were presented, and from that day there was never a magical Santa Claus for the boy."

Elsewhere, Houdini named this magician as Dr. Lynn, and placed the performance in Milwaukee. Dr. Lynn's famous trick was "Pali-genesia," in which a man is (apparently) chloroformed, cut up, his component parts tossed in the air, and is finally put back together again and produced whole and sound. The trick is in fact one of the "Black Arts" family, in which black-clothed assistants moving against a black background can "disappear" objects or parts of a body by masking them off. Dr. Lynn's poster read ANOTHER MAN CUT UP TONIGHT. The performer appeared with a large, dangerous-looking knife and invited volunteers to be cut up. No one would volunteer. So Dr. Lynn would usher in his own man, who was then securely tied to a door at the back of the stage. The framing of the stage was very brightly lit and the background to the trick matt black, so that the audience could only see objects that were brightly lit. In the course of the tying-up, the man's right arm and left leg were slipped behind the backcloth and a dummy arm and leg were hooked on, to be unhooked by an invisible black-clad assistant at the crucial moment. The man's head, when the time came to cut it off, would be thrust back into a trap door also covered in black material. When the head was "severed," a cloth was dropped over it and the head (in fact a head-shaped dummy) was carried away under the cover.

The boy was indeed "hypnotized" by this performance. The adult Houdini remained fascinated by mutilation: he possessed several grisly and much-thumbed photographs of Chinese executions by beheading and by the death of a thousand cuts. These were images which spoke to his adult obsessions. But those may well have originated in Dr. Lynn's terrifying show. "I really believed that the man's arms, leg and head were cut off," he noted in his diary years later. (In 1916 Houdini laid this particular ghost: he bought the illusion from Lynn's son and presented it himself.)

After this, young Ehrich's fascination with circus life knew no bounds. Various stories exist of his childhood exploits. According to one of these, his first public performance was at the age of nine, when he persuaded a visiting circus to pay him thirty-five cents to demonstrate his virtuosity at hanging upside down and picking up needles with his eyelashes. In another version he began as a contortionist under the title "Eric, Prince of the Air." "Thus, to any young man who has in mind a career similar to mine, I would say: 'First try bending over backward and picking up a pin with your teeth from the floor, and work up from that into the more difficult exercises.' "

It was at this time, too, that his fascination with locks began. Again the tale is wreathed in hyperbole. A publicity pamphlet tells how his mother locked up her larder so that her sons shouldn't raid it, whereupon Ehrich learned how to pick the lock, leaving Mrs. Weiss mystified when she found the door still locked and the pie plate empty. Or, his anxious parents plucked him away from the circus and apprenticed him to a locksmith. There, "One day the son of a prominent banker came in with several of his friends to have a pair of handcuffs removed. For a joke, they had slipped the handcuffs on him, but were unable to release him, as they had no key. I found that they had broken off a bit of wire in the keyhole. By the merest accident I discovered the way in which I could unlock the handcuffs, without a key. I took them off and thought no more about it." In another version, the local policeman had arrested the wrong man but was unable to release him and the locksmith left his apprentice to wrestle with the problem while he and the policeman went off for a drink.

The fascination with locks and magic was certainly genuine, and it persisted. When the family moved to New York in 1888, Theo got a job with a photographer who was an amateur magician and showed him a simple coin trick, which Theo in his turn showed Ehrich. Ehrich proved remarkably adept, and began to read everything about magic he could lay his hands on.

That same year he landed a steady job. Strolling down Broadway he saw a line outside H. Richter's Sons, necktie manufacturers. A board announced that an assistant cutter was wanted. He would never get the job if he waited in line—that was clear. So he walked to the front, took down the board, thanked the applicants for their interest and told them the position was filled. Then he walked in, holding the board, and got the job.

This cool and chutzpah were among the skills which would become the basis of his livelihood. He began to cultivate others. One of these was physical fitness. He was an excellent swimmer—good enough to try out for the American Olympic team. He joined the Pastime Athletic Club, whose field on Sixty-seventh Street and the East River was not far from where he lived. Athletics provided the first outlet for that driving necessity to be first, to be the winner—to defeat all competition—which was to colour the rest of his life. "I want to be first," he told a newspaper reporter in 1910, when he was at the height of his fame. "I vehemently want to be first. First in my profession, in my speciality in my profession. For that I give all the thought, all the power that is in me . . . When I can no longer, goodbye the joy of life for me! So I have struggled and fought. I have done and abstained; I have tortured my body and risked my life only for that—to have one plank on the stage where the imitators cannot come, and one spot where they all fall back and cry 'Master!' " This was the exact truth, then and always. He had not yet begun to push his body to those extremes which his later training involved. But he had begun his lifelong abstention from alcohol or tobacco. His father disapproved of them on moral grounds, and the coach at Pastime told him they would undermine his athletic capabilities. He never touched either. He became a good runner; at the age of sixteen he won a prize in the American Amateur Athletic Union mile race but was disqualified for having previously competed in some unapproved games—"Be very particular about this in future," admonished the chairman of the AAAU in a letter reinstating him.

Photographs taken at this time show a short, compact, well-knit young man displaying his physique in athlete's strip. He has the slightly bow-legged stance that was to become one of his essential professional assets, since it ensured that, however tightly he was tied up, he could always retain the essential minimum of slack which would enable him to free one hand. His grey eyes stare intently out of the picture. He looks very innocent. An innocent, in many ways, he would remain.

He made friends—Joe Rinn at the Pastime Athletic Club, Jake Hyman at Richter's tie factory—who shared his interest in magic and everything pertaining to it. Joe and he used to go to the theatre on passes sent by a friend or on tickets bought at a cut-price stall. Joe also went to séances from time to time, and one day he agreed to take Ehrich along. They went to see Mrs. Minnie Williams, a very fat lady who specialised in materialising the dead before the eyes of their loved ones. Mrs. Williams "held forth in a house on Forty-sixth Street which had been made over to her for one dollar by Mrs. Anderson, the widow of a tobacco dealer, who had been her devoted follower." Joe was a friend of Mrs. Williams's daughter Gertrude. The boys watched as Gertrude collected a dollar each from about forty people before the séance. They noticed that each spirit, on leaving, said "Gawd bless you!" in a hoarse voice, and that the boards creaked as the spirits walked. Ehrich was impressed—not by the performance, though he recognised the bulky Mrs. Williams's astuteness (particularly in not trying to pass herself off as female ghosts, who might be expected to be more ethereal), but by the easy pickings.

This was the year—1891, when he was seventeen—that Ehrich first read the memoirs of Robert-Houdin, the great French magician of the mid-nineteenth century. The book transfixed him. It is easy to see why. It is written with all the panache and elegance which its author reputedly possessed. But, more than that, Robert-Houdin's story might have been specially designed to appeal to the seventeen-year-old Ehrich Weiss. It tells of a young man, about Ehrich's own age, who finds himself abandoned and alone. He falls ill and is rescued by an itinerant magician whose pupil and assistant he becomes. Finally he strikes out on his own and, after many hardships and tribulations, becomes the greatest magician of his age, hobnobbing with kings and living in elegance and luxury.

Ehrich's identification with this mythic version of himself was deep and immediate. "My interest in conjuring and magic and my enthusiasm for Robert-Houdin came into existence simultaneously," he wrote some years later. "From the moment that I began to study the art, he became my guide and hero . . . What Blackstone is to the struggling lawyer . . . or Bismarck's life and writings to the coming statesman, Robert-Houdin's books were to me. To my unsophisticated mind, his 'Memoirs' gave to the profession a dignity worth attaining at the cost of earnest, life-long effort. When it became necessary for me to take a stage-name, and a fellow-player, possessing a veneer of culture, told me that if I would add the letter 'i' to Houdin's name, it would mean, in the French language, 'like Houdin,' I adopted the suggestion with enthusiasm.''

The "fellow-player" was Jake Hyman, his friend at Richter's, who now became his ally and partner in magic. They gave, with some success, magical presentations at private parties. Until Jake came up with his momentous suggestion, Ehrich was variously known as "Eric the Great" or (if he was doing card tricks, at which he was adept) "Cardo." "Houdini" was an improvement on either of these. Quite apart from its reference to Ehrich's hero, it had a definite ring to it. It also sounded vaguely Italian, which was appropriate, since Robert-Houdin's own two mentors in magic both took Italian names, although both were Frenchmen: it was always vogue-ish for magicians to have Italian names. Ehrich had already been Americanised to Harry for most of his friends.

So Ehrich Weiss metamorphosed into Harry Houdini in the great substitution trunk that was America. He and Jake Hyman (who now became Jack Hayman) decided to take to the road and try their luck as the Houdini Brothers. Richter's wrote him a reference in case of future need:

H. RICHTER'S SONS
502 & 504 Broadway

New York, April 3, 1891.
To Whom It May Concern:

We hereby certify that Mr. Ehrich Weiss has been in our employ for two years and six months as assistant lining cutter and we cheerfully recommend him as an honest, industrious young man.

H. Richter's Sons.

4

$\mathcal{A}$ARON'S ROD

 What rabbi would wish to see his brightest son throw up a steady job in the *shmatteh* trade, a business where Jewish boys traditionally make good (or at least make a living), in order to take up the uncertain life of a travelling conjurer? Rabbi Weiss had little time to brood: in 1892, almost as soon as the decision had been taken, he made the final abdication and died. Ehrich repeated to the dying man the promise that he had made on his twelfth birthday, about how he would always look after his mother. Then the Houdini Brothers (Jack Hayman was soon replaced by Theo as the subsidiary member of the duo) took to the road.

It appeared highly improbable that the promise would ever be fulfilled. No one was more keenly aware of this than Ehrich himself. When, many years later (in 1912), he finally achieved a salary of $1,000 a week in New York, he requested his first week's pay in gold, drove straight to his mother with the bag of coins and emptied them into her apron. (This melodramatic gesture is notably similar to the "Shake me, I'm magic" incident of his poverty-stricken youth.) He always described this moment, when he finally and so spectacularly fulfilled his promise, as the greatest thrill of his life. In 1892, however, his did not seem a realistic choice. My son the doctor—yes (that was to be Leopold, the youngest Weiss boy); my son in neckties—possibly; but my son the conjurer?

Yet young Harry, as he was henceforth known, was only following in an ancient tradition—as Rabbi Weiss might have realised. Do not conjuring tricks of one sort or another lie at the very roots of Jewish history? What else facilitated the departure from Egypt of the children of Israel? It will be recalled that Pharaoh was at first most unwilling to let them go and had to be frightened into doing so by means of a series of wonders, beginning with Aaron's Rod. "And Moses and Aaron went in unto Pharaoh, and they did so, as the Lord had commanded, and Aaron cast down his rod before Pharaoh and before his servants, and it became a serpent. Then Pharaoh also called for the wise men and the sorcerers; and they also, the magicians of Egypt, did in like manner with their secret arts. For they cast down every man his rod and they became serpents; but Aaron's rod swallowed up their rods."

Even though Aaron's rod thus demonstrated its superiority, Pharaoh remained unimpressed, which was hardly surprising, since his own priests had shown that they knew the same trick. (It is still to be seen in Egypt today, where snake charmers paralyse snakes by applying pressure to a point on the neck, when the snake uncurls and looks like a stick.) More powerful magic was evidently called for; so God weighed in with the ten plagues (frogs, lice, murrain, rivers of blood, the slaying of the first-born, etc.) and climaxed this performance with the parting of the Red Sea.

The earthly impresario of all this was of course Moses, Aaron's elder brother and the founder of the Jewish religion. Moses is best known as the deliverer of the Ten Commandments. But in surviving fragments of ancient alchemical and magical literature, he figures as the author of secret magical texts. His activities while he was leading the Israelites through the wilderness suggest that he was familiar with, among other things, what became known as natural magic— the use of natural laws to apparently magical effect. With the help of his young assistant, Joshua, he arranged terrifying phenomena designed to strike awe into the hearts of the Israelite masses and make sure they kept well away from the scene of operations. When God dictated the Commandments, "all the people perceived the thunderings, and the lightnings, and the voice of the horn, and the mountain smoking; and when the people saw it, they trembled, and stood afar off." This allowed Moses the forty days and forty nights he needed to produce the tablets of stone inscribed with the Commandments. Similarly, when the Tent in which Moses was to receive God's word was pitched some way from the Israelites' camp, only Joshua was allowed inside. "And it came to pass, when Moses entered into the Tent, the pillar of cloud descended and stood at the door of the Tent; and the Lord spoke unto Moses . . . face to face, as a man speaketh unto his friend." Or so Moses assured them. The Israelites were naturally terrified, and maintained a respectful distance. Joshua, however, remained inside the Tent throughout, stage-managing the effects. He later became an impressive performer in his own right, bringing down the walls of Jericho by blowing his trumpet. Jesus continued the magical tradition, raising Lazarus, performing his trick with the loaves and fishes, having his friends walk on water and, finally, resurrecting.

So the evolution of Houdini from rabbi's son to vaudevillian in nineteenth-century America was less bizarre than it seems. And a good many other rabbis' sons were following much the same path. In 1918 Houdini was to form the Rabbis' Sons Theatrical Association. Houdini was president, Al Jolson first vice-president, and Sergeant Irving Berlin second vice-president of this highly exclusive society. Its members had to be sons of rabbis or Jewish scholars. The original name of Jolson's family (it is tempting to say, their "real name": but under these circumstances, is any one name more, or less, real than another?) was Joelson. They were immigrants from Russia, his father an orthodox rabbi and cantor who, like Rabbi Weiss, was appalled by his son's chosen career. Irving Berlin's father, Moses Baline, was also a cantor, also from Russia. Other big show-business names shared the same background. Louis B. Mayer's father, though an unsuccessful businessman rather than a rabbi, solaced himself with religion; as a very young boy, Louis was expected, as was Ehrich, to act as both an emotional and financial prop to his father. Adolph Zukor, from Hungary like the Weisses, was the son and brother of rabbis. The Warner Brothers, the Shuberts, George Gershwin, Fanny Brice, all shared the rabbinical heritage.

It was not as if these people were products of a particularly theatrical tradition. The cantor's role is a fairly operatic one, but no more so than that of, say, a Greek or Russian orthodox priest. And the traditional Jewish fields of excellence had been in the classical and intellectual arts—music, science, mathematics, philosophy—not those of popular entertainment. These were the acknowledged routes out of the ghetto. "All the folk in our circle—brokers, shop-keepers, clerks in banks and steamship offices—used to have their children taught music," wrote Isaac Babel. "Our fathers, seeing no other escape from their lot, had thought up a lottery, building it on the bones of little children. . . . And in fact, in the course of ten years or so our town supplied the concert platforms of the world with infant prodigies. From Odessa came Mischa Elman, Zimbalist, Gabrilowitsch. Odessa witnessed the first steps of Jascha Heifetz."

What, then, impelled this particular group of people so supremely to express the popular soul of everyday America? Perhaps it was their extraordinary devotion to America, their desire to proclaim their Americanness. In 1917, when America joined the first world war, Houdini wrote to a friend: "I register tomorrow for enlisting. HURRAH, now I am one of the boys." He was by then forty-three, and was rejected on grounds of age; but that did not stop him doing his bit. He cut down on his professional engagements in order to give free performances at war benefits and for the soldiers in training camps and canteens. For two years he more or less devoted himself to this work, responding to all requests and usually travelling at his own expense. If he could not go and suffocate in the mud with the young recruits, he could at least give them a little fun—and something more tangible: his favourite trick for the boys was an old standby, "Money for Nothing," in which he produced an endless stream of coins out of thin air. Whenever he performed in front of men just about to sail for Europe, he would conjure up a succession of five-dollar gold pieces and present one to each of the soldiers. He managed to give away more than seven thousand dollars of his own money in this fashion; furthermore, by the time of the Armistice he had sold $1,000,000 worth of Liberty Bonds, singlehanded. Others were not to be outdone in their devotion to their homeland. Louis B. Mayer, like Houdini, adopted a symbolic American birthdate—in his case the most symbolic of all: his official birthday was July 4. So was George M. Cohan's (his real birthdate was July 3).

Although my own family's devotion to England, their adopted country, was and is exemplary, I can't imagine any of them expressing it in quite this way. It isn't the English style (and anyhow, what day would one choose? Shakespeare's birthday? The Queen's?). The gesture would seem ridiculous: *un*-British. It is hard for any Jew ever entirely to forget that he lives where he does usually because his family, in the recent or not-so-recent past, was thrown out of somewhere else. And in Europe, with its ancient and established national cultures, this does not make for a sense of belonging. Whenever a Jew—a politician, a businessman, a criminal—attracts too much attention, fellow Jews shake their heads and exchange significant glances. It is generally agreed that this is not good policy. Jews should keep their heads down, practise good citizenship, and feel grateful for being allowed to live peaceful, unpersecuted lives.

But this attitude is essentially European, not American. If the Jews in America had been compelled into emigration by forces beyond their control, then so had almost everybody else. When the Weisses and Balines and all the others arrived at Castle Garden, they were only the latest in an endless stream—of Irish, Poles, Germans, Swedes—all there for similar reasons; all striving to make their way. When the Jewish immigrants arrived in America from the ghettos of eastern Europe, they found themselves *for the first time* in a society where they were merely members of the ruck of common humanity: nothing special.

Houdini's generation knew what their parents' experience had been. They could never forget it: it was their family history. However much it was dressed up with stories about princes and royal connections, the Weiss family legend was about being thrown out of Budapest because they were Jews. But where this had been the central fact of Mr. and Mrs. Weiss's lives, for the children it was just a story. First-generation Jewish parents were irretrievably locked into the ghetto they carried around with them. But the children, triumphantly, uniquely, could escape into being Americans. Shocked by his first encounters with German anti-Semitism, Houdini wrote: "It may exist in America, but never that I have known. I never was ashamed to acknowledge that I was a Jew, and never will be, but it is awful what I hear from people that are Jew Haters, and do not know that I am a Sheeney." He may have led a particularly sheltered existence. But the fact remained that anti-Semitism could never become a part of semi-official policy in America, as it was almost everywhere in Europe.

Of course, American Jews might not seem as wholly American to their fellow Americans as they liked to think. When Ben Hecht asked David O. Selznick to sponsor an appeal for the formation of a Jewish army in Palestine to fight in World War II, Selznick refused: "I don't want anything to do with your cause for the simple reason that it's a Jewish political cause. And I am not interested in Jewish political problems. I'm an American and not a Jew." Hecht then challenged Selznick to name three people whom they would telephone and ask whether they considered him an American or a Jew. If one of them answered "an American," Selznick would win. None did.

But, because this was America, not Europe, how others might view them was a secondary matter. Houdini's Americanism was something he was as entitled to as anyone else, and his life's work became an expression of this new sensation, unique to his generation: the knowledge that he was, first, an American, and only incidentally a Jew. This was a matter of especial pride and hope for him. And when Houdini, the archetypal little man, took on authority in its grimmest and most symbolic form and stepped magically free from the most savage restraint, all Americans and a good part of the rest of the world rejoiced with him.

Not that the dream was unmixed with disappointment or anger. Many of these super-optimistic, super-American men were, at bottom, also very angry. Louis B. Mayer, the Cohns, the Warner brothers, were known for their bouts of uncouth fury. Irving Berlin became a recluse. Houdini's whole act could be seen as an expression of anger—anger at having been held down; an anger he would later turn against himself.

Thus, far from starting at a disadvantage, Houdini's pedigree could not have been more apposite for his time and ambitions. Nor could his character. The Jews who made it big in show business in the early twentieth century were driven men. Their drive was not just the common American drive to make money (though they had that as well). But there were a thousand easier, surer ways to get rich. No: they were driven to share their compulsions with the public. They needed a stage, in the most literal sense, to work out their inner lives. And, in the most literal sense, they found it.

Houdini began in the smallest possible way: by scraping up engagements in dime museums such as Huber's, on Fourteenth Street, which presented a series of acts—freaks, strong men—of the kind commonly associated with circus side shows. Then he ventured further afield. In Coney Island he worked with a strong man in a tent for "throw money"—that is, they had no entry fee to rely on but passed the hat round after the act.

After a while he saved enough to buy his first illusion. The magic press was filled with advertisements offering trick methods and equipment for small sums of money. Houdini himself, when he fell on hard times a few years later, produced his own catalogue of such offers. For the kind of money in question—amounts ranging from fifty cents to ten dollars—there would be no question of buying the exclusive use of a trick, although in the top echelons of the profession large sums changed hands, and there was always a lot of bad blood about infringements of rights and revelations of secrets belonging to other people.

Houdini's illusion was the trunk and rope-tie trick he called "Metamorphosis." This he presented, first with Jack Hayman, and later, when the two fell out, with his brother Theodore, or Dash—as he was generally known, possibly on account of his penchant for sharp dressing, but more probably because it was an anglicisation of his Hungarian name, Deszo. Harry and Dash travelled to Chicago, where Harry managed to get a booking at Kohl and Middleton's dime museum on the Midway at the 1892 World's Columbian Exposition. He gave twenty shows a day, for twelve dollars a week—sleight-of-hand, rope-ties of the kind used by spirit mediums and described in a number of books exposing the mediums' fraudulent ways, card tricks. By 1893 he had introduced a handcuff act: this marked the first appearance of "Harry Houdini, Handcuff King and Escape Artist." This personage, however, as yet held no interest for the public, any more than any of the other incarnations of Harry Houdini.

Still, he had made the great step out of the ghetto and into that other world he would henceforth inhabit. This was a world equally self-contained and removed from ordinary society: the nomadic world of the travelling entertainer whose home is a hotel room in whatever town he plays (once, that is, he has risen to the point where he can afford hotels). In a sense, Houdini had returned to his earliest roots. What was Moses but a travelling showman who, by sheer force of personality and skill of presentation, managed to lead his troupe forth from the unpleasant certainties of Egypt to a life on the road, replete with discomforts, uncertainties, and hope?

5

*T*WO LADIES

Unquestionably the most important person in Houdini's life was his mother. If he could have cloned her, so that she need never leave his side, how delightful life would have been! Magic, as so often, provides a metaphorical solution. Among the notes Houdini left at his death was a charming variation on the old trick of sawing a woman in half. In this, a long rectangular box is shown standing on a large square platform. The box has two doors in front and two doors on top. These are opened, and the platform turns around showing the box from all sides. Then a large woman steps into the box and the doors are closed. Two sawhorses are carried in and set in front of the platform. Each front door of the box has a window with a small curtain. The illusionist raises one of these to speak to the woman: it turns out to be the foot end. So he raises the other: her head is duly in place. The assistants carry the box to the sawhorses and saw it in two. When this is done the two half-boxes are turned with their open ends towards the audience. The half-lids are raised: out of each steps a girl dressed just like the original woman.

Reality being less easily manipulated, mothers are not readily sub-divided. So other steps must be taken. In 1894 Houdini had just turned twenty. He evidently concluded that the time had come when he ought to have a wife. So—abracadabra!—he found one. Traditionally, the magician sits his assistant on a chair, covers her with a cloth, waves a wand, and when he whips the cloth away—she has vanished. In Houdini's case it was the other way about. One moment, there was nobody; the next, there she was.

To say his marriage was sudden is an understatement. Houdini gave an account of it, emotionally true if factually inaccurate, in a magazine interview: "One day I was hired to give an exhibition at a children's party in Brooklyn. At the close a little girl, about sixteen, said to me very bashfully, 'I think you are awfully clever,' and then, with a blush, 'I like you.' 'How much do you like me?' I said, 'enough to marry me?' We had never seen each other before. She nodded. And so, after talking the matter over, we were married."

Mrs. Houdini's own recollections are different, though scarcely less abrupt. According to her, Houdini had arranged to give a show at her high school. Wilhelmina Beatrice Rahner (usually known as Bessie or Bess) was just eighteen. She persuaded her mother, who thought all theatre wicked, to let her attend. Mrs. Rahner and Bess sat in the front row. In the course of the show the young magician upset some acid on a table; it spilled over and, to Mrs. Rahner's fury, spoiled Bess's dress. Houdini was devastated. But Bess was smitten. Some days later, he came to the house and asked if he could have the old dress, as he wanted to get a new one to replace it and needed to be sure the replacement would fit. Since he had no money to buy a dress, Mrs. Weiss sat up nights for a week constructing one. When Houdini brought it round, Bess was thrilled, ran upstairs to put it on, then slipped out with Houdini while her mother was busy else-where. Houdini suggested they go to Coney Island. Bess, who had never been out on her own before, suddenly began to worry what her mother would say. "If you were my wife they wouldn't dare punish you," cried Houdini fiercely. Bess, not unnaturally, was startled at this sudden proposal—if that was what it was. No sooner said than done. They passed a second-hand jewellery store, and went in to try on wedding rings. Having selected one, Houdini found he had hardly any money. Luckily, Bess had some, so they bought the ring together. They then went to visit the local ward boss, whose name was John Y. McKane. At first he refused to marry them. But, when he saw their determination, his heart softened. They acquired a licence and were "properly married by the Boss of Coney Island, with two ward heelers as witnesses. The date was June 22, 1894."

Thus Bess's account of the affair in the biography of Houdini she commissioned and oversaw in 1928, soon after his death. But a few pages later she reproduces a newspaper clipping which indicates that the truth was something else again. The *Coney Island Clipper* reports: "The brothers Houdini, who for years have mystified the world by their mysterious box mystery, known as 'Metamorphosis,' are no more and the team will hereafter be known as the Houdinis. The new partner is Miss Bessie Raymond, the petite soubrette, who was married to Mr. Harry Houdini on July 22 by Rev. G. S. Loui, of Brooklyn. Harry has bought his brother's interest in the act, and he and Miss Bessie Raymond will hereafter perform it."

"Miss Bessie Raymond, the petite soubrette"? Can this be the same demure schoolgirl whose mother thought all "shows" were wicked? Yet another clipping gives yet another picture. The story was printed on the wedding date given by Mrs. Houdini, and the one the Houdinis always celebrated as their anniversary: 22 June 1894. "Risey [a local wag who had been persecuting the "Hunyadi brothers," a misspelling of Houdini] ran afoul of one of the Hunyadi brothers who was taking one of the Floral Sisters, 'neat song and dance artistes,' for a stroll between turns. He had heard of Risey's boasts and he glared at him. Risey passed the word about 'fakers and fake box tricks.' . . . The Brothers Hunyadi offered Risey $100 if he could fathom the secret of their box . . ." The Floral Sister was Bess, who had run away from her severe and joyless mother. The Floral Sisters were on the same bill as the Houdini Brothers. Dash had arranged to meet the sisters on the beach. Harry saw Bess: the *coup de foudre* ensued. For the next two weeks they were inseparable. Then they disappeared, and reappeared announcing that they were married. The marriage did nothing to reconcile Bess with her mother, an implacable and rigidly Catholic German lady who had to cope with eight other daughters and a son besides. Here was a son-in-law who was not only a magician, but Jewish! For years, she would sprinkle the pictures in her house with purifying holy water every time he visited. Even a second wedding ceremony, a Catholic one this time, could not mollify her. To cover all eventualities, they also got themselves married by a rabbi. "I'm the most married woman I know," Bess used to say. "I've been married three times and all to the same man." She and Mrs. Rahner were not reconciled until twelve years later, when Bess fell dangerously ill and wanted to see her mother. Houdini, supported by one of his brothers, went round to his mother-in-law's and camped in her front room until she agreed to come back with him. After that, "he was the same as a son to her."

In the meantime, however, Bess would not lack for a mother. She could have Houdini's: indeed, she would have to. Mrs. Weiss had not been present at the wedding. This was an omission so notable, given Houdini's emotional dependence on her, that it makes one wonder whether he would have been able to bring himself to marry at all if she—his first love—had actually been there with him. As it was, he had imperatively to obtain her immediate approval of this momentous step. Almost the first thing he did after the wedding was take his bride home to meet her.

Bess was afraid that Mrs. Weiss would be as horrified by her son's having married a Roman Catholic as Mrs. Rahner had been by her Jewish son-in-law. She need not have worried. She was welcomed with open arms into the Weiss household, poor and crowded though it was. "I was perhaps fortunate in that the Weisses had several sons and only one daughter," Bess commented. (The daughter, Houdini's little sister Gladys, was the youngest child.) The night they arrived, with so little room in the apartment, Harry had to sleep with one of his brothers, while Bess found a shakedown with some neighbours across the landing. They went on to find a furnished room. Mrs. Weiss had to lend Bess a skirt, because in her own clothes the new Mrs. Houdini looked so much like a little girl that lodging-house keepers became suspicious. She was tiny and slight with a sweet, childish face and curly hair, and looked about twelve years old.

"Two ladies," sings the M.C. in the musical *Cabaret*,

> Two ladies
> And I'm the only man.
> I like it
> They like it
> This two for one . . .

Did "they" like it? A letter from Houdini to his wife, written years later, indicates that relations between the mother and the wife were not always so easy. "My dear girl, where as I say you are mine, my mother claims me as her son. So the two loves do not conflict," he wrote. But the fact that he felt it necessary to reassure her shows that, on the contrary, in Bess's view conflict they did. How could they fail to? And how could Bess, the newcomer, the interloper, fail to feel jealous?

Here, as throughout their relationship, Bess's view may only be obliquely made out. She hints at her frustrations, but never directly expresses them. There exist hundreds of letters, notes and postcards written by Houdini to his wife, but none from her to him. This says as much about the compulsive nature of Houdini's letter writing as about Bess's mute acquiescence in the role he mapped out for her.

The two were rarely apart: Houdini would frequently write to her from another room in the same house. But it may not be entirely coincidental that notes in Bess's hand begin to appear in the Houdini papers only after his death in 1926. It is as if she only then could begin to emerge as a person in her own right.

There are, however, clues to Bess's view of her life with Houdini. They emerge in the biography she commissioned soon after his death, which was written by Harold Kellock, a professional journalist, with her full co-operation and assistance. Houdini enthusiasts dismiss this book as over-romanticised, "Bess's view of events." But for this very reason it is sometimes revealing. And although it may be romanticised—for the period just after Houdini's death was, as might be expected, the period when Bess's view of her late husband was least critical—the fact remains that the events it describes are events in which she participated.

There is nothing in the Kellock book to indicate any tension between Mrs. Weiss and Mrs. Houdini. Although there must have been difficult moments, it seems clear that there existed a genuine affection between them. "[Mrs. Weiss's] instant acceptance of me was the more beautiful because Houdini's love for his mother had dominated his life completely," Bess remarks. "After my coming there were of course two loves in his life, running parallel, so to speak. But never was there any sense of clashing or of division. As I look back at this, I realise that the perfect smoothness of our relationship was largely due to the mother's fine sense of human values and rare generosity of spirit. She kept her son's devotion and she made me feel that her life was enriched by my affection for her and by his happiness with me." As to this happiness, husband and wife both described it in fulsome and rather similar terms. "We were romantically in love to the end," says Bess, while Houdini, on their thirtieth anniversary, described his marriage as "still a Honeymoon."

A honeymoon! There's a word to take you back. In the days when honeymoons still happened, their gruesome nature was a byword. The orgy was licensed to take place at last: but all rarely went as it should have done when the music stopped and the guests went home and the inexperienced young couple were left face to face. "Honeymoon" is about moon and June and romance; the cold shock of reality is not catered for. Few married couples of thirty years' standing would describe themselves as "romantically in love," nor their relationship as "a honeymoon," and few would think that relationship diminished thereby. If they are still together, they have long since progressed to the pleasures of genuine intimacy. The Houdinis' descriptions of their marriage ring true, however. For the quality which most strongly characterised the emotional plane of this strange relationship was total unreality.

> Adorable
> Sunshine
> of my Life,
> I have had my coffee, have washed out this glass, and am on
> my way to business.
> Houdini
> "My darling I love you"

wrote Houdini to his wife in one of the countless notes he used to leave around the house for her to find; and the quotation marks around the expression of feeling perhaps convey more than was intended. Why should love exist only between quotation marks? It is as if he were suddenly struck dumb when it came to expressing his feelings—as if he could grope his way through the aphasia only by using someone else's clichés. Very often, in fact, he would literally do just that: he would clip some terrible piece of saccharine doggerel, the kind of thing you might find inside birthday cards or valentines, and paste it onto the end of his notes.

One might be tempted to conclude that the feelings thus expressed were as impersonal, as shallow and insubstantial, as the awful verses themselves. *(What is there in the Vale of Life / Half as delight-ful as a wife . . .)* But this is not necessarily the case. Houdini did exactly the same thing when writing to or about his mother; and of the depth of his feelings for *her* there can be no shadow of doubt.

As strange as their expression is the fact that his love letters to both his mother and his wife took exactly the same form. The qual-ity of his love for his mother, in tune with the role imposed upon him at such an early age by his father, was more than what is gener-ally associated with the filial. But the feelings he so laboriously and literally tried to spell out in his letters to Bess were something less assured—something much more self-conscious—than those which usually exist between husband and wife. The role of son came natu-rally to him; but the role of husband was one which he was forever gingerly trying out. In language and sentiment he could not differ-entiate between the two.

Bess's account of her early married life is fairly fragmentary. The first emotion she records is disorientation and alarm as she takes in the strangeness of the universe she has entered. Houdini's world seemed normal, natural and inevitable to him. His family were of course used to him; and as for his friends, they were all very young (Houdini was only just twenty when he married)—and boys of that age tend to accept their peers without giving much thought to the springs of character and motivation. But for Bess, this was to be no superficial acquaintance, and her first glimpse of life with Houdini did not reassure her. "Within a few days after my marriage," she wrote, "I began to realize that I had stepped into a world far differ-ent from my former well-ordered and sheltered life, a world of strange duties, strange contacts, and inexplicable happenings which my superstitious nature magnified into terrors."

This world was characterised, both physically and emotionally, by a scene which took place after the Houdini Brothers' last perform-ance together.

Houdini asked his brother and me to take a walk with him after the evening's work was over. He led us into the country on a dark, lonely bridge spanning some swiftly running black water. It was a weird-looking night, with a split moon that seemed to be dodging in and out behind heavy clouds. In the middle of the bridge he halted us, and there we waited for a time silently, I at least in growing trepidation.

Finally a distant bell tolled solemnly twelve times. As soon as the last beat ceased to reverberate, Houdini clasped his brother's hand and mine together, raised them aloft and cried: "Beatrice, Dash, raise your hands to heaven and swear you will both be true to me. Never betray me in any way, so help you God."

His brother and I repeated the vow after him. Then Houdini kissed me and shook Theodore's hand. "I know you will keep that sacred oath," he said.

This scene rings entirely true. Throughout his life Houdini was in the habit of demanding of his close associates that they swear undying loyalty on pain of death or worse. All his assistants had to sign such fealty oaths, couched in language as dramatic as Houdini could contrive. Through these scenes Houdini reassured himself that his interests would always come first, not only in his own mind but in the minds of all those who might be close to him. And in order to convince himself that this had been achieved, he needed to stage a drama, to script the scene as he would script a play; as he scripted all the important moments of his life; as he scripted, indeed, his love letters. This blurring of the boundaries of his private and his public life was to be one of the secrets of his charisma—that quality which ensured, from the moment of his first great success, that when he set foot upon a stage, audiences would be mesmerised by him. What the audiences were witnessing was the drama of the inner man. But the converse was also true: his closest friends, his brother, his wife, were faced with this curiously unprivate figure, who was unable to see his intimate life other than in terms of the role he should be playing and the roles *they* should be playing alongside him.

From the first, the marriage was conducted on this histrionic basis. Bess relates a couple of incidents which took place about a year after they were married. In one, she insisted upon going to see a show which Houdini, obsessively uncomfortable with any hint of the risqué, had forbidden. "He said the show was unfit for me and if I disobeyed him he would spank me and send me home. Naturally after that warning I went to the show. He followed me, carried me out, spanked me thoroughly, divided all our poor savings, led me firmly to the railroad station, bought my ticket to Bridgeport where my sister lived, and put me on the train . . . At the last minute, lifting his hat courteously, he said: 'I always keep my word. Good-bye, Mrs. Houdini.' My heart was breaking, and I was on the edge of hysteria, but the memory of the spanking rankled and enabled me to reply with a pretence of calm dignity: 'Good-bye, Mr. Houdini.' . . . Six hours later, at 2 A.M., the bell rang and I heard Houdini's voice. I flew to the door, and we fell into each other's arms, weeping. 'See, darling,' said Houdini, 'I told you I would send you away if you disobeyed, but I didn't say I wouldn't fly after you and bring you back.' " On another occasion, it was Bess who lost her temper. Whenever this happened, Houdini would walk round the block, return, open the door, and throw his hat into the room. If the hat flew out again, Bess was still angry. This time, the hat was promptly returned more than once. An hour passed; then a messenger appeared with a note "To be delivered in a Hurry to Mrs. Houdini, then Exit Rapidly." It read: "Mr. Houdini wishes to inform Mrs. Houdini that the globe fell out of his hands, but the second one slipped. He wishes to convey his sorrow, and promises that the one that fell will never fall again. Mr. Houdini, Friend Husband." Bess comments that "It was impossible to be angry very long with a husband like that." But the reader is left marvelling at the nature of this marriage in which, at the end as at the beginning, the protagonists addressed each other as "Mr. Houdini" or "Mrs. Houdini"—for this was still their habit right up until the day Houdini died thirty-two years later.

Bess was also struck early on by the double standards her husband applied in his dealings with the world. She gives an example: when a girl, Bess was deeply superstitious. "My own entire family believed in ghosts, witches, and the power of the evil eye and lived in a constant dread of supernatural evils." Houdini scolded her about this and set about teaching her the error of her ways. He did this by playing a trick which scared her half to death. Her father had died some years before; she had never told her husband his first name. Houdini told her to write that name on a slip of paper, crumple it up, and then burn it in the gas jet. After that, she was to rub the ashes onto his arm—and lo! the name, Gebhardt, appeared in letters of blood . . .

"I was paralyzed with fear. Then, slowly, a full realization of this diabolical thing dawned on me. In my early folk-lore, the devil, disguised as a handsome young man, lured girls to destruction. It was clear to me that I had married the devil . . ."

In fact this was nothing but a simple trick. If you write on your arm with a sharp instrument and then rub it hard, what you wrote will come up red. Houdini wanted to show Bess how it was done so that she would henceforth abandon her superstitions. He knew she was unaware he had found out her father's name (not hard to do, given all those sisters); and he knew, from his experiences of spiritualist séances, how effective such unexpected details can be.

But although he relentlessly attacked other peoples' superstitions, he was never a sceptic himself. Later in his life, he set about exposing false mediums, bringing all his habitual vehemence to that task; but the roots of his fury lay in thwarted hopes, not stony materialism. At the start of their life together, Bess realised that although he might denounce *her* superstitions, he cherished his own. For instance, he would not perform on Friday the thirteenth. Such inconsistencies never bothered him. He proceeded upon his sternly moralistic way as if his own lapses from the standards he imposed upon others simply did not occur. In his own mind, they did not: and that was all that mattered.

So Bess was expected to take her place as a member of Houdini's supporting cast—unquestioningly. Questioning was the one thing he would never put up with. It threw him into a fury. And yet in many ways their marriage was, more than most, a genuine partnership. Few married couples then worked literally side by side—indeed, few do so today. A magician, moreover, relies absolutely on his assistant. As a partner, Bess, small and lithe, was a considerable improvement on the large and lumbering Dash. There were those who thought that this was the principal reason for Houdini's wanting to marry her. Not only would she be a better performer, but half the takings would not have to be handed over to Dash. There may have been something in this; but it could never have been the whole story.

In Kellock's biography Bess recounts her shock when she first realised Houdini expected her to be his stage partner—though if she was already performing as a Floral Sister, this can hardly have been too overwhelming. True, the role of magician's assistant carried with it certain humiliations for a delicately brought-up young lady. She would be expected to wear tights, and her figure would be the object of dispassionate appraisal. The fashion was for bosomy, well-built ladies: "What the hell d'you think I'm running—a kindergarten?" demanded one burlesque-show manager when she presented herself. But on this level a true companionship developed between them. "It was pleasant . . . to practice tricks with Harry and to be initiated into the secrecy of his mysteries," she remembered.

Marriage is a bespoke garment: what fits one is unlikely to fit another. On its own terms, the Houdini marriage worked. Those terms were Houdini's. Within his world and according to his standards, Harry would do his very best to be a model husband. Those were the terms on which Bess either had to accept him or—what was totally unthinkable from his standpoint—not.

How he would have faced up to a rejection from Bess—whether he would have been able to survive it—we do not know, because it never happened. If she did not find their marriage easy, she did not leave it. Often moody and bad-tempered, her one effective recourse was to upset or worry him. This was the only way she could make herself felt. And her moodiness did upset him, deeply and genuinely, as his diary records on numerous such occasions: "Bess had a brain storm"; "Raised hell because I kidded on the phone to the operator"; "Bess very angry with me"; "Bess has been very sweet lately; hope she keeps it up," he noted once—but she did not, or not for long, for two weeks later he was lamenting again: "When I get home she is sore, and is sore for the night." Over the years, her discontent became more tangible. She increasingly took to drink. Towards the end of his life, while he was onstage performing, she would be in the dressing room complaining: "Listen to him! I, I, I! That's all I ever hear, I, I, I!" But Houdini's fulsome declarations of undying devotion would always coax her back into a good mood.

Children never came along to intrude their own peculiar brand of reality into this laboriously constructed idyll. Both Houdini and Bess deeply regretted this. They kept a succession of dogs, most notably the little Charlie, who travelled with them everywhere: his cushion was stowed in Bess's trunk along with her linen and "kitchen things." They doted upon him, and were heartbroken when he died. But dogs were a lame substitute for the real thing. Bess revealed after his death that "Houdini created a dream child, a son named after his own father, Mayer Samuel." In their large New York house Harry occupied the fourth floor while Bess's quarters were on the third. He was in the habit of sending Bess daily letters via the maid about Mayer Samuel's progress. The letters stopped only when this "son" became president of the United States. This was perhaps the best kind of son for Houdini. A dream child can never disappoint its parents. It is difficult to imagine how he would have coped with the obstinate realities of a flesh-and-blood child, especially a son. His view of fatherhood had been lopsided; his relations with younger men were always strained and resentful. It seems improbable that this would have been an easy or satisfactory relationship in the flesh.

One can only conjecture as to the reason for this childlessness.

Bess sometimes said her husband was sterilised as a result of over-exposure to X rays. Houdini's youngest brother, Leopold, became a radiologist in the early days of that science, before it was realised how dangerous X rays could be. He had his office and consulting room in the house Houdini bought at 278 West 113th Street, and Houdini enjoyed playing with the X ray machine. But the house was not bought until 1904, and by then Houdini had already been married ten X ray–free—and child-free—years.

Infertility is not uncommon. But my own guess, based on his effusive daily—sometimes thrice-daily—outpouring of love-declarations—is that Houdini may have been impotent. Why all those protestations? What was so wrong that he had to keep proclaiming his devotion? Why this constant need to reassure both Bess and himself? The month before he died, when they had been married thirty-two years, he was signing himself "your husband until and after the curtain rings down on our lives, e'en to the crack of Doom."

It is not hard to imagine that the kind of attachment Harry felt for his mother may have led to difficulties in normal relations with other women. He was uneasy with any reference to physical sex. His own fantasy heroine, as he describes her, was far different from the usual heroine of the kind of he-man movies he later aspired to emulate: "a girlish woman, or rather a womanly girl, one whose affections would spring from a mental attraction, rather than a physical or sex magnet." Bess, the only woman with whom he ever had a romantic relationship, was scarcely more than a child when they met. As Houdini was forever saying, she represented his ideal of womanhood: an unthreatening girl with as little as possible of the woman about her.

His relations with women other than his wife were stilted to an abnormal degree. One of the big difficulties in Houdini's movie career was his complete inability to so much as kiss another woman, even—especially—before the camera. "I'm afraid I'm not much of a ladies' man," he told a Hollywood interviewer in the understatement of the century, adding, typically, "I am so old-fashioned that I have been in love with the same wife for twenty-five years."

How, then, did he ever bring himself to marry? Perhaps it was in the nature of a dive for freedom, away from the debilitating thrall of his mother (whose absence from the ceremony we have noted) and into adulthood. The headlong speed with which he did it suggests a man who shuts his eyes, holds his nose and plunges in without daring to pause for thought. If he had thought longer, he might never have nerved himself to it. "I have uncanny feelings at times," he wrote to a friend twenty-two years later. "When I meet people [I] seem to know at once their whole pedigree . . . Never made a mistake. Saw a young girl passing down the board walk, she never gave me a 'look' three days after she was my wife, and thank the Almighty we have had 22 years of connubial Felicity." He had made his leap, and was absolved from having to think of such things again for the rest of his life. As for the notion of his wife looking at another man—the very possibility literally knocked him backwards. Once, at a party, Bess was invited to sit on the knee of one of their fellow guests, a colonel, and drink a glass of champagne with him. To tease her husband, she did so. But the idea that one might be able to joke about such sacred mysteries as sex, he found incomprehensible. Houdini completely lacked the detachment such jokes require. When he came in, he "stopped sharply in the doorway with an expression of incredulous horror on his face that his wife never forgot. His knees sagged as if he had received a knockout blow . . . He could hardly speak. She helped him into a taxi and into their lodgings. None of her explanations could lift him from his utter prostration of spirit." For weeks afterwards, the mere mention of the word "colonel" would reduce him to the depths of gloom. Such a nervous effort as he had made in acquiring a wife would not bear repetition. The possibility that she might leave him—that she might find some other man more attractive—was so terrifying to him that it was wholly unbearable. If he indeed was impotent, he would naturally have been unsure of himself. All those over-emphatic reiterations of his love—that Niagara of cliché—could hardly have compensated either of them emotionally for what he could not supply physically. And if Bess were ever to leave him on that account, or have an affair with someone else, not only his fragile self-confidence but also his act, which depended so strongly on the image of Houdini as a virile superman, would have been destroyed. What sort of Tarzan is it who can't keep his Jane?

In time, he seems to have achieved his real dream. He had, in a sense, two mothers. Bess recounts how she had to clean his ears for him, make sure he changed his underwear, try to get him to wear clean shirts. The fact that they did not have children meant that Houdini could play the child within his marriage without competition.

In 1924, testifying before a Senate committee which was looking into fortune-telling, the following extraordinary exchange took place:

> HOUDINI: Step this way, Mrs. Houdini. One of the witnesses said that I was a brute and that I was vile and that I was crazy . . . I will have been married, on June 22, thirty-two years to this girl . . . Outside of my great mother, Mrs. Houdini has been my greatest friend. Have I shown traces of being crazy, unless it was about you?
> MRS. H: No.
> HOUDINI: Am I a good boy?
> MRS. H: Yes.
> HOUDINI: Thank you, Mrs. Houdini.

Evidently, after over thirty years of marriage, Bess was still little more than an accessory to Houdini's self-image. Maybe, after all those years, she had lost any other perception of herself. She knew what was expected of her and she provided it. Those had always been the terms of the contract.

As for Houdini, it was all playacting for him—and all deadly serious: so serious that he only dared approach it by playacting. The only dialogues he could endure were predictable ones: those he had rehearsed with the other party, or which had been written for him by other people. Nor did he merely confine himself to reiterating romantic clichés: he acted them out. He would sometimes say to his wife, "Mrs. Houdini, you are a modern woman of liberal ideas. You will not be angry if I keep a date this evening. I expect to meet the most beautiful lady in the world at such and such a corner at six-thirty. I shall be home very late." Bess would know this was her cue to dress up in her best and keep the assignation. Houdini would pick her up like a grand cavalier and sweep her off in a taxicab to "some jazzy suburban roadhouse," where he would order a private dining-room and ply her with champagne (which he, of course, did not share). "That wasn't no lady, that was my wife"—might have been written seriously about these romantic escapades of Houdini's.

This was the man who took screen kisses so seriously that he could not perform them. For Houdini, the world was the stage, the stage was the world. He did not differentiate. As he himself once said, "All the world is a theater to me." And within this theatre, his marriage was the most enduring of scenarios. They were both in thrall to it. For Houdini, it provided the base of support, both emotional and practical, which he needed in order to feel able to deal with the outside world. As for Bess, on the day she married, she had agreed to surrender her life to Houdini. She had joined his cast, and could conceive of no existence outside the play.

6

FREAKS

Jack Flosso, whose father knew Houdini well, said to me: "Never forget that Houdini was a product of his early professional years. He thought the freak world was normal and the straights were freaks."

The freaks were among Houdini's earliest professional friends. "I have often sat at the table with Unthan the legless wonder, who would pass me the sugar, and the fat lady, Big Alice, would obligingly sit at the edge of the table so as to give poor little Emma Shaller, the ossified girl, plenty of room. Jonathan Bass, who was announced as his own living headstone, did not become the cemetery ornament he threatened to be. Blue Eagle, the man who broke boards over his head to show the solidity of his cranium, is running an embroidery shop in New Jersey. Mexican Billy Wells, who had cobblestones broken on his head, is soliciting for a photograph gallery." When the Houdinis worked dime museums, they appeared on what was known as the "curio stage," where the freaks were exhibited. They were a "working act," keeping the public amused until it was time for the freaks to appear.

The public, staring at a freak, senses something not quite of this world. Nature's aberrations inspire terror, and there is not much distance from terror to superstitious awe. But freaks do not *perform*, in the stage sense. They simply are. They exist: that is the extent of their performance.

Could Houdini, the performer par excellence, be called a freak? Certainly his world was the world of freaks. He never settled down in the conventional sense. He bought a house, but it was never much more than a pied-à-terre and a store for his vast collection of magical and theatrical memorabilia. He spent most of his life on the road, moving at first from rooming house to rooming house, later from hotel to hotel. His correspondence was conducted from his dressing room on a selection of hotel stationery. He went on touring literally until the day he died. In the world where people stay in one place, raise a family, wash the car on Sundays, he was always walking on eggs, always on his guard because he felt at a disadvantage. The necktie factory was the extent of Houdini's adult acquaintance with the straight world, and that did not last long or amount to much. He grew up with the freaks. And he felt at home with them, because Houdini *was* a freak in all senses of the word. His performance was Houdini on display. His act was himself as much as was any fat lady's or ossified girl's.

That self, as he perceived it—or rather, as he enacted it, for he precisely did *not* perceive it—was as much an outsider as any physical freak. The story of Houdini's rise to fame is the story of his self-discovery. The closer he came to the core of his inner self, the greater the crowds he drew. The fantasies he acted out before them were in a sense everyman's fantasies—of invincibility, of immortality. But his starting point was not everyman's. Most people feel themselves to a greater or lesser extent trapped by circumstance. But Houdini felt bound and gagged by it. He escaped from handcuffs, from straitjackets, from police cells and the various shackles of authority; naturally, for they were part of his act, the mise-en-scène from which the climax would be developed. But for Houdini they were more than that, just as the act was more than just an act.

A question often asked in relation to Houdini is why all the fame accrued to *him,* and not to some of the other equally competent escapologists who worked the halls at the same time? Perhaps part of the answer lies here. For them the act was an act, a job, work; but for Houdini it was not an act at all. Once again, the boundaries between his public and his private selves were indistinct. His marriage was set up as a continual performance; his stage show continually invaded his private life. One of the very first engagements of "Monsieur and Mlle Houdini" was at Huber's, a famous dime museum on Fourteenth Street, New York. On their first day there, they arrived simultaneously with another exhibit—the original electric chair. Huber had acquired it from the Auburn prison, where it had been used to electrocute a murderer named Kemmler in 1890. Fascinated by it, Houdini returned to buy it when Huber's was sold up in 1910. Bess hated it, and kept moving it down to the basement intending to throw it out—but "Houdini always missed it and had it brought upstairs again."

Murderers particularly fascinated him. One of his most vaunted escapes, performed in 1906, was from the condemned cell which had once housed Charles Guiteau, the assassin of President Garfield. This exploit—in the course of which he also freed all the other prisoners on Death Row and then locked them up again in the wrong cells—featured in countless publicity leaflets. But his interest in Guiteau did not end there. He collected Guiteau material—he owned, for example, the murderer's phrenological analysis. His drama collection included letters from Edwin Booth, the famous actor; but letters from John Wilkes Booth, Edwin's brother and (more important) the assassin of President Lincoln, also featured in the collection, and he was particularly proud of them. In his gaol breaks, he identified deeply with the prisoners who had languished, powerless, in those very places; and the worse the crime—the more it placed its perpetrator outside the bounds of society—the greater its fascination for Houdini.

The difference between him and the freaks he worked with, or the prisoners whose cells he temporarily occupied, was of course that he could do something about his condition. He could escape from it. But the condition itself remained—inescapably—in his mind. In 1901, in Germany, he was placed in a straitjacket from which it took him an hour and twenty-nine minutes to escape. "The pain, torture, agony and misery of that struggle will forever live in my mind," he wrote. He knew better than most what it felt like to be ineluctably trapped: forever on the margin.

Harry and Bess needed, when they began, to get onstage—any stage. They lost no time in producing the first of a series of flyers extolling the virtues of "Monsieur and Mlle Houdini" (or, on another occasion, "Mysterious Harry" and "La Petite Bessie") and their wonderful Metamorphosis act ("Exchange Made in 3 Seconds"). In the very first poster, the exchange took two minutes, and the poster concluded:

NOTICE TO MANAGERS
A STARTLING FEATURE
TIME OF ACT, 15 MINUTES
OUR ACT HAS BEEN FEATURED IN MASKELYNE
COOK'S EGYPTIAN HALL, LONDON
OXFORD, CAMBRIDGE AND ROBERT HOUDIN'S, PARIS
We will Forfeit $1000 if Any Detail of Our Act Given Herewith
is Misrepresented
Harry and Bessie Houdini

This was the first appearance of Houdini the publicist, a personage who never allowed mere fact to stand in the way of self-advertisement. Later, his stunts would rank him with Phineas T. Barnum: the two greatest publicists of their day. But no two men could have been more different. Barnum's achievement was essentially that of the successful tabloid editor. He knew how to catch the popular imagination, and exploited that knowledge cynically and shamelessly. Was he not the author of the immortal direction THIS WAY TO THE EGRESS and the equally timeless aperçu "There's a sucker born every minute"? Houdini, like Barnum, was obsessed with catching the crowds. But although he lured them with his tricks, he could never have spoken lines such as those. He was, like many freaks, an innocent. He always met any competition, real or imagined, in the most straightforward way imaginable: he came out fighting, shouted louder, and hit his man harder. The same applied to his publicity. In publicity as in everything else, attack was the best form of defence. The bigger the lie, the more self-righteous he was in defending it.

Nobody took him up on this one, perhaps because nobody noticed it. The trunk trick might have figured in Paris and London, but not under the auspices of Monsieur and Mlle Houdini, who had never set foot outside the United States. But despite their best efforts, work did not exactly pour in. They took what they could get, mostly in beer halls or dime museums. The beer-hall programme would generally begin with a melodrama performed by the ensemble: there was no rehearsal, but everyone knew the few stock pieces, such as the immortal *Ten Nights in a Bar-Room*. Then would come the various individual turns. Bessie did her song-and-dance act; Harry escaped from his handcuffs and did some sleight-of-hand; they performed the trunk trick. The dime museums were less rough and boozy than the beer halls, but still very hard work. At Huber's, the barker would shout, "Your attention towards this end of the hall! Here you will find a clever young man; he will mystify you if he can, escapes from everything, makes no bluffs. Houdini, look at him, the king of handcuffs." At Kohl and Middleton's, in Chicago, where they could usually find an engagement if all else failed, they were required to be onstage from ten in the morning until ten at night, giving ten to twenty shows a day. Speaking of those days "when I was playing Dime Museums, and being classed a 'freak,' "

Houdini said: "I generally kept very quiet, and tried to make a living, not knowing that I was developing my dexterity by working ten to fifteen times daily." When the museum closed, Harry would visit gambling houses and buy used cards cheap, and Bess would make up special packs for card tricks and sell them between the acts. On their very best week they might make sixty dollars between them—but this was unusual.

It looked for a moment as if the Houdinis would make good quickly. They were playing in a concert hall in the south when a wire arrived announcing that they were booked to play Tony Pastor's Theatre next door to Tammany Hall in New York. This was real fame. Tony Pastor's was the leading vaudeville house. Irving Berlin and Al Jolson would get their first big breaks there. Captain West, who owned the concert hall, advanced them their fare to New York, and they set off in high excitement. When they arrived, however, they found that their names, in barely legible type, were (as might have been expected) at the bottom of the bill. They were to play three times a day, at the worst times: ten-thirty in the morning, when the cleaners were still clattering around; twelve thirty-four P.M., in the middle of lunchtime; and six-thirty—dinnertime.

The management appeared not even to have noticed their presence. But just as they were getting ready for their third show, one of the big stars, a singer named Maggie Cline, ran into them on the backstage stairs. She kindly showed Bess how to make up properly, then went round the front and watched the act, taking Tony Pastor with her. Afterwards she said, "Say, you Great Houdinis, you are great!" Years later, in her last season, by which time Houdini topped every bill, they appeared together again, but however much they prodded her memory, she could not bring the evening at Tony Pastor's to mind. At the end of the week Mr. Pastor wrote them a testimonial: "The Houdinis' act as performed here I found satisfactory and interesting." This, however, gained them no engagements; and the critics, not surprisingly, had failed to notice them at all.

So—since a living must be made—the Houdinis joined the circus:

to be precise, the Welsh Brothers' Circus, "a ten-twent'-thirt' show without animals which toured the smaller eastern towns during the open season." Now they were really hitting the low spots. The circus, when they joined up with it, was in Lancaster, Pennsylvania. It was a black, rainy night, and they "stumbled about through ankle-deep mud for miles in the dark, trying to find the tent," Bess remembered:

> At last a voice from out of the darkness hailed us. "Is that the Houdinis?" Houdini shouted an affirmative, and the next instant we were pulled into what looked like a great black cave. It was the car—an old truck transformed into living quarters. In a minute a lantern flashed in our faces . . . [It] was Welsh, our boss.
> "Well, what do you want?" he asked, looking us over.
> "Anything," was Houdini's prompt reply.
> "The first thing you do with this outfit is to work in the sideshow," said the boss. "You do Punch and Judy; the wife, mind-reading. In the concert, Houdini to do magic, wife to sing and dance—then your trunk trick, and the handcuff act as the big feature. And of course, you are in the parade. Twenty-five a week and cakes."

The rules and regulations governing the Welsh Bros.' All-United Golden Shows were down-to-earth. Number one stated that "Artists asking exhorbitant prices that are not worth the salary agreed upon, must expect to be discharged after the first appearance . . . or receive a salary according to their worth." Number ten laid down that "Grumbling and growling will not be tolerated under any circumstances." There was a handwritten addendum: "All male members must go in daily street parades, if required." The contract mentions only "Metamorphosis" and "Miss Houdini's serio-comic specialties." In addition to their twenty-five dollars the Houdinis would get their meals (the "cakes") and accommodation in a cardboard cubicle in the "car." Bess was at first thoroughly disconcerted by all this, but after her first morning, when she awoke "to find the sun streaming through a little hole in the side of our cupboard" and was kindly shown to the breakfast tent by one of the two other women in the company, she soon felt at home. The circus poster advertised a Wild Man who never appeared and was generally not missed; but one day he was called for, and Houdini volunteered to be him. "The ringmaster, Clinton Newton, who could talk politely and sonorously about anything or nothing, made a preliminary address about the capture of the Wild Man in the depths of the Java jungle . . . and described how he lived on a diet of raw meat, cigarettes, and cigars. Then the cage was drawn in with Houdini growling and tearing at a bit of raw meat. The Wild Man was an immediate hit and became a permanent feature. He was a hit with the male performers as well as with the audiences, for the men showered him with cigars and cigarettes to hear him growl, and as Houdini did not use tobacco the rest of the men of the troupe enjoyed free smokes."

Only the handcuffs did not do well. They aroused not a flicker of interest in the audience, who simply assumed that Houdini must be using prepared cuffs. However, even they were not without their uses. One Sunday in a small town in Rhode Island the whole troupe was suddenly arrested for breaking the Sunday law. Mr. Welsh was in New York overnight, so they had no one to defend them and were summarily sent to spend the night in the lock-up. "In the lock-up the Fat Woman wept bitterly. Her cell was too small, and she was wholly uncomfortable and miserable. So after the sheriff had gone and everything was quiet, Houdini picked the locks of the jail and the whole company stole quietly back to the big tent. The next day Mr. Welsh arrived to fix matters with the sheriff, and we pulled up our stakes and went quietly away from there."

At the end of the season, since all their living expenses were met, the Houdinis had managed to save up a certain amount of money even though twelve of their twenty-five weekly dollars were always sent back to Mrs. Weiss. Houdini was persuaded to take a half-interest in a burlesque troupe called the American Gaiety Girls, the main feature of which turned out to be its debts. The show, possibly not helped by its new proprietor's loathing of anything resembling smut, sank into the mire, taking the Houdinis with it, until things got so bad they could scarcely afford to eat, let alone pay anyone's salary.

It was 1896, and they now joined up with a character named Marco. Marco, an erstwhile church organist, had put all his money into an elaborate travelling show, into which he incorporated the Houdinis. Their first trip took them to Nova Scotia. But this show, too, was a failure, and soon consisted only of Marco, the Houdinis and a man named Kearny, the "manager, carpenter, stage crew, actor and confidential adviser to Marco." Houdini decided to try a publicity stunt for the show: he would free himself from a running horse to which he had been roped. Unfortunately the horse turned out not to be the docile old nag he needed, but a young and frisky colt which dashed off with him into the fields, so that by the time it was safe to free himself they were miles away from any potential spectators. The show, like the horse, ran out of control—downhill. Marco decided to go back to the States and his church organ; Houdini took over. When they arrived at the point where renting a church for eight dollars broke them so that, unable to afford a room, they had to spend the night in a hallway, where the two men gave Bessie their coats to lie on, they decided the time had come for them to give up, too.

A boat bound for Boston lay at the quayside. Bessie spun a sob-story to the captain, and he agreed to give them their passage in exchange for a show for the passengers. But this, too, was doomed, for as soon as the boat began to move Houdini was prostrated. It was his first experience of seasickness, from which he would always suffer appallingly—the mere act of buying tickets for a passage made him nauseous. Tricks were out of the question. Bess agreed to try her hand at them, but with little success. She knew how they were done, but that did not mean she could do them. A kind passenger took pity on them and passed the hat round nevertheless. Bess was not sick but ravenous, and proposed to spend the money on a meal, but Houdini flatly forbade her even to mention food, let alone spend any money on it. The situation was saved by the same kind woman who took pity on her and treated her to a meal.

Then came more hard times. They travelled from one precarious engagement to another. In St. Louis, in cold weather, they found themselves stranded. Their baggage, including the precious trunk which was their only key to a livelihood, was held at the station with twenty dollars due on it. They had no engagements, and without their props, would not find any. They rented an unheated hall bedroom, containing only a cot and a rickety stove, for $1.50 a week, and lived on pilfered potatoes cooked on bits of old packing-case which they fed into the stove. Just before rent day, Houdini wangled them an engagement as "The Rahners—Harry and Bess—America's Greatest Comedy Act"—at Escher's Music Hall, thirty dollars a week. Unbelievably, this—mainly a compilation of old jokes cribbed from back numbers of comic magazines—went down well enough to secure them a second week "at a cut"—twenty-five dollars. At the end of this, Harry revealed to the manager that they were really "the Great Houdinis": the money had enabled them to redeem the trunk from the station. The manager agreed to book them for a third week, back on the original thirty dollars.

But three weeks' work was the exception, not the rule. In desperation, Harry set up "Professor Harry Houdini's School of Magic." "DO YOU WANT TO LEARN AN ACT?" inquired the flyer. "If you want to go on the Stage, travel with a Circus, play Variety theatres or Museums, you must first learn to do something to attract Attention." He sold some magic apparatus on commission for a Chicago manufacturer called Roterberg (who was to become a lifelong friend), and also some tricks of his own. At this point, it would have been possible to buy, for five dollars, the "Hindoo Needle Trick

. . . taught to me by Hindoos at World's Fair in 1893. The trick is to have committee inspect hands and mouth; you then swallow forty to fifty sewing needles, then a bunch of thread, and bring them up all threaded" and for a little more ("price on application") "Metamorphosis Substitution," "my original act." Luckily for Houdini, nobody seems to have wanted these two: they were still acclaimed as his most spectacular tricks until the day he died.

This exhausting and uncertain life went on, not for months, but for years. A manager in Milwaukee (that least auspicious of towns) swindled them out of some earnings. Houdini lost more in a dice game trying to retrieve the situation. Gambling was his vice. Ruthless in his abhorrence of anything which might lead to bodily weakness—he was teetotal; he never smoked; his refusal to admit that he might ever be other than perfectly fit was one of the compulsions which ruled his life—this might have been his Achilles' heel. Bess's fury on this occasion, spectacular even by her standards, made him cautious. "Even a small stake at cards is dangerous, for it cultivates the habit of gambling, which may soon become a passion," he wrote. Passion—which implies letting go and loss of control—was something Houdini sought to eliminate from his life. That life increasingly depended upon his taking no chances. Bess made him promise never to gamble again, which he did not—or not very often.

Then, at the end of 1897, came an offer to join Dr. Hill's California Concert Company, a travelling medicine show, at twenty-five dollars a week.

The format was simple. The troupe would arrive in a small town (they all travelled in a decrepit victoria large enough to carry a small organ, and played a different town each day) and set themselves up on a street corner. Dr. Pratt, Dr. Hill's partner, would play the organ, Houdini would play the tambourine, and Mrs. Houdini sang. A crowd would gather. When it was big enough, Dr. Hill would take the stage and tell everyone about his wonderful medicine, which he would sell to all and sundry. Then he would announce that the troupe would be giving a performance that evening in the local hall. The performance would open with a playlet. This would be followed by whatever acts the current ensemble could perform. Houdini gave a magic show: when Buster Keaton's parents, Joe and Myra Keaton, joined the show for a while, they did an Irish comedy routine. Bess liked the Keatons: she and Houdini claimed to have given Buster his name. He was just a toddler when they knew him, and Bess, in particular, seems to have been attached to him. When there was a fire in the hotel where they were all staying, she rushed up to the room where he was sleeping and rescued him. Perhaps she saw in him the baby she was still hoping for.

Medicine shows have a venerable history. In the sixteenth and seventeenth centuries they swarmed throughout Europe. They were little troupes of performers centred around a (supposedly) Italian doctor, or *dottore* (Italian doctors were famous; *dottore* is still a polite Italian honorific). The purpose of the show was to attract a crowd which could then be persuaded to buy the doctor's miraculous medicine. In order to attract the crowd, the troupe would stage a parade. The performers often included a monkey, a "turk" or "moroccan" to add even more exoticism, and a clown figure—the "Zanni" or "mountebank," or sometimes a harlequin. As time went on, the crowds became less interested in the medicine, and the show took on an increasing importance in its own right. Eventually, in the eighteenth century, it evolved into pantomime, the commedia dell'arte, with its stylised cast. The doctor, increasingly redundant in a medical sense, lingered on as the dominating, satanic master of ceremonies, or circus ringmaster.

In a sense, then, the American medicine show, like that which the Houdinis now joined, was a throwback. But its long history had earned it little status. In the world of vaudeville, there was a definite hierarchy. At the top were the established vaudeville theatres, such as Tony Pastor's, and the big theatre chains run by the Orpheum Circuit in the west and the Keith Circuit in the east. Then came the small music halls and dime museums like Huber's in New York and Kohl and Middleton's in Chicago. Below these were the beer halls. And at the very bottom were the travelling medicine shows.

There was a type of variety act at this time known as "Hebe comedy" (in which, as it happens, Al Jolson started out with his brother Harry). It consisted of dialogue: "You're a monkey." "Vot—you call me a monkey?" "Sure. You know what a monkey is? A monkey is a very fine person." "I know dat. Mine father, mine mother and mine brothers and sisters are all monkeys, too." Hebe comedy was to vaudeville acts as medicine shows were to vaudeville. So that to be a Jewish performer in a medicine show represented a theatrical depth below which it was virtually impossible to sink.

It was on Dr. Hill's suggestion that, when business turned slack, the Houdinis became spirit mediums. After all, strange powers and exotic, supernatural connections were all part of the medicine-show tradition. They agreed readily enough. Houdini had no special bee in his bonnet regarding mediums at this stage—his medium-busting was to come much later.

They turned out to be remarkably successful in their new calling. This was partly because, being the good professionals they were, they did their preparation properly. Bess soon learned to go into trances and use the special medium's voice and language. They had already worked out a "mind-reading" routine in which code words represented numbers:

Pray = 1
Answer = 2
Say = 3
Now = 4
Tell = 5
Please = 6
Speak = 7

Quickly = 8
Look = 9
Be quick = 10

Thus, if the mind reader needed to know the number on a dollar bill—say, 59321884778—Bess, holding the bill, might speak as follows: "Tell me, mind reader. Look into your heart. Say, can you answer me, pray? Quickly, quickly! Now! Speak to us! Speak quickly!" The number code could also, of course, be used to represent letters of the alphabet and spell out a word or phrase.

There were other established procedures. There was a special mediums' "Blue Book" giving relevant detail for a circuit of towns in the Midwest. When they arrived at a new town, they would go to the cemetery and memorise the names, which would be sure to make an impression upon the audience. They would listen hard to the gossip around the boarding-house dining table. And they would often employ a "tipster" who would relay points of interest about the audience as they filed in to the séance. Most impressive effects could be achieved using all these aids. So successful were they that, when the medicine show died early in 1898, they set up as mediums for a while on their own account.

Two coincidences finally frightened them off this line of work. The first took place in a town over the Canadian border. Bess, in her trance, was reading and answering sealed messages from the people at the séance according to the usual system. One of the questions read: "Where is my brother John? I have not heard from him in nineteen years. (signed) Mary Murphy." Instead of the usual evasive, generalised answer, Bess, suddenly remembering a Mrs. John Murphy who kept an ice-cream parlour near Sixty-ninth Street where the Weisses lived in New York, replied, "You will find your brother at—East Seventy-second Street, New York." She reckoned that, by the time Mary Murphy had written and received a reply, they would be safely in another town.

But Mary Murphy fooled them. She wired—and received a reply from, yes indeed, her long-lost brother. "There are an astonishing number of coincidences in life," mused Bess apropos this incident. The Houdinis suddenly found themselves celebrated as seers. They moved on, feeling shaken, but spiritualism was a much more certain living than vaudeville, so they persisted. The end came when Houdini noticed in one audience a mother whom he had recently seen scolding her little boy for riding his bicycle too recklessly. He told her he had a spirit message that her son would break his arm riding his bicycle. Soon after the woman returned home, the child was brought to the house with his arm broken. That was enough for Houdini. He gave up the medium business then and there.

After this followed a brief spell with a travelling theatre troupe specialising in melodramas, in which the Houdinis both played and did turns between the acts; followed in April 1898 by another six-month spell with the Welsh Brothers' Circus, where Houdini toyed with the idea of becoming an acrobat. He even went so far as to buy "pink tights and uppers" on 3 September. But acrobatics was not what he wanted to do. On 8 October the Welsh Brothers closed. Success, even of the most modest kind, seemed as far away as ever.

What Houdini really wanted to do was not acrobatics, which came so easily to him, nor supporting roles in melodrama, nor even card tricks, at which he was expert—but escapes.

The public was still resolutely uninterested in watching him free himself from handcuffs. But he already knew how this might be made more interesting. In 1895, while he and Bess were touring with the ill-starred Gaiety Girls, he conceived the notion of visiting police stations and challenging them to lock him into any handcuffs they cared to use: he would escape. He first tried this approach in Holyoke, Massachusetts. He was manacled at the police station, walked into an adjoining room, shut the door, escaped in less than a minute, repeated the feat twice, and received a handsome notice in the local paper. He did the same thing in other towns: more press stories followed. But these were very small towns, and the stories escaped the attention of the circuit bookings managers. In the larger cities, police stations were too busy to give Houdini the time of day, and journalists had more pressing copy.

In Chicago at the end of 1898, he decided to improve on this stunt. A certain amount of preparation was required. First, he made friends with some newspapermen. Then there was the question of gaining access to the police. If any police force in the country was liable to be too busy to listen to him, it was Chicago's. So he wangled an introduction to Andy Rohan, a lieutenant of detectives, the right-hand man of the police chief and a well-known Chicago character. He took Bess to the city gaol to visit Rohan: she kept him talking while Houdini wandered around studying the lock system of the cells. They were there a long time, but Houdini could not find what he wanted. The locks were too complicated. So next day, to Rohan's astonishment, they called again. Finally Rohan had had enough and threw them out. But by then Houdini had discovered what he needed. Next day, he told his reporter friends that he could escape from the city gaol after being handcuffed and locked in a cell. So they all returned to the gaol, where Andy Rohan was not averse to teaching Houdini a lesson in front of the newspapermen. He was locked up, and, a minute later, walked into the warden's office. But the reporters were unimpressed. They had heard about his previous visits, and assumed he had taken wax impressions of the locks and made his own keys. Houdini therefore offered to strip and be searched before he was locked up. They agreed; at his suggestion they even sealed his mouth with plaster. They left him handcuffed and naked; within ten minutes he was back in Rohan's office, dressed. A story! He even got his picture in the papers.

That was it! It was all he wanted. He spent everything he had on buying copies of the papers, cutting out the story and mailing it to everyone he could think of. The effort soon bore fruit. A few days

later he received a visit from a representative of the Hopkins Theater, Chicago's top vaudeville house. The headliner had died: could
the Houdinis fill in at short notice? They would have the star spot—
the one before the finale.

It was manna from heaven. But Bess was ill in bed with flu. She
was not particularly strong, and the hard life they were leading had
taken its toll. Houdini's letters frequently mention that Bess is not
well. But the "Metamorphosis" trick, the climax of their act, could
not be done without her. Terrified of going on alone but appalled at
the prospect of having to turn down such an offer, Harry began to
set impossible conditions. He wanted star billing; he wanted a hundred dollars a week; he wanted the star dressing room with a large
mirror. The representative agreed to everything—anything, if they
would only come along at once. What were they to do? Bess solved
the problem. "Get me to the theatre," she said. "I'll work."

The Hopkins engagement only lasted a couple of weeks; then
they returned to the dime museums. But the Chicago publicity was
still working, and Houdini persisted with the gaol-breaking stunts.
One evening in Minneapolis, a stranger approached him after the
show and invited him and Bess for a cup of coffee. During the show,
evidently thinking that Houdini's handcuffs might be specially doctored, he had (Houdini later wrote) "purchased a few pairs and sent
them on stage." The challenge had been dealt with in short order.
Once they were seated, Houdini asked him what he thought of the
act. He dismissed it all—except the handcuffs and the substitution
trunk. Everything else, all the little magic—card tricks, sleight-of-
hand, the production of pigeons, guinea pigs and a multitude of
other objects from a silk hat—only detracted from these two big
stunts at which Houdini excelled. Why not exercise a little showmanship and cut the rest out? Then he introduced himself. He was
Martin Beck, the booker for the Orpheum Circuit, the big western
theatre chain. He would try them out at sixty dollars a week, and if
they were a success, he would raise them.

"They are artists of the front line, and furthermore a lady and gentleman in all that the term implies and can always find room with any of our amusement enterprises," ran the encomium they had received from the Welsh Brothers at the end of their last circus engagement. "The Houdinis are truly great people." Was it really possible that they had put the world of the Wild Man and the Fat Lady behind them forever?

It was not. That was something they never could do, and never wanted to. Martin Beck had picked out the two items which were Houdini's own. They expressed, as nothing else expressed, the man himself. When he performed those two stunts, Harry Houdini, like the freaks, was putting his own oddities—his own psychological deformities—on show. He was a performing freak, but a freak nonetheless. He never lost his affinity with these companions of his early days; and at the time of his death, one of the many books he was preparing was a book about freaks.

$\mathcal{H}$ANDCUFF KING

"I started in the show business when I was a youngster, but my mother took me out and apprenticed me to a locksmith," Houdini told the Washington *Times* in 1906. "That is where I got my first knowledge of the weakness of locks. I discovered a method of opening them which I kept to myself." Elsewhere he retold the old story of how he was left by the locksmith to file a pair of recalcitrant cuffs off an unfortunate fellow marooned in them by a jammed lock. But he hadn't needed to use the file—there was an easier way: his "secret."

"Secret" was a word Houdini often used. There is something very attractive about it. Children have secrets. They huddle together over them and exclude everyone not privy to them. Exclusion, of course, is a large part of the attraction of any secret. It is also part of the attraction of the world of magic. Magicians, too, are clannish and exclusive. They have their societies and their publications—the Magic Circle, the *Linking Ring*, the *Sphinx, M.U.M.*—from which the general public are excluded. This is understandable: they want to guard their secrets. Exclusion, for them, affords more than simply pleasure: it affords a living. For magicians' secrets and children's secrets have this in common: revelation almost invariably means anticlimax. When you don't know how a trick is done, it seems magical. When you do, the pleasures of connoisseurship may remain, but the magic is gone forever.

Naturally enough, Houdini made much of his "secret." Various people tried to guess what it might be. One ever-popular theory held that he was able to contract his hand by dislocating the bones, so that it became smaller than his wrist. Houdini himself asserted that this was how he escaped from the German convict chain (by which German prisoners were shackled together). In fact he could not have done so: the feat is physiologically impossible. Another (and likelier) method of escaping from the chain is the old strongman's trick of bursting one of the links. To do this, the chain is previously prepared: one of the links is held in a vice and the metal is pushed back and forth until it is "fatigued" so that one more strain will break it. And here indeed is a "secret"—or one of them. Houdini always made much of the strength and impregnability of his chosen restraint, whatever it might be—a specially built packing case into which he would be nailed, to emerge as if by magic, leaving it to all appearances miraculously untouched; a fearsome convict chain. But he always made sure he had a good look at it first, and took any opportunity to effect a little careful preparation.

The contents of his famous "Trunk No. 8" reveal the full extent of that care and preparation. As Houdini became more successful, his baggage increased exponentially. But Trunk No. 8 was the secret of secrets. Only Houdini, Bess and his closest assistants had access to it. After he died, it passed with the rest of his magical effects to his brother Dash, who was by then known as Hardeen. It remained in the basement of his house in Brooklyn; and there it was found, after Hardeen died, by a magic collector, Dr. Morris Young. "It was opened in a very ordinary manner exposing a canvas-covered tray;

saws and other tools were attached inside the trunk lid . . . ," he wrote.

> Removal of the tray brought to light the large lower space that was crowded with what looked like a jumble of more tools. Straps attached to the bottom of the trunk served the purpose of holding some of the items . . . Two cigar boxes were labelled respectively "Handcuff and leg iron keys" and "Old Postcards Magicians, etc., Key Blanks." There were a number of metal cash boxes. One contained many packages of sewing needles (needle trick) and a small leather pouch, a coin purse, corn kernels, jeweler's rouge, soldering supplies, keys, a *Wohnungs Waechter* key, sealing and other waxes, chalk, crayons, buttons and thread. Another box was filled with small tools such as pliers, dividers, calipers, drills, leather and canvas sewing tools, glass cutters and a few lock picks. When laid out on tables, the tools and other objects found in the trunk formed an impressive array. Carpenters, plumbers, leather and canvas workers, and mechanics would have felt quite at home. There were five planes, mallets, hammers (one double-claw), an axe, wood and metal saws, chisels, gouges, gages, a spirit level, plumbs, spool of marking twine, abrasive papers, a portable grindstone, many files, screw drivers, a spokeshave, wrenches, small reamers and threaders, a large and small blowtorch with soldering irons (some electric), caulking tools, sailors' palms, paint brushes, rulers and measuring tapes, pliers, putty knives, oil cans, nail pullers, crowbars, vises, a small candlestick, and a bench cleaning brush. From amidst all these, two small books startled me. They turned out to be a 14th edition copy of Henry T. Brown's *507 Mechanical Movements, Embracing All Those Which Are Most Important . . . and including Many Movements Never Before Published (1884),* and a copy of Fred T. Hodgson's *ABC of the Steel Square and Its Uses* (1908).

And these were by no means all the tools Houdini carried with him.

What mere challenge could withstand such an array? If the packing case was displayed in the theatre foyer overnight as a "draw," Houdini or his assistant would take the opportunity to replace a few long nails or bolts with short ones, easily removed, or make some other relevant adjustment. The convict chain, by the time it reached the stage, would not be the chain it was when first it left its maker.

The secret of the handcuffs was of course a simple one. It consisted of keys.

Sometimes not even keys were needed: just a sharp tap in the right place might be enough to open a spring-loaded cuff. Houdini wore a sheet of metal underneath one of his trouser-legs to knock catches of this type apart. Otherwise, he made sure that all eventualities were catered for. A letter to one of his assistants detailed the keys he needed and the handcuffs and leg-irons they would open. Twenty-eight varieties of handcuff are listed, beginning with a "Double-lock twoer Ratchet," and ending with the Navey handcuff and leg-iron requiring two keys to open it. There are even more varieties of keys: sixty-one in all. Number eighteen is a master key for 95 percent of all regulation English cuffs. "The key in this set being split, allows you to really unlock almost any cuff of this pattern, as you simply insert the key, give it sufficient turns to catch hold of thread and bolts, and pull. This split key, which is the invention of Harry Houdini, who patented it in England, is the best master ever used on any style cuff." Not all obstacles are so simply overcome. Number twenty-one, the "Master English Plug, also known as the Slave Iron . . . will require two teeth on top to remove the plug, before it is possible to insert the key. Some of the plugs unscrew to the right, and some to the left. When the cuff is being locked on you, watch which way they turn the key." The last key on this list, number sixty-one, opens the Nova Scotia Leg-iron, found by Houdini in Nova Scotia in 1895 (on the ill-starred Marco tour). "Scarce," he remarks laconically.

When it came to locks, he never stopped learning. "In Berlin," he wrote, "I knew a locksmith, Mueller, who has a shop on Mittle Strasse, and he was more than willing that I should work for nothing, and I commenced repairing locks for him. He soon discovered that his 35 years of experience was nothing as compared to my trick in opening locks, and he soon had a thriving trade for his young man to open locks. In order that I should know the exact heights of the various locks used on the police chains, he ordered a great gross, and soon exchanged them for another great gross of other patterns, etc.

In that way I would pass 6 to 10 hours daily picking locks and soon, with the assistance of the four marked picks, I could open any lock that contained the 5 or 6 Chubb levers. The 'gate ways' were never made close, as is the case in the very fine lever locks, so it became a very simple matter for me to open each and every lock which was made on that principle."

He acquired an ever-growing collection of special keys of his own design which were carried around in their own case. But possessing the keys did not by itself ensure success. Just as important—perhaps even more so, as one commentator remarked—was the ability instantly to identify which key was required, "for it is obvious that the audience cannot be kept waiting until the performer has tried all forty-five keys in every one of the locks." Then it was necessary to know where to conceal them "in spite of the searching which is sometimes insisted upon"—or, in Houdini's case, invited: this was one of the essentials of his routine. And even after all this, other skills were needed. Manipulating the key in the lock was no easy matter. "The primary lesson is, to learn to use both hands with equal facility, as . . . one hand washes the other, but in this case one hand releases the other," wrote Houdini, adding: "The method adopted by me to acquire this end was, when at table I practiced to use the left hand persistently, until I could use it almost as easily as the right." His toes were almost equally dexterous, although presumably he did not exercise them at table.

There were other important details, too. One of these he learned at the start of 1899, just after the Hopkins Theater engagement, when Sergeant Waldron of the Chicago police department locked his special cuffs around Houdini's wrists at Kohl and Middleton's Museum. Houdini was quite unable to extricate himself. He struggled with the cuffs for more than an hour. The audience began to jeer, and moved on to the next freak. He was still struggling when the museum closed at ten o'clock. Bess wept; Houdini stood disconsolately on his platform. Only Sergeant Waldron remained. He explained that he had dropped a lead slug into the cuffs, so that the lock was jammed. There was no way of opening it: Houdini would have to be sawed loose.

In future, clearly, he must never accept a challenge without first seeing the challenge cuffs locked and unlocked. That was the lesson. But would there be a future? Houdini, after this fiasco, was sure there would not. The world had ended for him when he failed to break free from Sergeant Waldron's doctored cuffs. The Chicago *Journal* carried the story: WAS AN UNFAIR TEST: MAGICIAN HOUDINI SAYS SERGT. WALDRON PLAYED A JOKE ON HIM.

Marooned at the centre of his own universe, Houdini was convinced that this was the end of his career. It did not occur to him to wonder who was going to notice a small-time mishap to a small-time performer in a dime museum. Next morning he was suicidally dejected. Mr. Hedges, Kohl and Middleton's manager and a staunch friend of the Houdinis, laughed and told him to get a move on or he'd be late for the opening performance. But the dejection, which seemed so extreme and exaggerated, was important. It was another pointer to Houdini's *real* secret—the secret that would ensure his name remains, after all these years, a byword; that, in his prime, would pack the halls and sell out his every performance. What, after all, was it that Martin Beck thought he had spotted? A man escaping from *handcuffs*?

There used to be an escapologist who performed on Tower Hill, just outside the Tower of London. I saw him once when I was a child. He stood in an open space struggling with chains. The performance seemed rather pointless, although it was evidently to some extent memorable. But even the child I then was recognised that the escapologist was not an enviable figure. He struggled on, isolated on his bleak hill. No triumphal future beckoned. It just seemed a rather odd way to make a living.

I remember the escapologist as a Laocoön-like figure, fighting with his chains as the prodigious statue fights with its snakes. But

Laocoön had no choice in the matter: his fate, his fight, was ordained by the gods. By contrast, the escapologist's occupation seemed somewhat arbitrarily chosen. Houdini, however, had as little choice about what he did as Laocoön. The struggle dominated his imagination.

In an extraordinary article written in 1908, he describes his first view of a straitjacket. This took place in St. John's, Nova Scotia, just after Marco had skipped off back to Bridgeport leaving the Houdinis to carry the show alone.

While in St. Johns I met a Dr. Steves, who then was in charge of a large insane asylum, and received an invitation from him to visit his institution, which I accepted. After showing me the various wards, he eventually showed me the padded cells, in one of which, through the small bars of the cell door, I saw a maniac struggling on the canvas padded floor, rolling about and straining each and every muscle in a vain attempt to get his hands over his head and striving in every conceivable manner to free himself from his canvas restraint, which I later on learned was called a strait-jacket. Entranced, I watched the efforts of this man, whose struggles caused the beads of perspiration to roll off him, and from where I stood, I noted that were he able to dislocate his arms at the shoulder joint, he would have been able to cause his restraint to become slack in certain parts, and so allow him to free his arms. But as it was that the straps were drawn tight, the more he struggled, the tighter his restraint encircled him, and eventually he lay exhausted . . .

Previous to this incident I had seen and used various restraints such as insane restraint muffs, belts, bedstraps, etc., but this was the first time I saw a strait-jacket and it left so vivid an impression on my mind that I hardly slept that night, and in such moments as I slept I saw nothing but strait-jackets, maniacs and padded cells!

Bewitched by this vision, Houdini could not wait to try out a straitjacket of his very own. What an impression that would make upon the public! "The very next morning I obtained permission to try to escape from one and during one entire week I practised stead-ily and then presented it on the stage, and made my escape there from behind a curtain. I pursued this method for some time, but as it was so often repeated to me that people seeing me emerge from the cabinet after my release, with hair disheveled, countenance cov-ered with perspiration, trousers covered with dust and ofttimes even my clothes being torn, remarked, 'Oh, he is faking, it did not take all that effort to make his escape,' that eventually I determined to show to the audience exactly what means I resorted to, to effect my re-lease, and so did the strait-jacket release in full view of everybody." (In fact it was Hardeen who first realised that this was the most effective way to present a straitjacket escape.)

The drama of Houdini's act lay not just in his skill and showman-ship but in the figure he presented. In the challenges—to police departments, to handcuff enthusiasts, to constructors of impregna-ble packing cases—he was that irresistible hero of a thousand fairy-tales, the little man who takes on all comers. Escaping from the straitjacket, he was psychodrama made visible. He very soon learned what he must do in order to be effective. Once he had realised the essentials—that the straitjacket escape must be presented in full view; that the handcuffs must not be allowed to seem too easy, or the act would be dismissed; that he must take on, not just inanimate restraints, but living authority—he was launched. The sheer sus-pense—Would he do it? Would he be defeated this time?—could hold an audience spellbound while nothing, or virtually nothing, was happening on stage. And of course the reason the audience cared was that Houdini himself cared so enormously. For him, the question of whether he freed himself or not really was a matter of life and death.

One of Houdini's more improbable aficionados was Edmund Wilson, America's most distinguished man of letters. Wilson was a keen amateur magician; but he observed and admired Houdini as a phenomenon who transcended his calling. Writing about him in the

New Republic, Wilson observed, "He lived his own drama and had otherwise little of the actor about him—so little that . . . one has the feeling that, in his role of public entertainer, he was always a little out of his orbit." When the apparently trivial is endowed with the weight of emotion Houdini brought to his act, it is no longer trivial; and nor, therefore, is the performer.

Beck started them with a booking in Omaha in April, at sixty dollars a week. The routine consisted of escapes. On the stage were some chairs, a table loaded with chains and manacles, the substitution trunk in a corner, and a cabinet of steel tubing, curtained on all four sides and over the top (Houdini had learned this lesson from a circus giant who had been able to peek over the top of a previous cabinet). A committee was invited onto the stage from the audience, to inspect the cabinet for hidden aids and check over all the cuffs and irons to see that they really did lock. Houdini's skill as a magician, which meant that he could palm, misdirect attention, and hide his picks in unlikely places, came in useful here. A favoured hiding-place was his thick, wiry hair. When he had to strip naked, he sometimes hid a small pick in the thick skin on the sole of a foot—not a spot that would ordinarily be searched by even the most rigorous police surgeon.

A feature was made of challenges from the audience, such as Martin Beck had sent up on the night he had booked them. In Omaha, Houdini freed himself from five pairs of regulation handcuffs and a set of official leg-irons supplied from the police. MANACLES DO NOT HOLD HIM, gasped the Omaha *World-Herald.* "The entire handcuffs and leg-irons of the police department were on exhibition and all of them were used that could be worn conveniently, or rather inconveniently . . . In less time considerably than it took to adjust this array of jail 'jewelry' he returned from an adjoining room, where it was impossible to conceal a confederate, relieved from the entire paraphernalia and having the same linked together, forming a chain."

He also performed the needle act (which had not sold when Professor Houdini had attempted to lure the public to buy it). He made a hit. The Nebraska Clothing Co. ran a series of ads featuring him: "The ad man put a pair of handcuffs on Houdini and locked them. Houdini got out of them in less than two minutes and had them interlocked without the aid of a key and without leaving the office. The ad man sent out and bought a deck of cards, having loaned his last deck to a missionary who was going to the Philippines and wanted to go as a deck hand. Houdini opened that deck and counted out 52 cards; he turned them over and showed that there were 52 queens of hearts in it, and next moment counted out 52 aces of spades . . . He unlocked a fine door lock without a key, using a wooden toothpick to pick it, and finally picked up a cigar off the ad man's desk, where there wasn't any cigar, and picked a match out of a black ink well . . . As Houdini is out at Fairmount park this week the ad man invites him to come in and find a few more cigars on his desk, for he can't. Give Houdini a few more years and he'll have cigars to burn and money to burn as well."

That was what Martin Beck thought, too. He raised the Houdinis to ninety dollars and sent them off to begin a tour of the West Coast Orpheum circuit, starting in San Francisco. This time they took a room at six dollars a week, with running water and a gas stove. Unfortunately it also had fleas; and, on their first morning, there was an earthquake. Houdini was not to be put off. He successfully challenged the San Francisco police department. The usual routine followed: he was strip-searched, weighed down with fetters, and left to do his worst—only to walk into the office hot on the heels of the complacent police sergeant and all the pressmen. There followed a week's successful run at the San Francisco Orpheum, followed by an article by one Professor Benzon in the *Examiner*. The professor pooh-poohed the act and explained that the secret lay in a key which Houdini concealed in his mouth. Professor Benzon, given the same facilities, could replicate all Houdini's handcuff feats. Houdini did not let this heaven-sent opportunity pass. He offered to let Professor Benzon strip him, seal his mouth and lock him in a cuff. If he could not escape he would forfeit a hundred dollars. Then he would lock the professor in a cuff and give him the key. If he could not escape, he must give Houdini a hundred dollars, and must also let him shave off the professor's long black beard. This challenge was not taken up: but the public flocked in. A fellow performer advised the Houdinis to ask for a raise. They were worth at least two hundred dollars. Two hundred dollars! A week! Finally they plucked up courage to ask Beck to raise them to a hundred and fifty. He did so at once. Houdini went straight out and bought Bess a fur neckpiece for thirty-five dollars. It was, as Winston Churchill remarked in other circumstances, the end of the beginning.

The Orpheum tour ended in the autumn of 1899. It had been hard work: every week a new location, with vast distances to be covered between houses in the huge spaces of the American West. Bess and Harry were undaunted: they asked nothing more than to carry on indefinitely with this terrifying schedule. But if they hoped to repeat their triumph in the East, they were disappointed. The new century found them picking up a week here and a week there. They played the first week of February at the New York Theater, Manhattan, but suffered a debacle when Houdini mislaid the key that released Bess from the "Metamorphosis" trunk at the end of the act. Bess, inside in the dark, was terrified and began to shout. The theatre manager arrived with a fire axe with which he was about to attack the trunk when, in the nick of time, the keys were found. When the mishap was not repeated, New York lost interest. "Reengaged for next week Keith's, Phila," recorded Houdini triumphantly on 9 February from Boston; but the Keith's circuit would not send him on a regular tour as had the Orpheum circuit. From Philadelphia they moved to Toronto, where they were so broke that Houdini had to write to a friend excusing himself for not sending some handcuffs—he had forgotten to do so in Philadelphia, and to send them from Toronto would involve paying duty, "so I trust you will not be angry if I wait until we leave Canada and send the cuffs to you from the States."

The engagements continued to come in steadily, but after their triumphs in the West the previous year, there was a definite air of anticlimax about it all.

What was to be done?

Early in 1898, Houdini had written to the famous London magician J. N. Maskelyne to ask if he could join his show at the Egyptian Hall. Maskelyne sent a curt refusal: "I have no room for any addition to my company. I seldom change my artists." But things had changed in the two years since then. They were proven crowd-pullers. "Who created the biggest Sensation in California since the Discovery of Gold in 1849? WHY! HARRY HOUDINI! The ONLY recognised and Undisputed King of Handcuffs and Monarch of Leg Shackles," blared a publicity broadside. The time had come for the Handcuff King to conquer some fresh fields. Some time towards the end of April or beginning of May, Bess and Harry decided to try their luck in Europe. On 21 May they still did not know exactly when they would leave—"Possibly we may sail in the early part of June as I have just landed in N. Y. and am rushed fixing things." On 30 May 1900, with no engagements arranged, the Houdinis set sail for London.

8

WITH ONE BOUND
HE WAS FREE

The most famous Bound Man in history was Prometheus. (There were of course countless Bound Maidens, chained to rocks and guarded by dragons. But that is a very different kettle of symbolic fish.) Prometheus annoyed Zeus, King of the Gods, by suggesting that if men had the gift of fire this would be of immense value to them. Zeus, mean-spirited as usual, demurred. He thought that once they had fire men would become conceited and would begin to consider themselves the equals of the gods. Prometheus, regardless, took a reed, lit it on the sun, and returned to earth with the flame. Zeus, looking down, saw the earth studded with thousands of flickering stars. In his fury he sent Pandora to punish mankind with her box of miseries and diseases. As for Prometheus, he was chained to a rock, where every morning a great eagle came and pecked open his body and ate his liver. Every night the wound healed and the liver grew again. Prometheus suffered inexpressible agonies. But, not possessing Houdini's skills (even though he was a demigod), he was unable to free himself. He had to wait hundreds of years until finally he was unchained by Hercules.

Houdini, though a mere mortal, needed no Hercules. In him (this would undoubtedly have been his own view) Zeus would have found an altogether worthier opponent. The reception he received in Europe confirmed his uttermost hopes and expectations.

The Houdinis did not sail for Europe entirely unprepared. They had no bookings, but they knew there were possibilities. In 1899 T. Nelson Downs, the King of Koins, who came from Iowa and was an old friend of Houdini's (they first met in Chicago at the Great Columbian Exposition seven years earlier), had secured an engagement at the Palace Theatre just by mailing some reviews to the management. His coin manipulation act had gone down well. He became a "headliner," made a star-billed tour of Britain, and went on to triumph on the Continent "at the salary of an ambassador." Other American magicians had also done well in London: Howard Thurston the card manipulator; Billy Robinson, who had been Herrmann's old stage manager and who had now set himself up as a "Chinese Mandarin Magician" under the name Chung Ling Soo; Horace Goldin (another old acquaintance from Chicago days), who specialised in "rapid-fire" stage illusions. Houdini, too, sent his reviews—but to no effect. So he decided to see what he could achieve in person.

They arrived in London after a crossing during which Houdini was so seasick that Bess had to tie him to his bunk during the brief periods when she left him, for fear he would try to throw himself overboard. They reached dry land, recovered, found lodgings and set out to assault theatrical agents and managements. At first they had no success. Downs had hit the right moment; the Houdinis had not. Another escape act, Cirnoc, had disappointed the management of the Oxford Music Hall. And some recently billed challenge acts had also bombed. The Bullet-Proof Man had lost all appeal, together with his life, when a marksman shot him in the groin and it transpired that his bullet-proof vest (padded with powdered glass) did not reach down that far. Annie Abbott, the "Georgia Magnet," had faded overnight when a newspaper disclosed that the failure of five men to lift her was attributable to the laws of physics rather than supernatural powers. Faced with Houdini, agents were polite but unforthcoming.

The Houdinis' break came when an agent they were supposed to see was called away. Instead, they met his assistant, Harry Day, a young man just starting out in theatrical management. The two Harrys immediately took to one another—so much so that Harry Day was to represent Houdini for the rest of his life. Day persuaded the manager of the Alhambra, C. Dundas Slater, to give the Houdinis an audition. Slater was impressed with the substitution trunk act but dubious about the handcuffs. He could not really believe that Houdini could get out of any handcuffs presented to him. Cirnoc, for example, had insisted on using his own. If Houdini could get out of Scotland Yard's handcuffs, then he might consider him.

This was what Houdini had been waiting for. An appointment was made with Superintendent Melville for 14 June. The usual routine followed. Melville was altogether dismissive of Houdini's claims. He took a pair of regulation cuffs, locked Houdini's arms around a pillar and led Day and Slater off to his office. They would leave him to cool his heels for a couple of hours. Houdini had freed himself before they had so much as opened the door. On the strength of this, Slater booked him for two weeks at the Alhambra at sixty pounds a week.

A special press performance was arranged before the opening night, during which Houdini was surprised to see a total stranger walk down the auditorium, climb on to the stage and denounce him. Not only was Houdini a fraud, said this person; he was not even an American. *He,* on the other hand, was the Great Cirnoc, and he was the original Handcuff King.

At this point a man in the audience stood up and said, "That is not true. I know that young man is an American. I also am an American and I saw him several years ago doing his handcuff act." He identified himself as Chauncey M. Depew, a distinguished lawyer and politician. Houdini was saved. He whispered to Bess, "Get me the Bean Giant."

The Bean Giant was his showpiece. Its inventor, Captain Bean of Boston, had offered five hundred dollars to anyone who could release himself from it. Houdini had won the bet but forfeited the cash, as he would not reveal his method. The lock of the Bean Giant was so placed that, even given a key, it was impossible to release oneself. "Properly presented this is a good trick for exhibition purposes," Houdini explained some years later to an assistant, "that is to carry a cuff of your own, and show to the public how difficult this handcuff is by locking it on one of your committee's wrists, giving him the original key and asking him to unlock the cuff." In this case, Cirnoc was the "committee." He insisted that, first, Houdini free himself from the cuff. Houdini promptly did so—inside his cabinet and using his own key, "a long one, as it is impossible to reach the handcuff with the regular key and with the aid of the extension you are enabled to reach the keyhole with ease and facility." Then he locked Cirnoc into the cuff and presented him with the regulation key, which, of course, was useless to him. Finally he had to ask Houdini to release him. Next day, the papers were full of the story.

Cirnoc, far from destroying Houdini, had done the opposite. Houdini, however, felt no gratitude for this involuntary assistance. He could never forgive intending competitors. A little less than three years later, while he was playing at the Pavilion, Leicester Square, he received a telegram from his brother Dash: "Cirnoc is dead." Houdini noted: "My most unscrupulous imitator. He died on his way to Australia on my opening night at Alhambra. He tried to ruin my show but only succeeded in making my opening night a sensation."

After this welcome publicity, the Alhambra engagement was a smash hit. It began in early July and was extended to the last week in August. Every night, sceptics brought along their various unbeatable manacles; every night, Houdini beat them. Suspicion grew that he had an assistant hidden inside the cabinet. One night he agreed to do his escape outside it. Police challengers chained and fettered him and fastened the various restraints together behind his back with another handcuff so that he was forced into a kneeling position. He stipulated only that he be allowed to keep his hands out of sight; he escaped within five minutes. He became so famous that Lord Northcliffe, the famous newspaper proprietor, came to his dressing room to ask if he might consult Houdini upon a number of subjects of American interest. Houdini's views would be published in his paper. "It appears he must have thought it over, for they never appeared," Houdini noted.

His engagement would have been extended even further were it not that he had agreed to take his act to Germany.

He was to open at the Central Theatre, Dresden, where he was supposedly booked for the month of September. The Herr Direktor, Gustav Kammsetzer, was, however, still sceptical about the real potential of the act, even though it had gone down so well in London. He explained to Houdini before he went on that when German audiences didn't like something they whistled. If the public whistled, he was to come off at once. "You can well imagine my feelings," Houdini wrote later. "This manager had brought me to the Continent with a contract which enabled him to close me right after my first performance if I was not a success, and I was not aware of that fact until just before going on . . . I had never addressed an audience in German before. I must have said some of the most awful things to make them believe I was good."

There were no whistles. The audience rose and cheered after his very first handcuff release. "When that audience rose in a solid mass . . . I knew I was going to stay my full engagement. And above all the din and noise and shouts and screams of the public, I heard Herr Direktor Kammsetzer's voice shouting like a madman. He ran to the middle of the stage and applauded. He took off his hat and cheered. In fact, I have no fear of saying that I recorded with him the greatest triumph of any artiste he had engaged." He went on to escape from leg-irons and manacles from the Mathilda Gasse Prison, held by heavy locks forty pounds in weight. The house was sold out for the entire month: the takings broke all records. Herr Kammsetzer wanted to keep Houdini for another month, but the Wintergarten, Berlin, where he was to play October, refused categorically. They had already covered Berlin with flyers reading simply:

Wintergarten
HOUDINI
im
OKTOBER

His success in Berlin was even greater, if that were possible, than in Dresden. Everyone wanted to see Houdini. Tickets to the Wintergarten were sold out days ahead: the police intervened to prevent more being sold. The fire department was on alert in case of some catastrophe. The management wired ahead to Ronacher's, Vienna, which had booked him for November, to ask if the opening could be delayed for a month. The Ronacher manager replied that if the Alhambra, which had secured a return booking in December, would also agree to a delay, he was willing: but Dundas Slater refused. The Wintergarten management, desperate not to lose this extraordinary new draw, agreed to pay Ronacher's the equivalent of Houdini's salary for a month—DM4,000 or $1,000—in order to keep him. Triumphantly, Houdini printed a flier—"THEATRICAL NEWS FROM GERMANY 1900"—detailing all this, topped with an elaborate triptych of posed photographs, signed "Kindest regards and well wishes, Respectfully yours, Harry Houdini"—which he sent to everyone he could think of.

Meanwhile, imitation handcuff acts were sprouting like mushrooms. Cirnoc had opened at the same time as Houdini in Dresden, but had failed. In Berlin, the Circus Busch offered to pay Houdini's fine if he would leave the Wintergarten: having failed to secure him, Herr Busch engaged a rival *ausbrecher* named Hermann. Houdini immediately set about undoing this rival. He attended one of Hermann's performances, rushed into the ring when Hermann called for a committee from the audience, ascertained that Hermann's cuffs were not regulation police ones and made his own challenge. He would give Hermann five thousand marks if he could escape from a set of Houdini's cuffs, another five thousand if Houdini failed to escape from the ones Hermann was about to use, and yet five thousand more if the German could replicate Houdini's latest feat—an escape he had made while stripped stark naked in Berlin police headquarters. Hermann, in a fury, resorted to abuse and xenophobia. He accused Houdini of trying to deceive the audience. He was not even an American, he was a "low-life Hungarian."

Not an American! Houdini flourished his American citizenship papers and his passport and yelled, "This brands one of us a liar!" The crowd roared, but the newspapers sided with Hermann, "because he is a *native* and I am a foreigner."

Clearly, however, the vogue for escape artists was such that the market would easily support more than one—so long as it was always beyond question who was in control. Why not keep it in the family? Harry sent a wire to Dash in New York: "COME OVER THE APPLES ARE RIPE."

Dash lost no time in acting on this suggestion. He had been working as a nightclub bouncer, and rumour had it that he had gone too far one night, and someone had died. He arranged to leave for Germany on the first available ship, the *Deutschland*. Harry met him at the Friedrichstrasse station. He had set up the equipment for a duplicate act, including a trunk, handcuffs, straitjacket and musical score. But what was Dash to be called? There could only be one Houdini—and yet there needed to be some echo . . . He played his first theatre as "Harden" (this was supposed to sound English to German ears), then added another "e" to become "Hardeen," which he remained. "Hardeen has made a wonderful reputation in Europe," reported the magic magazine *Mahatma* some time later. "[He has] made quite a sensation coming right after his brother, and is acknowledged as the best copy of Houdini in the profession today."

Copy is the key word here. A sense of uniqueness was essential to Houdini's equilibrium. His immediate destruction of Hermann and Cirnoc was not merely professional—it was compulsive. It was never enough for Houdini merely to defeat a rival. He had to stamp on him, jump up and down on his head, and leave him for dead. He even felt equivocal about Hardeen, who after all had been entirely his own creation. In a complaining letter to another magician whom he thought had been trespassing on his territory, he wrote, "Why, you have acted worse than my brother. He calls himself Hardeen, but not Harry Hardeen."

In a German newspaper dated 9 December 1900, Hardeen is referred to as "Theo Hardeen . . . genannt HOUDINI der Zweite"—with HOUDINI in huge letters while "der Zweite" can hardly be seen. If Houdini was—just—able to accept Hardeen, it was because he never had been and never would be known as anything but an acknowledged copy. This was true even when in fact it was Houdini who was copying Hardeen. It was Hardeen who found out how the straitjacket escape should be presented. It takes quite a time to wriggle out of a straitjacket, and if it is done inside a cabinet there is nothing to prove that there was no assistance. A bored and hostile audience once let Hardeen know this is no uncertain manner. So he promised to repeat the challenge two nights later in full view. The theatre was sold out, and when Hardeen finally accomplished his feat, the crowd went wild. Hardeen sent Houdini the press clippings, and from then on Houdini's straitjacket escapes were all performed on the open stage, to much greater acclaim than Hardeen's. Even so, Houdini's fear that Hardeen would forget himself and step out of his agreed role always loomed edgily between them. In 1907 they were booked to appear in the same cities by rival American circuits. "I don't think that I have anything to fear," Houdini noted, "as I am the originator, and he is like the rest of my imitators, with the exception that he is my brother (and a dam good brother at that.)" But as late as 1911, when he had been world famous for years, Houdini was transported with fury when he arrived in England to find that Hardeen had just completed a tour of his own which appeared to have gone down only too well. Bess had to play the secret peacemaker: "My Dear Bro. Dash . . . Just heard that you are not coming over here *and the reason why,* now Dash please do come over and if Harry does not pay the difference I will. Harry does not know that I am writing this. Now I want to tell you why he is sore, you know we are playing all the towns that you played, and of course there are plenty of guys always ready to tell Harry about your challenges and what you did, and Harry told me you had promised not to do the challenges, etc. Of course he is sore now but I am sure if he sees you he will forget all about it . . . I am as ever your loving sister Bess."

Sir Arthur Conan Doyle, who was to become a good friend of Houdini's, remembered with appalled astonishment his introduction to Hardeen. "He did it by saying, 'This is the brother of the great Houdini.' This without any twinkle of humour and in a perfectly natural manner." It was a revelation to Conan Doyle, that ultra-English gentleman, that such a sentence could be uttered without irony. But irony requires self-consciousness, detachment, self-awareness, and Houdini was sensationally free from any of these qualities. He was merely informing Conan Doyle of Hardeen's role in Houdini's world. An old family friend wrote, equally without irony, that "When Harry passed on, Hardeen really came into his own." The fact was that *until* Harry passed on, there was not the slightest possibility of his doing any such thing.

Leaving Hardeen in Berlin, Houdini filled in a free ten days with the now-customary triumphant sellout at Magdeburg, and then returned to London where Dundas Slater was impatiently waiting. This time he was actually featured above the costly ballets for which the Alhambra was famous, *"which is something unheard of."* "It would be boastful to tell you how big a hit we are over here," he wrote disarmingly to an old friend in Boston (thus telling him nevertheless). From there he moved to the north of England and played a week in Bradford, where on one evening, 8 February 1901, standing room was sold for ten shillings, seats were sold on the stage, and hundreds were turned away. Then they returned to Germany. "We closed a *20* weeks engagement at Alhambra London and jumped here to Germany and stay here at least 6 more months, and at an excellent salary no not an excellent salary but an *'exhorbitant'* or newspaper salary," he wrote triumphantly from Leipzig.

For any performer, such a progress would be astonishing. The only contemporary capable of generating comparable hysteria was Sarah Bernhardt. But Bernhardt was a great actress with many obvious attractions—beauty, spectacular presentations, a scandalous reputation. Houdini, on the other hand, escaped from handcuffs.

It was not as if, at this point, his act was in any way as slick and spectacular as it was later to become. An act such as Houdini's is routinely a team effort. In magic and illusion, part of the essential misdirection lies in the assumption that the performer's assistants are innocent stooges when, on the contrary, they are vital collaborators. As he himself put it: "To avert suspicion from our assistants we make them seem as awkward and clumsy as possible. We have them drop things, stumble over chairs, and make mistakes of a minor nature. We want you to get the idea that these men play no real part in the performance of our tricks; whereas, of course, they are most important cogs in our work. Once I was sitting next to a woman who kept exclaiming at the clumsiness of one of the cleverest assistants I have ever seen. Instead of the magician doing the work, the assistant was really doing nine-tenths of the tricks. Yet he acted his part so well that this woman finally said, 'My! how clumsy that man is! I wonder why the magician keeps him?' " The essential jobs performed by Houdini's assistants and never suspected by the public included dealing with awkward customers who showed up obstreperously in the wings and would not be dissuaded (they were knocked out and woke up some time later elsewhere) and dealing with difficult challenge cuffs by substituting a more tractable set en route from challenger to performer.

Later on, Harry Day had a form letter printed which set out all the elaborate requirements for the Houdini show. These ranged from "Bill Matter (The World-Famous HOUDINI, the original HAND-CUFF KING & JAIL-BREAKER—The only living being who ever escaped from the SIBERIAN TRANSPORT VAN in Russia . . . **Everybody Invited to bring their own Padlocks**)" to an elaborate plan of the "STAGE PLOT for HOUDINI'S Death Defying Mystery, the dressing-room requirements and property list (**DO NOT get anything that is to be Charged to me**)." And Houdini had a form printed up which would enable him to keep track of his reception and working conditions in the different towns he visited, with such headings as OPPOSITION: WEATHER: COMPLAINTS: RECOMMENDATIONS: REMARKS REGARDING BILLING: WORKING OF SPECIAL NIGHTS.

But at this stage there was only Bess, the trunk, the handcuffs and the straitjacket. And the strain was beginning to tell. In 1901 Houdini was only twenty-seven; but although he was emotionally still almost childlike, in point of knocking about the world, he was already a weary veteran. "I am not well," he wrote in March 1901, "as the *prepetual* worry and excitement are beginning to tell on me and I am afraid that if I don't take a rest soon Ill be all done up. You know for the last 11 years Ive had the same strain over & over day in & day out & before this luck streak I had to do 8 to 12 shows a day."

Life on the road in England was eased by the network of "digs" available in every town. Years later, Houdini would ruminate nostalgically on the virtues of British theatrical landladies: "The 'digs' for my wife . . . and myself never cost more than £6 per week, including tips, often considerably less, and the table and service was in some ways superior to the best hotels, including, as it did, pheasants, cream, and all the 'fixins' . . . To my mind no more comfortable form of housing for the itinerant has ever been devised." But conditions in Germany were a good deal less luxurious. "It was the custom for acrobats to travel fourth class. This class of cars then had no cross seats, but were furnished with benches along the sides and during night runs the thrifty tumblers would spread their tumbling pads on the floor and sell sleeping privileges at so much per." In Germany, Houdini was forced to hire a typewriter for the first time: a challenger from Krupps, the armament manufacturers, had hurt his right hand screwing a cuff sadistically tight and he was unable to hold a pen. "To tell the truth I had to get it to attend to my Correspondence, as I do all of my own booking."

He also arranged his own publicity. Houdini was passionate about publicity. In Paris on this first trip to Europe, he had seven men sit in a line along a café terrace on the pavement. Every so often all these men would remove their hats and bow their heads, which were revealed to be quite bald and each inscribed with a letter— together spelling H O U D I N I. From the very beginning, his career may be followed in a trail of posters, flyers, publicity handouts and every kind of stunt imaginable. The smallest details fascinated him. When he began distributing his own films, he sent out meticulous publicity hints. He instanced as a possible advance stunt "Letters starting with I am droping this out of the window, am hemmed in by fire, must die and hope this will reach etc. The next line states that this is the way letters might come if the city was not protected with such an efficient fire department." He added approvingly, "Boasberg took the letters placed them in an airtight box, burnt the corners and smoked them, so they smelt firey." The letters were then sent to all the local chiefs of police.

His detractors point to this avalanche of self-promotion as part of the reason for his enormous fame. This is true insofar as the urge to self-advertisement was a part of his compulsive nature. Just as he had to do what he did, so he had to tell the world about it. But no publicity stunt could in itself account for his success. Publicity was no use without the goods to back it up. And it is at this point, before there were any elaborations to obscure it, that one of the most fundamental aspects of Houdini's appeal is clear to see. Houdini's act did not merely involve Houdini. The audience was in it with him.

There was an occasion in Blackburn in 1902 when audience involvement threatened to get seriously out of hand. Houdini had made his usual offer of twenty-five pounds to anyone who could lock him up successfully. It was taken up on this occasion by one William Hope Hodgson, who had been a soldier, had left the army, and was now trying to get a physical culture school going in Blackburn. Hodgson stipulated that he was to use his own irons and was to fix them himself. Houdini agreed, and deposited the money with the local paper, the Blackburn *Star,* as was his habit (it ensured capacity news coverage).

The two met at ten in the evening of 24 October. The hall was packed. Hodgson was carrying six pairs of heavy irons with clanking chains and padlocks. Houdini examined them. He stated, to a buzz of disappointment, that his claim was that he could escape from "regulation" irons. These, he said, had been tampered with—the iron had been wrapped round with string, the locks altered, and various other steps taken to impede escape. But nevertheless (cheers) he was prepared to try. Hodgson riposted that challengers were to bring their own irons, which was what he had done. Houdini agreed to take him on: but he would need a little extra time. There were more cheers.

Hodgson, with the help of a friend, began by fixing a pair of irons over Houdini's upper arm and pulling his arms tight behind his back with the chain. Then he took a pair of cuffs, pulled Houdini's hands forward and fastened them in front of his body. Such was the pulling and tugging that Houdini reminded Hodgson that he was to fix the irons himself—the challenge did not mention any assistance—and that it was no part of the bargain that his arms should be broken. The assistant stepped down. More cuffs were fastened and pad-locked; Houdini's arms were trussed to his sides; and, to finish, a pair of leg-irons was passed through the chains binding his arms together at the back and then fixed round his ankles. Another pair of leg-irons was added. Then the cabinet was placed over Houdini, and the waiting began. Strict watch was meanwhile kept over Bess and Hardeen, who were at the side of the stage.

After about fifteen minutes, the cabinet was lifted to reveal Houdini lying on his side, still securely bound. He indicated that he wanted to be lifted up. Hodgson refused; the audience hissed and booed; Hardeen lifted his brother to his knees. The cabinet was replaced.

After another twenty minutes the curtain was lifted again. This time Houdini said his arms were numb from the pressure of the irons and asked to have them unlocked for a minute to restore his circulation. Hodgson refused. "This is a contest, not a love match," he said, amid howls from the audience. "If you are beaten, give in." A doctor, examining Houdini, said that his arms were blue, and it was cruelty to keep him chained up in that way any longer. Still, he would not give in, and asked for more time.

Fifteen minutes later he reappeared and announced that one hand was free. There was terrific cheering. The curtain was dropped again. Houdini reappeared at intervals to let the audience know how things were going, and shortly before midnight, he emerged with torn clothes and bleeding arms to throw the last of the shackles on the stage. The huge audience, which had been sitting watching the cabinet for almost two hours, "stood up and cheered and cheered, and yelled themselves hoarse to give vent to their overwrought feel-ings. Men and women hugged each other in mad excitement. Hats, coats and umbrellas were thrown into the air, and pandemonium reigned supreme for fifteen minutes."

Houdini could never have allowed himself to fail a challenge of this kind. He would have seen it as the end of his career. He had to be invincible. And the more he was in the public eye, the more failures mattered. He was no longer a mere dime-museum freak-show performer; neither was he so well-established that he could have passed a failure off. Failure, moreover, would have broken him not just professionally, but personally. As much as any gladiator, he was fighting, each time he appeared, for his life. This was the terrible tension that held the audience during those long intervals when he was invisible in his cabinet. Houdini's actual appearances onstage constituted an astonishingly small proportion of his performance time.

The peculiar intensity of the Blackburn occasion lay in the fact that he was here confronting another desperate man. William Hope Hodgson was a bright lad who had never done very well since he had left the merchant navy. The physical training school was his last throw. If he could defeat Houdini, what a boost that would give him! So he, too, was fighting for his life—something of which the local audience must have been well aware. After this failure, his school came to nothing. (He later took to writing, and became an early practitioner of the science-fiction and fantasy genre.)

Both men were drained by the encounter. But Houdini was not so exhausted that he could not learn the important lessons it held for him. One was that (as when Sergeant Waldron had trapped him with the immovable cuffs in Chicago) he must never again lay himself so open to defeat. The second was that nothing generated the intense emotions upon which his act relied so much as suspense. If he could really get people biting their nails then they would sit and wait happily for hours. But for this to happen the suspense must be—at least in the public's mind—real. The merest notion of a put-up job would destroy him as surely as a defeat. What he gradually learned was to generate the suspense without really facing the defeat.

In 1904, two years after the Blackburn contest, there was a very similar happening at the London Hippodrome. This time the challenger was the *Daily Illustrated Mirror*. A reporter from this paper produced a pair of handcuffs which it had taken a Birmingham blacksmith five years to make and whose lock could reputedly never be picked. Houdini accepted the challenge for the following Thursday afternoon.

Four thousand people crowded into the Hippodrome to watch the contest. At three-fifteen Houdini entered his cabinet, his wrists fastened. Twelve minutes later he reappeared. The crowd cheered: but he was still secured, and said he just wanted to look at the lock in the light. He disappeared; the orchestra continued to play. Twelve minutes later he appeared again, still bound. His knees hurt: could he have a cushion to kneel on? This was granted.

At ten past four, almost an hour after he had begun, he appeared again. He was crumpled and perspiring. Could he be unlocked in order to take his coat off? The reporter, like Hodgson, refused, saying that Houdini only wanted to see how the lock worked. The cuffs would only be unlocked if he declared himself beaten. The crowd, as in Blackburn, jeered. Houdini, with difficulty, extracted a penknife from his pocket and, bringing the coat over his head, ripped it to pieces while the audience cheered. Then he reentered the cabinet. Ten minutes later he reappeared, free. The audience went wild and carried him shoulder-high round the arena.

What really happened on this occasion? One version has it that Houdini really was beaten and that, after he had cut his coat, he called for a drink of water which was brought to him by Bess. In the glass was a key; Houdini, while drinking, let this slide into his mouth. But the *Mirror*'s own report states that "Mrs. Houdini was present, but was so overcome that she had to leave the Hippodrome just before Houdini ripped the coat."

Had Houdini, as it seemed, nearly been caught out again? After his previous experiences, it seems improbable. A third commentator, who claimed that he had evidence to prove his statement, said he believed that the whole challenge was Houdini's idea. He knew the blacksmith, knew there would be no problem with the cuffs, and paid him to offer them to the reporter. After that, he paced the show in just the way that had been so effective in Blackburn—frustrated appearances, begging for mercy, the cruel opponent, the dramatic gesture—and it worked again.

There is no way to be sure. A correspondent who has examined the *Mirror* cuff asseverates that "there was no gaff built into [it]. It contains two genuine Bramah rotary locks which operate in sequence and which contain fourteen active tumblers between them. It's one snazzy piece of hardware." In any event, there could be no more outings for this particular format, or things would start to look suspicious. But it is well-known that later in his career, after he had made a successful escape in three minutes, Houdini would sit behind his screen for half an hour more, calmly playing cards or reading the paper while the band played and the audience on the other side bit its lips, sat on the edge of its seat and wondered whether this time, at last, Houdini had been unable to break free. And when the tension had just become unbearable there he would be, dripping with what looked like sweat but was really water with which he had just doused himself.

But if the difficulty was faked, the anguish was genuine. Houdini's audiences suffered with him because they sensed that they were witnessing not just his body, but his soul. Perhaps this spiritual nakedness—the absence, between performer and audience, of those walls of reserve generally imposed by detachment and professionalism, that sense that the performing and the private selves are separate entities—is the essence of charisma. Houdini, for the same reasons that he lacked all irony, was entirely lacking in reserve. His every peculiarity tended towards this essential confusion and conflation of what was public and what private. If he was de-tached, it was from what should have been his private life. Con-versely, everything that went on in the theatre was terrifyingly personal. It was a revelation of that inner self which escaped him at all other moments. He could reach it nowhere else; there was no-where else it could express its yearnings. The true charismatic, whether actor, politician, or escapologist, is acting under compul-sion—not because he is mad but, on the contrary, *to preserve his equilibrium*. This is the nature of the psychodrama sensed by the audience. The script, naturally, varies.

But it was not just his own drama that Houdini was acting out in his escapes from gaols and handcuffs. It was also the drama of his audience.

Houdini's was a time when relations between performer and au-dience in the theatre had become very formalised. In earlier days there had been no such hard-and-fast separation. In the circular theatres of Elizabethan England, the actors were surrounded by the audience. In the theatres of eighteenth-century Europe, members of the audience not only sat on the stage but reacted noisily to the play and characters. The gap between theatre and life was rather narrow: while the theatre was relatively *informal*, role-playing in everyday life was, on the contrary, so formalised as to be almost theatrical. A person's dress, demeanour, language, were an infallible guide to his place in the world. Moreover, within this hierarchy the actor's place was as a subordinate, a kind of higher servant. In a very real sense, the actors were at the beck and call of their audience. For its part, the audience felt free to express its views of what was going on on-stage—and of what ought to be going on—at any time during the performance.

All this was possible because the urban playgoing public was very small. Audiences were drawn from a narrow band of the well-to-do. They met frequently, attended all the plays, caught all the refer-ences. Performances—even public performances—were intimate affairs; and many performances were not public but private, financed by a patron and given for a select aristocratic audience in a private theatre. But by the nineteenth century this was a vanished world. Shop-bought clothes meant that the lady and her maid, the lord and the bank clerk were not immediately distinguishable on the street. Huge masses of people moving from the country to the city, from the old world to the new, further softened hitherto sharp distinctions. They also vastly increased the potential size of audiences.

The old intimacy, possible only amongst a small and cohesive society, began to disintegrate. The stage presented an increasingly stylised spectacle which, more and more, played out not the life of the audience but its fantasies. Actors and actresses were no longer varieties of upper servants, there to do a job to the satisfaction of their masters, but foci for these fantasies. So the spotlight turned increasingly upon individual performers, giving rise to a new breed: the star, who could successfully embody countless individual dreams.

The first of these superstars was Sarah Bernhardt: Madonna as Phèdre. The fact that she was mobbed by thousands of people wherever she went made her an object of suspicion to the theatrical establishment. But what was proved beyond a shadow of doubt was that there were tens of thousands of people out there who desperately needed someone to adulate—someone like Sarah.

As time went on, Sarah took to appearing, not in full-length plays in a straight theatre, but in excerpts in music halls. This was seen as a humiliation by the world of classical theatre. But it was an entirely logical progression. For Sarah spoke to an audience classical theatre could never satisfy. They came to see her, not the play. Her appeal went beyond culture and education. Her dazzled audiences, for whom she was a kind of deity, were largely drawn from the new urban masses all over the world. They were the kind of people who in an earlier era would have found their entertainment in fairgrounds and travelling shows of all kinds. They were too numerous now to be satisfied with that. So the fairground was brought into the theatre, as vaudeville; and in the few years of its heyday—before it was swamped by the rise of the cinema—it had all the vibrancy, all the assurance of a genuinely popular art form—which the theatre lacked. It was no accident that, in Sarah's view, the greatest English theatrical figure of her time was Marie Lloyd.

Mass communications (ensuring not only national but international publicity) had created Sarah: and the stage was set for the creation of other idols of popular culture. Harry Houdini, who could have flourished in no other milieu than vaudeville—for was his not the archetypal fairground act?—had, in the space of a few months, taken his place in this select band. He was one of those little men—physically small, metaphorically powerless—who were to dominate popular entertainment in the early years of the century. Charlie Chaplin and Mickey Mouse had their distinctive ways of triumphing over authority. Houdini did so in the most direct way it is possible to imagine—by literally breaking free of its shackles.

The fact that this was a large element of his popular appeal is clear from the pattern of his success during this part of his career—the part that was dominated by handcuff and gaol escapes. His popularity was greatest where authority was harshest. In the United States, where most people did not feel particularly oppressed, he did not manage to establish himself until some years later, when his act and its resonances were rather different. In paternalist industrial Britain he did well. But in the two most authoritarian states in the world—Germany and Russia—his success was phenomenal.

This was deeply resented by those who were responsible for keeping the hatches battened down—even though they could not help being fascinated by him. In Germany, where he made frequent appearances, Houdini found himself often at odds with the police. Germany was full of petty regulations which forbade, if they were strictly enforced, almost anything one might wish to do. Houdini ignored them. "It does seem strange," he wrote in 1901, "that the people over here especially Germany, France, Saxony, and Bohemia fear the police so much, In fact the Police are all Mighty, and I am the first man that has ever dared them, that is my success."

The first brush with authority had occurred soon after he arrived in Dresden, in 1900. Houdini wanted to try a new stunt: to be thrown from a boat handcuffed and free himself under water. The police refused to permit this on any account. Houdini did it anyway, and emerged to find a furious policeman on the scene. He was brought before the magistrate, who decided that the only charge-able offence he had committed was walking on the grass, for which he was fined a few pfennigs. The incident (to say nothing of his continuing practice of challenging the police to lock him up wherever he went, invariably to escape) did not endear him to them, and in the following year (1901) there was a more serious difficulty. This time they pursued him with regard to the very strict regulations which then obtained relating to misrepresentation. These had been used before to prosecute entertainers who were not what they set themselves up to be. Now Schutzmann Werner Graff of the Cologne police denounced Houdini as a swindler and published a story to this effect in the *Rheinischer Zeitung* which put Houdini in a very bad light.

Houdini demanded an apology, but was simply laughed at. So he engaged the best lawyer in Cologne and went to court. There were three trials. In the first, Houdini charged Graff with slander. Graff told the judge and jury that he could easily prove his case: he would chain Houdini up so that he could not release himself. Houdini was chained: and to demonstrate just how easy escape was, he agreed to show the judge and jury (but nobody else) exactly how he opened the lock. He won his case, the police were fined, and Graff had publicly to apologise to Houdini "in the name of the Kaiser." He declined to comply, however, and took the case to a higher court. Here he produced a lock which had been specially made by a master mechanic so that, once it was locked, nothing, not even the key, would open it.

The case came to court in July 1902. Houdini escaped from the restraint in four minutes; Graff was ordered to pay all costs (which were heavy, since the case had now been running more than a year) and insert an advertisement in all the Cologne papers proclaiming his punishment "in the name of the Kaiser" and apologising to Houdini for slandering him. Once again he could not bring himself to comply, and took the case to the *Oberlandesgericht,* the highest court, from which there was no appeal. His argument now was that Houdini said he could open safes, and although he had opened handcuffs and cell doors, he had never opened a safe in Germany. The judge decreed that Houdini should try the safe in his office. He was taken there, shown the safe and left alone with it. He was nervous, never having tried a German safe lock before. He gave it a good pull, just to see—and the door swung open: it had not been locked. After "a decent interval" he presented his feat to the judge, who found in favour of Houdini. Graff was fined thirty marks and had to pay the costs of the three trials, as well as the rest of the punishment. Houdini, triumphant, published long descriptions of all this in his publicity releases.

Meanwhile, he was invited to Moscow, to appear at the Establishment Yard cabaret. This was not easy, as he was a Jew and Moscow did not welcome Jews. Bess filled in the papers for both of them, stating that she was a Roman Catholic. They arrived, and Houdini rehearsed his opening speech. He always liked to address audiences in their own language. So before leaving Berlin, where he had been playing at the Wintergarten, he had got an interpreter to teach him a Russian speech, which he had learned by heart. The manager in Moscow, however, was appalled. "My God, we should be ruined!" he yelled at Houdini in German. "That isn't Russian. You are speaking in Polish, which is forbidden, and with a strong Yiddish accent, which makes the offence much worse!" He wrote the speech out again, with the correct phonetics. Houdini went to say it over to himself in a nearby park. When he finally had it ready and turned to go, some policemen leaped from the bushes and frog-marched him to a cell. They were taking no chances with this suspicious, muttering stranger. Houdini was not rescued until the manager, mystified by his nonappearance, got in touch with the police himself.

However, he had used his time to make friends with the police, and now issued one of his usual challenges. He had noticed the Russian prisoners herded through the streets, "carrying their black bread and a pot to cook their beloved *chey,* or what is known in English-speaking countries as common tea." They were transported to Siberia in travelling gaols known as *carettes.* Houdini persuaded Lebedoeff, the chief of the Moscow police, to let him try to escape from a *carette.*

The attempt was set for 11 May 1903. It was a cold day. Houdini was stripped naked and searched—more thoroughly than he had ever been searched before. He was laid on a table, and one man worked upwards from feet to head while another worked in the other direction. Then he was turned over and searched again. He was led into the prison yard, and the *carette* was searched in its turn. Two iron bands joined by a short metal bar were padlocked around Houdini's wrists, and his ankles were fettered. Then he was locked inside the transport cell. Only after this was he informed that the only key that would open the door was in Siberia. If he failed, he faced a long, cold journey. The *carette* was then, at Houdini's request, turned so that its back, containing the door with its one small, barred window, was against the prison wall.

According to one account it took him forty-five minutes to get free; another gives the time as twenty-eight minutes. But free himself he did. The door of the *carette* was still locked; his shackles were on the floor. Lebedoeff was furious. Houdini was searched again, and so was his assistant, Franz Kukol, who had been held at some distance from the proceedings. (Houdini had engaged Kukol, an excellent mechanic and musician, in Germany: the beginning of that team which was to become ever more essential to him.) Nothing

was found. Lebedoeff had promised Houdini a certificate if he succeeded in this escape, but now refused to give it to him. Needless to
say, no newspapermen had been permitted in the prison yard. Nevertheless the story got about, and Houdini became a popular hero,
because everyone hated the secret police. His engagement at the
Establishment Yard was extended from four to eight weeks.

How was this escape effected? Harold Kellock, presumably on
Bess's authority, says he worked through the window aperture. "On
the inside the door was merely a smooth sheet of steel, without any
sign of a lock, but with a little high window six inches square,
crossed by four bars. The lock was on the outside of the door, about
thirty inches below the window." But J. C. Cannell, in his *The Secrets of Houdini,* says Houdini pierced the metal floor of the *carette*
with a "cutter," folded back metal, removed the wooden plank-
ing beneath, and slipped out. The magician Milbourne Christopher
inclines to the window theory. "The lithograph which he had made
to publicize the feat in other countries, shows the window smaller
than it was and higher above the lock. A showman would not give a
clue to his method in his advertising." Certainly he used the door-
hatch in various of his gaol escapes. In Salford in 1904 the trap-door
through which food was passed to prisoners was left open at his
request, to enable him to reach the lock outside the door. And once
he could reach the lock, the only tool he needed was a tiny pick or
piece of wire.

Houdini remained in Russia, playing various engagements, until
September 1903. In that seething and ironbound dictatorship, he
was sensationally successful. "The superstitious court went mad
about me," he told a journalist years later. "The Empress with her
love of mysticism refused to believe that there was a scientific and
mechanical explanation for my magic. The Empress begged me to
stay and give her the benefit of my gifts, but I refused. I attended a
court function where wine was served. It so happens I am a teeto-
taller. I did not know the elaborate court ceremony. It seems that a

refusal to touch the wine served by the emperor is an insult to Russia. I promptly lost my standing at court." During one week in Moscow he earned $1,750. "Have managed to send home a small ship-load of Russian Roubles, so there is no complaint on this side of the question," he wrote from Nijni-Novgorod in August. "Things are still booming with us, and we have never been in such demand as at the present moment. It may be a long time ere we will work America, as I am actually asking for $1000 weekly salary, and to tell you the truth, I am not even anxious to accept that work at that salary. Over here I stay one, two and even 6 months in one City, and have a G R E A T reputation, and in America it means every week jump to another city!! So I will nures Europe as long as it will accept HOUDINI, and then come home to America, and retire." But he was glad to leave Russia, in spite of the money. "After you leave Russia, you feel as if you had yourself come out of some sort of mild prison." He never went back.

Houdini was now established as one of the world's leading performers. By the end of his first year in Europe, he was able to fulfil every immigrant's dream, which is to return in triumph to the place he left in ignominy.

In January 1901 he saw in a London shop window a gown that had originally been designed for Queen Victoria, who had just died. He was by then missing his mother dreadfully, and the sight of the gown made him miss her even more, since the two ladies were very much of a size—small and dumpy, although Queen Victoria was fatter than Mrs. Weiss. So Houdini marched into the shop and offered to buy the gown. The shopkeeper was reluctant to let it go, but relented when Harry offered him fifty pounds for it and explained that it was for his mother. Then he wrote to his mother inviting her over for a visit: he had a fine surprise in store for her.

She arrived while he was playing in Hamburg, in time to watch a special benefit performance at which he was presented with a silver bowl. At the close of the engagement, the party entrained for Budapest. Despite his success, Houdini had not much money. He was never good at business, and was not yet demanding the salaries he could have commanded. He had not learned the lesson of that occasion when Martin Beck had been so happy to raise his salary—but only when he was asked. So the Houdinis and Mrs. Weiss had to sit up all night in a second-class compartment. But once they had arrived, all that changed. The finest hotel in Budapest was the Royal Hotel: this was where Houdini was determined to give a party for his mother. He wanted to book the palm-garden salon for it, but the management refused to let him have it. It was not let out for private parties. Houdini took the manager aside. "After listening patiently to his remonstrances, I revealed to him my plot to crown my little mother and allow her to be Queen Victoria for a few fleeting hours. He immediately consented to become my confederate, for my scheme appealed to his sportsmanship, and he said, 'My boy, for so worthy a cause you may have the room for nothing.' Accordingly the stage was set."

The party was a magnificent one. All the families on both sides were invited, including the most snobbish of his mother's relatives, her Uncle Heller, who had sternly disapproved of her imprudent marriage, and all his parents' friends. The manager entered into the spirit of the game by putting on the clothes he wore only to receive royalty, and bowing all the guests into the salon personally. "How my heart warmed to see the various friends and relatives kneel and pay homage to my mother, every inch a queen, as she sat enthroned in her heavily carved and gilded chair," continues this extraordinary account of rococo wish-fulfilment. "That night, Mother and I were awake all night talking over the affair, and if happiness ever entered my life to its fullest, it was in sharing Mother's wonderful enjoyment at playing a queen for a day. The next morning, after having lived two ecstatically happy days, I escorted the Fairy Queen Mother en route to America." Then he borrowed the carfare back to Germany.

With one bound he was free—from poverty, from humiliation, from entrapment. And, unlike Prometheus, he had loosened his own shackles. But his spirit was not assuaged.

9

THE DISAPPEARING FATHERS TRICK

One of the wittiest and most beautiful tricks in the history of magic was presented by Houdini's literary mentor Robert-Houdin in November 1846, for Louis-Philippe at the château of St-Cloud. It was called the "Disappearing Handkerchiefs." Here is his description of it:

I borrowed from my noble spectators several handkerchiefs which I made into a parcel and laid on the table. Then, at my request, different persons wrote on the cards the names of places whither they desired their handkerchiefs to be invisibly transported.

When this had been done, I begged the king to take three of the cards at hazard, and choose from them the place he might consider most suitable.

"Let us see," Louis Philippe said, "what this one says: 'I desire the handkerchiefs to be found beneath one of the candelabra on the mantelpiece.' That is too easy for a sorcerer, so we will pass to the next card: 'The handkerchiefs are to be transported to the dome of the Invalides.' That would suit me, but it is much too far—not for the handkerchiefs, but for us. Ah, ah!" the king added, looking at the last card, "I am afraid, M. Robert-Houdin, that I am about to

embarrass you. Do you know what this card proposes? . . . It is
desired that you should send the handkerchiefs into the chest of the
last orange-tree on the right of the avenue."

"Only that, sire? Deign to order, and I will obey."

"Very good, then. I should like to see such a magic act. I,
therefore, choose the orange-tree chest."

The king gave some orders in a low voice, and I directly saw
several persons run to the orange-tree, in order to watch it and
prevent any fraud. I was delighted at this precaution, which must
add to the effect of my experiment, for the trick was already
arranged, and the precaution was too late.

I had now to send the handkerchiefs on their travels, so I placed
them beneath a bell of opaque glass, and taking my wand, I ordered
my invisible travellers to proceed to the spot the king had chosen.

I raised the bell: the little parcel was no longer there, and a white
turtle-dove had taken its place.

The king then walked quickly to the door, whence he looked in
the direction of the orange tree, to assure himself that the guards
were at their post. When this was done he began to smile and shrug
his shoulders, "Ah! M. Robert-Houdin," he said somewhat
ironically, "I much fear for the virtue of your magic staff." Then he
added . . . "Tell William to open immediately the last chest at the
end of the avenue, and bring me carefully what he finds there—if he
does find anything."

William soon proceeded to the orange-tree . . . He carefully
removed one of the sides of the chest, thrust his hand in, and
almost touched the roots of the tree before he found anything. All
at once he uttered a cry of surprise, as he drew out a small iron
coffer eaten by rust.

This curious "find," after having been cleaned from the mould,
was brought in and placed on a small ottoman by the king's side.

"Well, M. Robert-Houdin . . . here is a box; am I to conclude it
contains the handkerchiefs?"

"Yes, sire," I replied with assurance, "and they have been there,
too, for a long period."

"How can that be? The handkerchiefs were lent you scarce a
quarter of an hour ago."

"I cannot deny it, sire, but what would my magic power avail me
if I could not perform incomprehensible tricks? Your Majesty will
doubtless be still more surprised when I prove to your satisfaction

that this coffer, as well as its contents, was deposited in the chest of the orange-tree sixty years ago."

"I should like to believe your statement," the king replied with a smile, "but that is impossible, and I must therefore ask for proofs of your assertion."

. . . Louis-Philippe unfastened a ribbon [from the neck of a turtle-dove] that held a small, rusty key with which he hastened to unlock the coffer. The first thing that caught the king's eye was a parchment on which he read the following statement: "THIS DAY, THE 6TH JUNE, 1786, THIS IRON BOX, CONTAINING SIX HANDKERCHIEFS, WAS PLACED AMONG THE ROOTS OF AN ORANGE TREE BY ME, BALSAMO, COUNT OF CAGLIOSTRO, TO SERVE IN THE PERFORMANCE OF AN ACT OF MAGIC, WHICH WILL BE EXECUTED ON THE SAME DAY SIXTY YEARS HENCE BEFORE LOUIS PHILIPPE OF ORLEANS AND HIS FAMILY."

"There is decidedly witchcraft about this," the king said . . . "Nothing is wanting, for the seal and signature of the celebrated sorcerer are placed at the foot of the statement, which Heaven pardon, smells strongly of sulphur . . . But," the king added, taking out of the box a carefully sealed packet, "can the handkerchiefs by possibility be in this?"

"Indeed, sire, they are; but before opening the parcel, I would request Your Majesty to notice that it also bears the impression of Cagliostro's seal."

"It is certainly the same," my royal spectator answered after comparing the two seals. Still, in his impatience to learn the contents of the parcel, the king quickly tore open the envelope, and soon displayed before the astonished spectators the six handkerchiefs which, a few moments before, were still on my table.

As a famous magician put it, "Any unprejudiced person will agree that the effect of this trick was as close an approach to real magic as it is humanly possible to achieve." The main principle upon which it is based—that of predicting which hiding place the king was likely to choose from a selection forced upon him, so that all preparations might be made in advance—is clear. But the skill and artistry of the presentation, down to the key hung round the dove's neck and the smell of sulphur emanating from the box of the devilish Cagliostro, go far beyond such elementary principles. They make it easy to see why Robert-Houdin achieved the success he did in his lifetime—and why his memoirs so enchanted, among others, young Ehrich Weiss. "My interest in conjuring and magic and my enthusiasm for Robert-Houdin came into existence simultaneously," he wrote. "From the moment that I began to study the art, he became my guide and hero . . . I . . . reread his works until I could recite passage after passage from memory. Then, when Fate turned kind . . . I determined that my first tour abroad should be dedicated to adding new laurels to the fate of Robert-Houdin."

But alas! Things did not turn out as Houdini had hoped. "My investigations brought forth only bitterest disappointment and saddest of disillusionment. Stripped of his self-woven veil of romance, Robert-Houdin stood forth, in the uncompromising light of cold historical facts, a mere pretender, a man who waxed great on the brainwork of others, a mechanician who had boldly filched the inventions of the master craftsmen among his predecessors."

Thus the erstwhile disciple vilified the man he had so revered. He did so in a book published in 1909 after several years of preparation: *The Unmasking of Robert-Houdin.*

What had happened to occasion this startling reversal? The sequence of events is—I use the word advisedly—childish.

When Houdini, in London, was first struck by the thunderclap of instant celebrity, the effect upon both his character and his circumstances was profound. Materially he had, for the first time in his life, the means to indulge his predilections. Fame's other gift—at least in his own mind—was a universal entrée. If he wanted to meet somebody he had only to introduce himself and they would—he assumed—feel themselves honoured.

He was still very young—only twenty-six. Events were moving at an extraordinary, a truly magical, pace. In little more than a year he had been transformed from medicine-show barker to the most potent vaudeville draw in Europe. Is it surprising if he saw himself as his own publicity depicted him?

Others were less impressed. In London, during his first heady success there, he decided to visit Charles Bertram, then the most popular magician in London. He got himself up in the height of fashion as he conceived it—top hat, morning coat, striped trousers, spats and stick—and announced himself to Bertram: "I am the Great Houdini." Bertram replied crushingly, "Well, and what of it?" Years later he confided, "You know, Bertram did not like me. In fact, at that time, I was just a swell-headed kid." When it happened, however, he was less philosophical; and even in later years the slight rankled, so that he could not resist denigrating Bertram and his book *Isn't It Wonderful?*—even though Houdini was by then world-famous and Bertram all but forgotten.

By the time Houdini reached Paris in 1902, Robert-Houdin was long dead (he died in 1871, before Ehrich Weiss was born or thought of). But this fact had not registered with the majority of Parisians, who told the inquiring American that he was running a small theatre on the Boulevard des Italiens. This was indeed the Théâtre Robert-Houdin, but it was now occupied by Georges Méliès, the pioneer of film. Méliès was a noted magician, and many of his brief movies feature tricks facilitated by the camera and performed by himself. "At that time," Houdini recalled, "[it] was on the style of a Fair Ground show. They gave performances with moving pictures every time they had a crowd. On Saturdays, at the Theatre Robert-Houdin, they gave Magical entertainments, and I saw Mons. Méliès, who was very interesting to me, and he managed to make quite a hit with the Harlequin the afternoon I was there." Méliès, evidently, was sticking to the traditions of his location. The Théâtre des Italiens, just down the road, had housed the original commedia dell'arte, that theatrical development of the magical medicine show, with its Dottore and Arlecchino—the ancestor of all theatrical magic shows.

From Méliès, Houdini learned that Houdin's daughter-in-law was living in the Paris suburbs. Houdini had a little time on his hands. He had been booked to appear at the Folies-Bergère; but on the day of his arrival its owner had been committed to an asylum and his wife had sold the theatre. The owners of the Olympia were anxious to book him, but the contract would take a few days to work out. He therefore decided to seek out Mme Emile Houdin. He began his campaign with a letter, sent by messenger, with instructions to deliver only to the lady herself and await a reply. The letter ran: "I, as a representative of American Magicians, do hereby kindly ask your consent to permit me . . . to place a wreath on the tomb of Robert-Houdin, also to grant me a few moments, so that I may have the pleasure of thanking you in person for your extreme kindness. Thanking you in advance for your awaited for letter, I do hereby sign myself *Harry Houdini.*"

All this flowery language, however, was unavailing. The letter was delivered, but the lady declined to reply. Later she let it be known that she was ill and did not wish to be disturbed.

Houdini was hurt by this rebuff, but he persevered. Robert-Houdin's tomb was in Blois, his home town, where his daughter Rosalie and her husband still lived. Houdini set off for Blois. Rosalie, a sculptress, was busy when he arrived and did not want to be interrupted; but her husband, Henri, welcomed the young magician. "What a great difference to the reception, or attempted reception, of Mme Emile Houdin," he commented, (the word "reception" here being used in an unusual transitive mode: to reception). "I was soon placed at my ease and shown a great many 'Grandfather Clocks' . . . Although at the time I thoroughly believed he had made them, I would not now be at all surprised if Robert Houdin had bought them and had his name engraved on the various articles."

Henri pointed out that there was nothing to stop Houdini visiting his father-in-law's tomb with or without the family's permission. So Houdini went there, stood for half an hour, returned to Blois to order a wreath inscribed "Honor and Respect to Robert-Houdin from the Magicians of America," collected a photographer, and had himself photographed at the tomb. He sent himself a postcard from Blois to his Paris address, 32 rue Bellefond: "Visited the grave of Robert-Houdin this date. Photographed same. I mailed this P.C. to myself to remember the date." It was 28 June 1902.

But although he had succeeded in his mission, his treatment at the hands of the Robert-Houdin family rankled. When he visited Russia the following year, he met a Frenchman living in Moscow, a M. Bolin, who specialised in building stage illusions. Bolin knew a great deal about magical history, and told Houdini that Robert-Houdin, whom he had met, was by no means the great magical innovator he had made himself out to be in his memoirs. Houdini latched on to this information and set about expanding it. He was himself obsessively interested in the history of magic. From the moment he was able to do so—that is to say, from the moment of his arrival in London—he spent all his spare time and cash fossicking around curio shops and secondhand book stalls in every city he visited. This was the beginning of his great library of magic.

He now set about combining these two obsessions. He would avenge himself for his shabby reception at the hands of the Robert-Houdin family by finding out the history of all the great magician's principal illusions, thus exposing his claim to be a great original for the lie it was.

The task proved uncommonly absorbing. It led Houdini into the byways of magical history, where he was henceforth to find his greatest happiness. Magical illusions generally have venerable pedigrees. Originality lies more often in adaptation and presentation than in pure invention ab initio. In this sense, Robert-Houdin was a real innovator. He was the first to see the possibility of using electric current to produce apparently magical effects. And, as the handkerchiefs trick shows, his presentation was exquisite. He, like many magicians, presented a levitation act, which he called *"suspension ethéréenne."* Who but Robert-Houdin would have thought of pouring ether onto a hot shovel behind the scenes as the levitation began, so that its smell permeated the theatre?

Houdini's diligent searches gave him great satisfaction. He began publishing his findings in 1906, as one of the features in a new enterprise: the *Conjurer's Monthly Magazine,* his first literary venture.

The *Conjurer's Magazine,* whose first issue appeared in September 1906, kept going for two years. In its pages, that cast of persons and obsessions which were to remain with Houdini for the rest of his life are already apparent. Here they all are, waiting to be moved to the foreground and magnified as circumstance dictates. Here is his great collection, choice selections from which are used to illustrate the magazine. Here are the veteran adversaries, unfortunates whose slights (real or imagined) were noted years before, never to be forgotten. An early occupant of this role was Horace Goldin, first met at Kohl and Middleton's on the Midway in Chicago when the Houdinis were trying to supplement their income by selling card tricks and Goldin was already earning seventy dollars a week. He was not helpful to the newcomers and Houdini never forgave him. "Horace Goldin has arrived with his 9,000 assistants and 4,000 pieces of luggage, and the railroad companies are happy. So are all magical apparatus manufacturers, as Goldin is buying all the tricks in the world, as fast as they are turned out." Here are the spirit exposés, railing at the inclination of prominent persons to see the supernatural in every conjurer's repertoire: "W. T. STEAD FOOLED AGAIN . . . Credit certainly must be given to the Zancigs for so completely fooling and pulling the wool over the eyes of this well-educated, worldly man." Here are the old friends, as tenaciously remembered as the old enemies: the magazine's London correspondent was Joe Hayman, whose brother Jack had been Houdini's first partner.

And here are the joys of authorship, which Houdini was now discovering for the first time. The year 1906 also saw the publication of his first book, *The Right Way to Do Wrong*. And the *Conjurer's Magazine* was the vehicle in which he organised the materials for his next two publications: "Handcuff Secrets Exposed" and that excursion into magical history and paranoia, *The Unmasking of Robert-Houdin*, whose publication marked the end of the magazine.

The *Unmasking*'s language is so violent that the unbalanced nature of the whole project is immediately evident. "The master-magician, unmasked, stands forth in all the nakedness of historical proof, the prince of pilferers. That he might bask for a few hours in public adulation, he purloined the ideas of magicians long dead and buried . . . That he might be known to posterity as the king of conjurers, he sold his birthright of manhood and honor for a mere mess of pottage, his 'Memoirs,' written by the hand of another man, who at his instigation belittled his contemporaries, and juggled facts and truth to further his egotistical, jealous ambitions. But the day of reckoning is come . . ."

What has all this ranting to do with the graceful, genial performer who gave only pleasure to those people fortunate enough to witness him? The answer, of course, is—nothing. *The Unmasking of Robert-Houdin* is not about Robert-Houdin. It is about Houdini. He *had* to write it, just as he *had* to perform in the way he did. On 19 July 1907, just before he finished it, he noted in his diary: "Wrote until 2.30 a.m. on Houdin book. This is a labour of love. I shall be happy when it is finished as it will take a lot of worry off my mind."

The first clue as to what was going on is the dedication. The book is *"affectionately dedicated to the memory of my father, Rev. M. S. Weiss, Ph.D., LL.D., who instilled in me love of study and patience in research."*

The overt intention of this is clear and simple. Houdini is presenting himself, as always when he speaks about his father, as a scholar and the son of a scholar. That was the defunct rabbi's role in the Houdini cast-list. To this end, he endows Rabbi Weiss with distinctions he never possessed (far from holding any higher degrees, he turned to religion because he could not make the grade as a lawyer). But the underlying meaning is equally clear. Houdini's father had failed him—failed to educate him, failed to support his beloved mother. Worse, perhaps—that mother had never ceased to be in love with him: their marriage had been "heaven." In this dedication he is associated with a book whose purpose is the destruction of another father figure: Houdini's father in magic, Robert-Houdin, whose name he adopted. Samuel Weiss had failed in his responsibilities towards his son. Robert-Houdin, through his family, had rejected his magical ward. So now Houdini was rejecting *him*. The shrill tone of the book is that of the aggrieved child determined to get his revenge.

Part of the failure of Houdini's real father lay in the fact that the land of his ancestors, in both the physical and the intellectual sense, was closed to his son. Ehrich, who was this father's son, could return to Hungary as a visitor, but the rooted life he might have led there was not available to him, because his father had fled from it. And the intellectual territory of Jewish tradition, which his father inhabited, was also barred to him, because of his lack of education and because there was no place for it in the life the Weisses were forced to lead in America. So he chose his own territory—the land of magic—which he peopled with its own lore and ancestors: the history of magic and the old magicians who had practised it. In this land, he was Harry Houdini.

These two—Ehrich and Houdini—can be seen battling it out in his correspondence. His most personal letters to Bess in the early days are still signed "Ehrich": "Darling Kadaria Wilhelmina Weiss, In the train I woke up—looked for you and our love—Yours till *Death*—Ehrich," reads one written from Dresden in 1903 in a moment of loneliness. Even at the very end, Ehrich still survived—just. In September 1926, a month before he died, he was "your husband until and after the curtain rings down on our times, e'en to the crack of Doom—Harry Houdini (Ehrich)." But the Ehrich signature became increasingly rare. Why inhabit an insignificant and unsuccessful persona rather than a famous and successful one? It was not long before Houdini was Houdini even to his wife. This was not entirely unselfconscious. After one particularly elaborate Houdini signature in a note left for Bess he added, "The rare signature only found on his cheek and in his heart letters to his *wife*." On legal or quasi-legal documents, such as the numerous directions he left for the disposition of his assets after his death, he appended both signatures. But before long, Ehrich Weiss was more or less obliterated. "My legal name is Houdini, not my real name as you say it. That name was the name under which I was born," he explained to a friend in 1917, leaving the position as obscure as ever.

One of the many advantages Houdini had over Ehrich was that, if one father failed him, others were there for the taking. If Robert-Houdin had feet of clay, there remained all the other old magicians. There they all were, just waiting for him.

Where?

In their graves, of course!

Q: What kind of magicians did Houdini like best?

A: Dead ones!

This was in every sense the literal truth. He could never abide competition, and his relations with his compeers were always uneasy. But once they were dead, he loved them. For Houdini, life and death were always seamlessly elided. Death was a vivid presence—increasingly so as time went on, but always there even at this period, when he was still in his twenties. His letters to Bess allude to it constantly—"yours till Death," "yours till the crack of Doom." As soon as he had any worldly goods, his concern was their disposition in the event of his death. The first will I am aware of was made in September 1901, when he was twenty-seven: it divides all the monies in his German bank account between Theo and Bess ("The money mentioned here shall apply only to that deposited in the Deutsche Bank in Berlin"). And even while his friends were living, the prospect of their funeral was always pleasantly before him. Harry Kellar was a famous magician who had taken a paternal interest in Houdini (but with whom he did not fall out). At Kellar's retirement party, Houdini, presenting a bouquet, said: "We have decided not to wait until he has passed to the Great Beyond for his flowers, may he be with us for a long time, but we will give him his flowers whilst he is with us, for you cannot appreciate flowers when you are at rest in the cemetery."

No, indeed.

Henry Ridgely Evans in *The Old and the New Magic* describes Houdini, whom he knew well, as the "Old Mortality of Magic" after the old covenanter in Sir Walter Scott's novel who "went about the country, from one churchyard to another, refurbishing and cleaning up the tombstones of the Puritan martyrs who were killed during the persecutions in Scotland in the reign of Charles II. On account of his pious labors, he was denominated 'Old Mortality' by the peasantry. Now Houdini has a similar penchant, but for the graves of his predecessors in conjuring. He hunts them out; often employs people to fix up the time-stained tombstones, and enacts the part of an Old Mortality of Magic." He invariably had himself photographed by the laboriously sought-out tombs. Robert-Houdin's was only the first of many. There are photographs of Houdini standing in some reverent posture by the graves of Heller, Bosco (which he discovered in Dresden in a state of disrepair, and, the lease on the plot having expired, about to be exhumed: Houdini bought the plot, and deeded it to the Society of American Magicians), John Henry Anderson, the wizard of the North, Lafayette, William Davenport, and countless others.

What do people see in cemeteries?

This has always puzzled me. I can see that such a fascination exists, but I am unable to share it. My parents, whom I loved, are dead: it would never cross my mind to visit their graves. For me, those graves and my parents are entirely unconnected. I could not even bring myself to go back to the cemetery and erect headstones there, as Jewish custom requires, a year after the death. Yet I cannot be so very different from all those people who draw comfort from these actions. On the contrary, the distress I feel at the thought of that meaningless place where my parents lie buried would seem to indicate that one ought to be able to feel something in cemeteries: that the absence of feeling is, in some sense, a deep insult.

The essence of cemeteries is surely that they are, or should be, in some sense *thresholds*. Here, if anywhere, is the point of contact between ourselves and other worlds: the world of the dead, centred upon the recent grave; the world of our ancestors, in the graves all around. Spiritualists sometimes speak of the "borderland," where we may speak to the dead. If "borderland" has a location, it is surely in cemeteries.

But if cemeteries are about roots and ancestors, they are also rude reminders of their absence. Nothing tells me that my roots are *not* here more pointedly than cemeteries. Every poetic country churchyard cries out that my ancestors are nothing to do with this. Would I feel more amid *their* graves—wherever those might be? In that cemetery described by Babel, perhaps? "The cemetery of a little Jewish town. Assyria and all the mysterious stagnation of the East . . . Carved grey stones with inscriptions three centuries old. Crude high-reliefs hewn out in the granite. Lambs and fishes depicted above a skull, and Rabbis in fur caps—Rabbis girt round their narrow loins with leather belts . . . The memorial stone, all overgrown with green, sings of them with the eloquence of a Bedouin's prayer."

It might equally have been Houdini's ancestral cemetery: and he had no more contact with it than I have. Nevertheless, he loved cemeteries—and loved them precisely because they are about ancestors. These cemeteries he everywhere visited *did* contain his ancestors—not his Hungarian ancestors, but his ancestors in magic.

Beside these graves, he was able to orient himself spiritually: to place himself where he belonged. Standing by the grave of some old and all-but-forgotten magician he felt . . .

What did he feel? It was not something he was ever able to express in words. The words that seem to crop up among cemetery-lovers are *serene* and *peaceful*. (They are, as it happens, the words Bess used about the comfort she found in visiting cemeteries after Houdini's death.) Perhaps there was something there of that timeless peace which he otherwise sought in his library. Indeed, one collector drew the comparison directly. "It's a bit like collecting," he said. "There they all are, with their granite."

But for Houdini, there was more to it than that. The clue is in his life: that paradoxical conjunction of compulsive vitality and an obsession with death. It was as if he sucked his life from the jaws of death: and this, in cemeteries, was especially the case. He danced on the graves of those old magicians, and their power passed into him. "Cemeteries," says Elias Canetti, "induce the triumphant feeling that, uniquely among the dead, one is still alive—the moment of exhilaration because of survival." In that sense, Houdini was a sort of antivampire, the least sinister of figures. The stake through the heart, in his hands, blossomed and flourished.

This search for ancestors was not confined to the dead. He set out, throughout his life, to contact as many old magicians as he could. Old is the operative word here. Houdini was able to relax only with older men. *He* was supplanting *them,* which was as it should be. He was always edgy with his contemporaries, and saw younger magicians only as rivals, ready to push him into obscurity and the grave. He had potential threats such as Blackstone and Dunninger expelled from the Society of American Magicians, which he ruled with a rod of iron from the moment he was elected president in 1914.

Some of these older men, like Harry Kellar, became fast friends, even though they were still celebrated. Others had been celebrated in their day but now languished in obscurity: Henry Evans Evanion, whom he met in London and who helped him start his magical collection; Ira Davenport, the old spiritualist performer, in New York State. Houdini took a particular pleasure in seeking them out. He treasured the memory of the time he spent with them just as, later, he saw to it that their graves were not forgotten. Here were living father figures who could replace Robert-Houdin.

Perhaps the most bizarre of these encounters was with Wiljalba Frikell, who had been a very famous magician in the nineteenth century, but who had long since retired. "I have had an argument with FATE," Houdini wrote Dash from Dresden in October 1903; and, for once, he was not exaggerating. Here is his account more or less in full, complete with his habitual misspellings:

Last Feb. just before I left for Russia, I discovered to my astonishment that the old time and well known magician, Dr. Wiljalba Frikell was alive and well. And living in Kotschenbroda. Well—I took the long ride from Berlin to Kotschenbroda which is about six hours, and arrived early in the morning. [He arrived in fact at three A.M. and spent the rest of the night on a park bench, since the station was all closed.] I waited until ten, found the house and rang the bell. Herr Frikell refused to see me. He refused even to come to the window, so that I could have a look at him. Informing me through his wife, that he had made enough bad experiences through his life, and that he wanted to be left alone. Mrs. Frikell said he was not well, and under no circumstances would he allow me to even have a glance at him. I begged and pleaded all day, but in vain. I searched the town for assistance, and even his relatives refused to speak for me. That is I mean an adopted daughter that he has. At any rate I went to a photographer, engaged him to come along with me to Frikell's house, to take a photo . . . Greatly disheartened I left Kotschenbroda, went to Berlin and wrote him a long letter. I sent him (to look at) some of the old time lithos that he used to make use of when he was active. One being spelled wrong, that is his name on it, he corrected same and returned it to me. In this way I managed to open up a correspondence with him, sent him some Russian tea from

Moscow, in fact really became very frienly with him through our letters.

We corresponded regularry, and after my trip to Russia, I returned and brought him another lot of tea. Eventually while I was in Dodrecht Holland playing an engagement with Circus Carre, I was greatly surprised to receive a letter from him to the effect, that he is pleased and honored at the interest I have taken in his welfare, and would like very much for me to pay him a visit. This was in the middle of September, so having a contract with the Central Theatre in Dresden, I made all arrangements to visit him during my stay in Dresden.

I wrote him whilst in Dresden and invited him to come and see me, as I would not be able to get to Kotschenbroda until Thursday. My Lithographer Zier from Leipzig having journeyed to Dresden to show me some new samples of lithos that I was desirous of having for England. Well Thursday came, and found that we gave no performance that evening, so took the opportunity to go to Berlin.

But again wrote him that I would positively call Saturday. In the mean time he came to Dresden, monday looking for me but failed to locate me. He is 87 years of age and rarely leaves his home. At the Theatre they refused to tell him where I was stopping and he went to the Konig Kaffe, and waited several hours, but finally being unable to see me, he went back home. Yesterday morning Sat. I took the 1.14 train for Kotschenbroda, as that place is only 20 minutes' journey from Dresden.

Arrived about 1.35 and as my appointment was for two o'clock I walked very slowly towards his Villa. I did not wish to arrive too soon. (and I did not)

I slowly reached the house, I rang the bell, it seemed to ring with a peculiar shrillness, I felt a something in the air which I atributed to the fact of being able to see Frikell when a lady came to the door and said "You are being waited for."

I entered, and found to my great and unspeakable astonishment that Wiljalba Frikell had died two and a half hours—while waiting for me!!!!!!

I saw the man—but he was dead.!!! He was not cold yet. he had died of heart failure. Mrs. and Mr. Frikell had dressed up especially to greet me, but Death forestalled my visit . . . Well my dear brother—can you imagine my feelings.

There lie the man who had sworn he would not see any stranger as long as he lived—and Fate compelled him to keep his word.

His wife informed me that he was all worked up on my expected visit and the day before (Friday) had cleaned up everything and had written down a lot of dates for me . . . There lay the old man lifeless and not even stiff or cold. His well groomed form lay on the lounge, where his goodwife had placed him when he grasped at his heart crying "My heart, what is the matter with my heart, O—" that was all he said. His face was still wet from the Cologne that his wife had thrown into his face, trying to revive him, and the wet sheets were still on the floor, . . . I never was so completely defeated in all my life. This had an awful effect on me, and I remained about two hours, then left meditatingly for Dresden. He will be buried tuesday and I shall attend his funeral. Will send a wreath for the S.A.M. [Society of American Magicians] and one for myself.

. . . last Monday he went to the photographers, and had his photo taken, something that he had not done in years. The proof he had taken was crooked, and thursday Oct 8th he had another sitting, saying that he wanted to give Houdini a good photo, in return for his . . . Madame Frikell will let me have it as soon as it is finished.

Characteristically, Houdini mailed two postcards back to himself in Berlin so that he should not forget the date.

Later, Mrs. Frikell told Houdini why her husband so obstinately refused to see him on his first visit. "It appears that he once had an assistant, a lady for the suspension, and they had a natural son. He was under the impression that I was a grandson, and wanted money."

Still, the supply of father figures did not run dry. The next year, 1904, Houdini was in London. He caught a severe cold which threatened to turn into pneumonia, and for the first time in his life was forced to cancel some performances and stay in bed. A newspaperman who called on him printed a piece about a number of old programmes and playbills which he had picked up and which were scattered around the bedroom. The day the article appeared,

Houdini received a note on a stained piece of paper from Henry Evans Evanion. Evanion said he had some articles which might interest Houdini; Houdini, always a prompt correspondent in a case of this sort, replied at once asking him to call at one the next day.

One o'clock came and went: there was no sign of Evanion. At about four in the afternoon the doctor told Houdini he was allowed to walk once around the block in the mild sunshine. As he left the hotel, the porter told him that an old man had been waiting to see him since one o'clock, but that he was such a disreputable-looking character that they had not allowed him to go up. He was still there, huddled in a corner, a bent figure clutching an enormous portfolio. They sat down on a sofa to examine it. Inside was a treasure-trove of materials—original programmes of all the great magicians of the last century, engravings, lithographs . . . Next morning, without his doctor's permission, Houdini took a cab to Methley Street, where Evanion lived in a dark basement. There they spent the day over a succession of cups of tea poring over Evanion's collection, until Dash and Houdini's disgusted doctor tracked them down at midnight and dragged Houdini away.

Over the next few months, Houdini bought the bulk of Evanion's collection, which somewhat eased the latter's financial situation. A year later, while he was playing in Wigan, he heard from Mrs. Evanion that her husband was dying of cancer of the throat. Houdini dashed back to be with his friend during his last days, and to see that he had every comfort. A fortnight later, Evanion's funeral took place. "Poor Evanion," Houdini noted in his diary that day. "He certainly was the greatest collector of magical material in the world. Although I advertised the funeral in the papers, no one was there but four old women and two nieces, with Mrs. Evanion. Paid funeral expenses." He also went on helping Mrs. Evanion—the first of a long string of pensioners he was to amass as his life went on.

For Houdini was always keenly aware of the transitory nature of luck. Things might suddenly change for the better, as they had with him: but all that good fortune might as suddenly vanish. "For every conjurer who died well off," he wrote a few years later, "we can name many that died in actual want . . . the magician who is enjoying a little meed of success should take warning from those who have gone before. Tomorrow may bring a better trick—by another man—but today is the time to save against the morrow when popularity wanes." Poor old Evanion might be a vision of his own future. Perhaps he saw his pensioners as a sort of amulet, a bargain with Providence: if I do this, I shall be spared that. (As he was.)

These good deeds went unremarked; sometimes even he was unaware of his commitments. He was once joyfully greeted by a man who, when Houdini pushed him aside and said he didn't know him, protested, "But you have been paying my rent for the past eleven years!"

As the years passed, stories began to circulate to the effect that Houdini regretted the tone he had taken in *The Unmasking of Robert-Houdin*. Not everyone thought this. One friend commented, "In my many conversations with Houdini on magical history, I never knew him to depart one whit from his statements regarding Robert-Houdin." Nevertheless, it seems clear that his sense of outrage had somewhat abated, and he saw that he had made a fool of himself. But his retreat was to self-justification, more than regret. "When a magician advertizes a trick as his version like you do the coin ladder that is *permissible*," he wrote to a magician friend. "But Robert-Houdin announced them all as his own tricks, and that is where the imposition came in . . . The older I get the more I know Houdin never invented his feats. The only mistake I made was in calling my book Houdin Unmasked. It ought to have been History of Magic from 1800 to 1850. In this way it would have shown Magic as it ought to have been known." But in that case, Houdini would still have felt compelled to unmask Robert-Houdin.

10

ALL IN THE MIND

Perhaps Houdini's single most famous exploit was the Detroit Bridge Jump. This took place on 27 November 1906, when he jumped, manacled with two sets of handcuffs, from the Belle Isle Bridge into the Detroit River. What happened next was told and retold a thousand times. The river, ran the story, was frozen. A hole had been cut in the ice for Houdini. He freed himself successfully from the handcuffs, but when he surfaced, he found that the current had carried him away from the hole.

Among the spectators, panic mounted. His team knew that Houdini could not hold his breath for more than three and a half minutes under water. The arrangement was that if he did not appear after three minutes, a roped man would jump in after him. But the assistant was understandably chary of committing himself to the ice-bound river. Instead, he threw a rope down through the hole. Bess, who had not been able to bring herself to watch the jump and was in her hotel room, heard the newsboys below her window shouting, "Houdini drowned! Houdini drowned!"

Houdini, meanwhile, had realised that he could survive, while he swam round looking for the hole, by breathing the air which was trapped between the water and the ice. Then he saw the end of the rope. He swam towards it and clambered out. Cheers resounded. Bess welcomed him with tears. He spent the next several hours thawing out and, that night, played to a packed house.

So runs the tale. But there have always been difficulties with it. One of these is that on that day, 27 November, the temperature, although cold, was above freezing. So Houdini's publicists moved the date of the jump to 2 December, when the temperature did not rise above 30°F. But in order for thick ice to form on a big river, the temperature would have to be much colder for much longer.

Was the jump, then, simply a figment of Houdini's publicists' imaginations? James Randi, the magician and Houdini enthusiast, assured me that this was the case. He met Gladys Weiss, Houdini's little sister, at a party on Long Island in 1953, when Gladys had with her a huge pile of postcards sent her by her brother while she was still a schoolgirl. After she told him how the girls at her school collected postcards, especially foreign ones, he sent her a postcard every day for two years while he was on tour. On the date in question, said Gladys, Harry and Theo were both in Europe, and she had the postcards to prove it. Houdini's publicists had put the story about in order to keep his name before the American public. Houdini was furious with them, because he reckoned that the truth, if it got out, could be severely damaging to him. But in those days long-distance communications were not what they are today. Nobody thought to check, and the story just passed into legend, as had been intended.

In fact the question of whether he did or did not actually make the jump, whether he did or did not actually fight his way through the ice, is of little consequence. The myth has its own reality, more solid than that of any mere happening. Houdini himself adapted the story freely in his lifetime. In a piece written for the *Strand Magazine* in 1919, he places the exploit in Pittsburgh, has himself shut in a trunk as well as handcuffed, and specifies that the ice was seven inches thick. Perhaps someone pointed out to him that the Detroit River, which is very fast-moving, never entirely freezes over.

As it happens he did make that jump—or a jump—from the Belle Isle Bridge that November day. Despite the evidence of Gladys's postcard collection (perhaps it was Theo who was sending them— he remained in Europe while his brother returned to the States) Houdini certainly was in Detroit at that time. He was booked for two weeks at the Temple Theater. And on 27 November 1906, the story appeared on the front page of the Detroit *News:*

"HANDCUFF KING" JUMPS MANACLED
FROM BRIDGE

———

Handcuff King Houdini Performs Remarkable
Feat and Comes Out Safely

———

Had a Rope Tied Around his Waist and Tied
to Bridge to Safeguard against Accidents

Tied by a lifeline a hundred and thirteen feet long, handcuffed with two of the best and latest model handcuffs in the possession of the Detroit police department, nerved by the confidence of a lion in his own powers . . . Houdini, the wonder worker at the Temple theater, leaped from the draw span of the Belle Isle Bridge at 1 o'clock this afternoon, freed himself from the handcuffs while under water, then swam to a waiting lifeboat, passed over the unlocked and open cuffs and clambered aboard.

Such is prosaic reality.

The bridge jump was part of a desperate campaign he was then conducting to bring his name to America's attention. It worked, or something did: that week broke all attendance records at the theatre. But Houdini, at this time, was by no means the draw in America that he was in Europe. From Europe in 1902 he wrote to a friend: "If I don't come to America this summer, it will be at least three years before I will again land my small feet on the land of the free and the home of the dollars. I am booked up so far that it seems to me that I am booked for life . . . by the time I have my work all played, I think I can sit back and look at the world from my chair . . . I talk German or French, as well as Hungarian or English, but you ought to hear my pronunciation, that is the whole secret of my success in foreign countries. It makes them all friendly with me ere I have performed a single trick." In 1904 it was still the same story. "There is no possible chance of me working America, until season of 1905–6, and if I dont work America then, will N E V E R play at all," he observed. He was engaged for months ahead and could, if he so wished, engage himself for several years.

But he missed his mother, and the number of flying visits that could be made across the Atlantic was necessarily limited (especially given his terrible seasickness). Besides, he was American, not European. He would have to try his luck at home sometime. In 1904, on a quick visit, he acquired a home base in New York. It was a twenty-six-room mansion at 278 West 113th Street, in the respectable "German section" of Harlem. It had been built ten years earlier, but Harry and Bess were its first occupants. Harry's bathroom, with its eight-foot square mirror before which he could practise and its out-size tub in which he could rehearse under water escape techniques, was worked with a mosaic H; Bess's, on the floor below, with a B. There was also a basement laboratory-workshop where he could build his equipment. Into this house Harry moved his mother, who was thus finally able to quit the flat on Sixty-ninth Street, and the already enormous collection of theatrical memorabilia which he had acquired from Evanion and countless others, and which had been following him around Europe, expanding all the while.

He also made time, during this visit, to plan for the future and revisit the past. He acquired a burial plot in the Machpelah Cemetery, Cypress Hills, to which he moved the bodies of his father and brother Herman. He took the opportunity to inspect the corpses: "Saw all that was left of poor father and Herman; nothing but skull and bones," he noted in his diary. "Herman's teeth were in excellent condition." And he paid a flying visit to Appleton, where he had been happy. He was interviewed there by the young Edna Ferber, who was to become known as the blockbusting author of *Cimarron* and *Showboat,* but who was then a cub reporter on the *Appleton Crescent.* She failed to find him at his hotel or the theatre, but ran into him by chance outside a drugstore opposite her office. "He is a quick nervous chap, inclined to jump when an unexpected noise is heard and to shut his eyes until they are almost closed, when speaking under excitement," she noted. She found him "pleasantly and very interestingly dressed in the conventional light grey summer suit, oxfords, flowing tie and sailor hat. One would never think him of the 'profesh' unless, maybe, his diamond shirt stud might speak. But then, Armour wears diamond shirt studs too . . . The reporter was allowed to feel his forearm, which is amazing, as massive and hard as a granite pillar. His neck, too, is large, and corded." He confided to her his future plans. "I think that in a year I may retire. I cannot take my money with me when I die and I wish to enjoy it, with my family, while I live. I should prefer living in Germany to any other country, though I am an American, and am loyal to my country. I like the German people and customs. Why don't I go then? Why it is too far away from my mother, who lives in New York City with a couple of my young brothers." Miss Ferber asked him about the secret of his wonderful escapes. "My secret? Well, certainly it is a trick of my own," he replied enigmatically. He confided that, while he was in England, he had been offered "an enormous sum of money" if he would consent to establish a school of burglary. But he had declined. At the end of the interview, he dropped a metal object into Miss Ferber's hand. It was the padlock to the vending machine full of chocolate and chewing gum against which he had been carelessly leaning. "Better give this to the drugstore man," he said. "Somebody'll steal all his chewing-gum." The reporter left to write up her story, "tottering with admiration."

Then it was back to Europe, where Harry Day was now insisting that he be paid on a percentage basis, which, as he almost invariably played to capacity audiences, substantially increased his earnings. His much-vaunted retirement was postponed again (as it would be until he died): an American tour was arranged for the following year. "Then I will return to Europe for my last trip, as I will be well pleased to retire on what I have managed to collect."

While he had been unknown, Houdini's outstanding characteristic had been his unwavering, almost absurd certainty that he was unique and would be famous. Now that this, as if by magic, had actually happened, he was plagued by insecurity. "A rich man," says Canetti, "collects cattle and hoards of grain, or the money which stands for them. A ruler collects men . . . whom he can make die before him, or take with him when he dies. A celebrity collects a chorus of voices. All he wants is to hear them repeat his name."

In the showbusiness community, insecurity such as Houdini's was the rule rather than the exception. George Burns said of Al Jolson, "It was easy enough to make Jolson happy at home. You just had to cheer him for breakfast, applaud wildly for lunch and give him a standing ovation for dinner." The movie kings demanded constant flattery and unquestioning kowtowing. One of the many reasons for this was that their success had a miragelike feel to it. At any moment the whole thing might melt away and they would be returned to the dismal realities of the ghetto. Both Adolph Zukor and Louis B. Mayer were plagued by nervous skin rashes. When Mayer met important people he was often terrified. He would stand with tears in his eyes until his secretary calmed him. And spending his now-plentiful dollars did not come easily to Mayer. He did not build a home of his own until 1925, seven years after his arrival in California; and when he did, it was not in Beverly Hills among the stars but in Santa Monica, because then he would be near the ocean and would not have to spend money on a second vacation home.

Houdini, the essence of whose public persona was boundless

courage, was debarred from showing any of the fears he may have felt. But those fears were nonetheless real. He never made any secret of his insecurities regarding money. The prospect that he might wake up one morning and find himself returned to poverty never ceased to plague him. It was one of the recurring themes of the *Conjurer's Magazine*. Ten years later, in 1916, addressing Rotarians in Cincinnati, the same refrain was still running through his mind. They should not think that a high-priced artist might take things easy. "You should rather say he has a temporary spurt of prosperity . . . The moment an artist loses his personality and magnetism, the moment his secret leaks out, the curtain comes down on his prosperity. He is not like a businessman who can bequeath his business to his son—for the artist cannot fasten his personality and powers upon another."

The poverty terror, it will be noticed, is inextricably linked with another: that of his "secret leaking out." Just as Houdini sucked in strength and power from his contact with those old magicians whom he visited so assiduously both before and after their deaths, so he lived in constant terror that others, rivals and imitators, would purloin his methods—his "secret"—and debase his currency. They would drain his powers—his magical powers, and hence the most magical power of all, the power to earn money—away from him. He was always on the alert for this, and when he spotted some sign of it, the blackguard in question had to be compulsively and comprehensively destroyed.

A scene of this kind took place in Glasgow, where he was booked to perform at the Zoo on his return from New York in 1904.

It might have seemed improbable, to judge from the reception he received there, that he should be worried about imitators. "The Northern District of the city was in a state of uproar last night," reported the *Glasgow Herald*.

. . . You might have walked on the heads of the surging, struggling, swaying mass of people almost from George's Cross to the Normal

School. A stranger within the city gates might well have wondered what strange happenings were abroad to bring out such a curious congregation. And yet the explanation was simple. Houdini, the Handcuff King and Prison Breaker, was announced to have accepted a most unique challenge which he would try in front of the spectators in the Zoo . . . It was evident that only a small proportion of the huge crowd could gain admission. There was no turning back, however, and the mass pressed on, obstructing the car traffic, and giving the police who endeavoured to preserve order a rough time of it . . . Inside the crush was as great as the regulations of the Police Act allow. When "The Manacle Manipulator" appeared, with his small stature, coal-black hair and eyes, and his deliberate articulation, with only a tinge of the American accent in it to give it flavor, there was an ovation. Excitement was rife, and for the distinction of securing a seat on the stage something like 50 people paid five shillings each.

Houdini does not boast too much to the audience. He told them simply that he meant to get out of the box which Messrs. J. & G. Findlay had specially made in order to test his ability to do so. Of course, he said, he could not say he would, but he would try . . . When he had asked for volunteers to come on the stage and "put a nail in his coffin" without receiving any response, eight carpenters set to work. They nailed and roped the box. With the driving of each separate nail the excitement increased . . . Afterwards the casket was placed inside the curtain on top of the raised platform to show that there was no trap-door trickery.

Houdini was left to his thoughts—and his trappings; the audience were left to their curiosity and conjectures. For an interval of about 15 minutes the spectators, consumed with curiosity, waited for something to eventuate. The "man who knows and doesn't care who knows that he does know" was just beginning to throw out hints that "Houdini's fairly boxed this time" when—Houdini himself appeared before him to disprove his statement. Covered with smiles and sweat, the mystifier was minus his hat and boots, while his clothes and collar were crumpled. Houdini had all evidence of a stern struggle, safely negotiated, but the box was left as if untouched. Not a nail was loosed, nor was one of the three binding ropes tampered with. It was all very mystifying. If the cheering of the audience can be taken as an indication, they certainly obtained full value for money and the fancy prices many of them paid for admission; prices being doubled and trebled.

That performance took place on 22 September. A greater triumph can hardly be imagined. But a week later, Houdini found that a rival—evidently hoping to capitalise on his extraordinary success—was advertising an escape from "an unprepared coffin." He could not let this pass. On 30 September, in front of a house jam-packed as always, he had a coffin brought onstage and demonstrated just how his rival had lied and cheated. The coffin was far from being "unprepared." It had been tampered with between the time it was left in the lobby for inspection and the time it appeared on stage. In the intervening period, the long screws holding the ends in place had been removed and short screws substituted. Houdini lay down in this coffin, had the lid secured, and showed how he could get out by pushing the ends out. Then he prepared the coffin on his own account. All the screws were replaced and tightened. He got in, had the lid clasped down, and invited a committee to add screws of their own anywhere they chose, and then to seal them so that any tampering would show. Some pasted stamps over the screwheads and inscribed their initials; others pasted stamps across the crack between the coffin lid and the sides. Then the cabinet was lowered over the coffin. In a few minutes Houdini emerged: behind him was the coffin, apparently untouched.

The psychology of such a performance is rather subtle. It turns on the inherently absurd notion that there is such a thing as an honest trickster. Houdini always presented himself as the one perfectly straight man in a crooked world. In a typical example, he talks about P. T. Barnum and his motto that "The American people want to be humbugged." He comments: "In my own particular work I find there is so much that is marvelous and wonderful that can be accomplished by perfectly natural means that I have no need to find recourse to humbugging the public."

Houdini was always at great pains to emphasise his absolute freedom from dishonesty. His frequent recourse to nakedness was a sort of metaphor for this. The impression of straightforwardness was reinforced by the straitjacket escapes, which he performed in full view and which were demonstrably not tricks, but feats of strength and suppleness. His incorruptibility was something he continually stressed. In 1906 *The Right Way to Do Wrong: An Exposé* discussed the methods and motives of a variety of thieves and tricksters, as revealed to him by police chiefs he had met in the course of business. In it, he takes a sternly moral line: "Disgraced, they are ruined for life, often ruining all their family. It is a terrible thing to have the finger of fate point at you with the remark, 'His father is serving time for doing so-and-so' . . . To those who read this book, although it will inform them 'The Right Way to Do Wrong,' all I have to say is one word and that is 'DON'T.' " And this impression of straightforwardness was no mere mask, cynically assumed. Houdini himself was entirely convinced by it. In Bradford a challenger had suggested that Houdini let himself be tied up so that he could not escape. The challenger would bet a large sum on the outcome, and they would divide the winnings. Houdini rejected this out of hand. He wrote contemptuously in his diary: "Guess he didn't know how I was brought up."

Because he was himself convinced he was able to convince others. He presented himself as an exemplar of straight dealing because that was how he saw himself. His self-righteousness was an essential part of his armoury. Yet how was he able so shamelessly to ignore his own deceptions?

"A despot," observes Canetti, "is always aware of his inner malevolence and therefore must dissimulate. But he cannot deceive everyone in this way. There are always others who desire power and who do not acknowledge his claims, but regard themselves as his rivals . . . He waits for the right moment to 'tear the mask from their faces'; behind it he finds the malevolence that he knows so well in himself. Once they are unmasked he can render them harmless." But Houdini was never aware of his own despotism. He was too much of a solipsist for that. In his world, all rivals were unconscionable villains, and he did not hesitate to destroy them by breaking the first rule of showbusiness solidarity—the very act for which he himself condemned so many of his compeers to the outer reaches of his displeasure: he betrayed their techniques. In *his* case, however, that was all right. "I am induced to take this step for the manifest reason that the public of both hemispheres may, through ignorance of the truth, give credence to the mendacious boasts and braggadocios of the horde of imitators who have sprung into existence with mushroom rapidity of growth, and equal flimsiness of vital fibre, and who, with amazing effrontery and pernicious falsity, seek to claim and hold the credit and honor, such as they may be, that belong to me," he fumed.

How did he know about those techniques which he revealed with such relish? Because, of course, he used them himself, time and again. Those techniques belonged to him, so he was free to reveal them if he chose. In the case of the coffin exposé, replacing long screws with short before a performance was one of the standard methods by which he himself had escaped from a variety of containers. On the Glasgow occasion, however, that method was ruled out. Houdini had to find some other way. The implication was that he did not (like his rival) use trickery. How, then, was it done? By magic? This, indeed, was the impression given by his performance.

So he sowed the seeds of a confusion which underlay that extraordinary power he exerted over the public imagination. Houdini always insisted in stentorian tones that he had no magic or supernatural powers. He had his "secrets"—that word he so often used—and naturally he was not telling anyone what those might be. They certainly had nothing to do with the puny secrets of his dastardly rivals. These "secrets" of Houdini's acquired a public life of their own. There is a rumour that, like Pandora or Joanna Southcott, he left them locked in a box, not to be opened until a certain number of years had elapsed after his death.

Most of these secrets were in fact known in Houdini's lifetime. He tended to make them public when they began to leak out, or when he had replaced them with something better—which had the added advantage of making things more difficult for hopeful competitors. They had, as he always said, nothing to do with magic. In the case of the Glasgow coffin, the secret was in the screws attaching the *bottom* of the coffin to the sides. These were good, long screws. They attached the coffin bottom to lengths of dowel inserted into the thickness of the sides. When Houdini wanted to get out, he turned over onto his front, crouched on his knees and levered the top away from the bottom by bodily force. Then he carefully stood the coffin on the dowel pillars and forced it down by jumping on it while the band played to cover any noise he made. His real advantage over his rivals lay in his prodigious capacity for misdirection, for controlling his audience, for devising new techniques—that, and the terrible innocence with which he exposed himself, body and soul.

Such secrets as he did possess were not the sort which could be bought, sold and finally "revealed." They were the kind of thing he discussed with an Australian reporter a few years later (in 1910): "I am strong, as you see; strong in flesh, but my will has been stronger than my flesh . . . I have done things which, rightly, I could not do, because I said to myself, You must; and now I am old at 36 . . . If the thought is intense enough, the pain goes—for a time. It is good for me that I am not a tall man. Why? Because I must be quick! quick! and a tall man is always slow. It is so through all professions. The best men are not too high . . . All the mean, cunning men that I have known—short! All the keen, eager, ambitious men—short! And for work—the tall man has too much to carry, he is too far from the ground, he cannot lose and recover balance as is necessary—in a flash."

In the fall of 1905 he opened in the Colonial Theater, New York, as a top-liner, the start of a six-week tour for which he was to receive $5,000. This was the tour which would make or break his American reputation.

Never had he tried harder. He devised spectacular feat after spectacular feat with which to catch the headlines.

In New York he performed Robert-Houdin's beautiful trick with the vanishing handkerchiefs. In Houdini's version the handkerchiefs were sent to the foot of the Statue of Liberty. He did not pretend to have originated this trick, but—perhaps ashamed of acknowledging its true provenance, since he was at that very moment writing *The Unmasking of Robert-Houdin*—said he had learned it from old Henry Evanion.

In Washington, D.C., he performed an exploit which especially appealed to him and which featured in all his publicity thereafter. This was the Guiteau escape. The warden of the tenth precinct gaol challenged him to defeat his new lock system. Houdini was particularly interested in Murderers' Row, which comprised seventeen cells, then containing eight prisoners awaiting judgment or execution. He asked to be locked into Cell No. 2, which had once housed Charles Guiteau, the assassin of President Warren Harding. Notorious assassins always fascinated him: he was particularly gratified to step, if not into Guiteau's shoes, into the cell which had seen his last days. This was now the home of one Hamilton, who was alleged to have smothered his wife and then sat up all night beside the body celebrating. Houdini, naked as always, was locked inside while Hamilton cowered in a corner.

Can any more bizarre scene be imagined? The small, naked man is locked inside the cell. The warden stomps away. From their hiding places—in his bushy hair, between his prehensile toes, stuck with a blob of chewing gum to the underside of a ledge—Houdini retrieves his miniature picklocks and the pieces of wire which serve as handles and levers. He frees himself. Then, still naked, he runs to the cells housing the other inmates. Quickly he lets them out of their cells—too astonished by this strange vision to protest, too alarmed to take advantage of the situation—and locks them up again in cells not their own. "As I was stripped . . . the prisoners thought the devil, or someone akin to him, was in their presence, and, trembling with fear, they obeyed my command." Then he finds his clothes, dresses, lets himself out of the wing and rejoins Warden Harris. E. L. Doctorow, in *Ragtime,* transposes this scene to the New York Tombs and gives it a distinctly sexual flavour. In his version, the society convict, Harry Thaw, in prison for murdering his wife's lover, undresses as Houdini dresses, and waggles his penis at him through the bars: a scene which acknowledges the sexual agenda underlying Houdini's insistent professional nudity.

Naked gaol escapes were one constant feature of his publicity. So were bridge leaps. There were escapes from safes. There were strait-jacket escapes. There were escapes from special challenge contain-ers: in Washington, D.C., September 1906, from a zinc-lined piano box; in Boston, early 1907, from—yes—a coffin whose lid was nailed down by members of the audience; from a paper box (razors and glue were his tools for working with paper); from a ladder to which he was locked; from an iron boiler; from a glass box. Another boiler, in Toledo, Ohio, nearly defeated him; in San Francisco, a government mail-pouch held him for twenty-five minutes. In De-troit the river was not frozen; in Rochester, in his first bridge leap the following year (after a series of conditioning baths in cold water) a drunk jumped in after him, and waded safely ashore; in Passaic, New Jersey, the pollution was nearly too much for him; in Pitts-burgh, forty thousand people watched him leap, handcuffed, from the Seventh Street bridge.

But despite all this, Houdini was not prospering as he had in Europe. His very success meant that he had to face increasing num-bers of rivals. In Detroit, a young Canadian handcuff artist opened at a rival house on the same night and was adjudged by the Detroit *Times* critic "unquestionably better" than Houdini (who pointed out that the Temple Theater, where he was playing, never advertised in the *Times*). Houdini destroyed him in characteristic fashion. In San Francisco he had to face an erstwhile friend, Brindamour, who now called himself "King of all the Handcuff Artists." He, too, was successfully destroyed. But each imitator detracted from Houdini's novelty. In January 1908, he was in St. Louis and noted in his diary: "Manager Tate informs me, 'You are not worth a five-dollar bill to me.' I told him, 'I hope you are mistaken.' We shall see." A few weeks later things were even worse. "Arrived in Cleveland seven o'clock. Am not featured. Is this week the first step towards oblivion? No attention paid to me." The spectre of what might happen if he failed was, as always, solidly before him. "Downs has retired, and is landlording in Marshaltown, Ia. He could not change his act and so died theatrically," he noted (T. Nelson Downs, the King of Koins, had preceded him to London in 1900). He had his pension roll of once-great vaudevillians, a constant reminder, an offering to fortune, an amulet to protect himself from their fate. But lucky charms do not always work.

Something new was needed: and on 5 January 1908, it appeared. It was a galvanised-iron can shaped like an extremely large milk can—large enough to hold a man: Houdini.

The can was filled with twenty-two pails of water. While this was going on, Houdini left the stage to change into a bathing suit. On his return, he announced that a man can only live a certain time "deprived of life-sustaining air." He then entered the can, and before disappearing under water, challenged the spectators to try to hold their breaths as long as they could. Then the can was topped up and he vanished from view. Houdini, who had been practising this kind of thing for years, was naturally able to outlast the fittest spectator. By the time he finally reappeared, they were awestruck and long since breathless. (Later he would challenge swimming champions to test out the can and see how long they could last in it. Houdini could hold his breath for three minutes under water; few professional swimmers were able to match this.)

Having made his point, Houdini had himself handcuffed. He bobbed under the water; the can was filled to the brim; then the lid was screwed on and padlocked down with six padlocks. The curtain was drawn. The orchestra played "Sailor, Beware." Half a minute, a minute, a minute and a half went by. At this point Franz Kukol appeared, wielding a fire axe. He went up to the curtain, put his ear to it and listened intently. At the end of three minutes, by which time the audience's lungs were bursting, he raised the axe. And at this point, Houdini appeared, dripping but triumphant. The can was revealed, filled to the brim, all its locks intact.

The new act was a sensation. It brought in the crowds, and it defeated the increasing army of handcuff kings. From now on, handcuffs were merely an accessory to Houdini's other tricks rather than a draw in themselves. "I never do handcuffs, always something ELSE. I . . . change my show on the month about 12 to 15 times," he wrote a little later. By 1911 his baggage included no fewer than four cans—one "1910 New York Can," one "Duston Challenge Can," one "Gamage Can" and one "Can 1910 unprepaired."

Much was made of the Milk Can's uniqueness and its dangers. "This stunt was a bit too dangerous to attract imitators," wrote Harold Kellock, Houdini's first biographer. "It required rare agility combined with under-water endurance, and complete equanimity of spirit. Houdini had to practise it for months before he dared risk it on the stage."

This was certainly true, since any illusion requires painstaking practice before it can be successfully presented. But the Milk Can was just that—an illusion. The committee Houdini invariably invited on stage checked out everything except the real escape mechanism. The seams of the can were all riveted and soldered in order to be watertight. It was shaped like a normal milk can, with a shoulder, a lid and two handles, except that it was much bigger—it stood forty-two inches high. The can sloped in about an inch towards the floor, which seemed to kill the possibility that it was simply a double vessel, constructed so that, once Houdini was inside, he had simply to stand up to lift off the outer covering.

As it happens this was precisely the principle on which the can was built (it had been made, to Houdini's own design, in Chicago). Only the shoulder, however, was doubled. It was apparently riveted to the body—and the handles attached to it, by which the can was carried on to the stage, cunningly reinforced the impression that it was solidly attached. The rivets, however, were fakes. Inside were dummy ends of rivets which the examining committee could feel with their fingers. But in fact the top of the can was attached to the body only by two trick rivets. The can was filled with water; Houdini stepped inside, unscrewed the two rivets, scrambled out and re-placed the top without ever touching the padlocks. There were tiny airholes in the lid so that he would not suffocate if something should go wrong.

The danger with any illusion of this sort is that it can be repli-cated. There were, inevitably, a few imitators. August Roterberg, his old magical supplier from the days when Professor Houdini was try-ing to make a few cents selling his tricks, wrote from Hamburg, where he was on holiday, describing one. Naturally it could not hold a candle to Houdini's: "His act is indeed compared with yours a schwindel." And Houdini's was never the only Milk Can in exis-tence. At the time when he was making such a hit with it in America, the British magic dealer Will Goldston had in stock a Milk Can which he had bought from a French mechanic. He was an old friend of Houdini's, and refrained from advertising the effect. Neverthe-less, a potential rival found out about it and made an offer for it. Goldston refused, mentioned the matter to Houdini, and let him have the apparatus at cost price in order to forestall other imitators. In 1909, however, Houdini was much perturbed to find that Hor-ace Goldin, that voracious consumer of illusions, had just bought a Milk Can. He wrote to his old rival in typically aggressive mode. Goldin wrote a mollifying reply: "To ease your mind, I once more tell you that my intentions were not to ever perform it or let anyone else do it, when I bought it, it was bought merely for curiosity. I have never copied anyone else's tricks, and I appreciate an original one."

But Houdini was not appeased. He took it for granted that, if he performed an illusion, or even took an interest in it, it was his by right. Will Goldston told a story about how Houdini admired a picture Goldston had just acquired. He would certainly have bought it himself if he had seen it. But he had *not* seen it, and Goldston had bought it. However, at the end of the evening Houdini simply picked the picture off the wall and walked off with it. Such was his assumption of right that Goldston let him get away with it.

Houdini's power, which was something more than a mere show-business creation, depended absolutely upon what went on in people's minds. It was of no account that, when he did the bridge jump in Detroit, the water wasn't frozen and he had a rope tied round his waist; or that he used picklocks and, sometimes, dollar bills applied in the right place, to make his gaol escapes; or that he got the better of his imitators simply because he was more ruthless and better at showmanship and deception than they were. However much he protested the contrary—*the more* he protested the contrary—in people's minds he was becoming a magical figure endowed with super-human powers. And now—in people's minds—when he lowered himself into the Milk Can he was confronting the most terrifying adversary of all. He had brought Death to share the stage with him.

11

THE DEATH AND RESURRECTION SHOW

Death had never been far from Houdini's thoughts. He was only twelve when his eldest half-brother, Herman, died of consumption in New York. Bernard Meyer, the Freudian analyst, points out that it was only a few weeks later that he ran away from home. The ostensible reason for this was in order to make some money, since his father had charged him with the care of his mother. Was this simply the last straw, yet another emotional burden at a time of life which is anyway difficult enough? At any rate, Houdini never forgot the anniversary of Herman's death, any more than that of any other death that mattered to him. Wherever he might be, he sought out a synagogue to say Kaddish on the anniversary of his father's death—the only Jewish ceremony he kept. He noted other anniversaries in his diary much as you or I might remind ourselves of birthdays:

February 24, 1914: Brother Herman died twenty-nine years ago.
February 25, 1915: Aunt Sally passed away. Only outlived my beloved mother one year, seven months and nine days.

May 30, 1915: Trip to cemetery with Dash, Sam and Fanny G., etc. Sam's father died eighteen years ago today.

As his act developed, so this preoccupation became increasingly apparent. He had haunted cemeteries for years. Now he seemed set upon finding out personally what it felt like under there. Specially built coffins were frequent accessories. He gave careful thought to the special problems a "buried alive" act would present. Getting out of the box would be only the beginning, for earth, unlike water, is not easily displaced. In some notes written in 1911 on board a steamer near Cherbourg (he often made use of time on board ship to work out new methods, when he was not too seasick) he suggested a special type of end trap in the box. Two loose boards are held by a catch in the top of the box: the release of the catch allows them to drop inward, leaving a large opening for escape.

He finally accepted a challenge in California in which he was to be buried alive, manacled, under six feet of earth. A spot near Santa Ana was chosen where the earth was light and sandy and the vegetation scarce. They began by burying him one foot deep, then two: gradually progressing to six feet. The first two tries were easy enough, but by four and five feet he was experiencing some difficulty. The challengers were for leaving it there. Houdini, however, insisted on going for the full six feet.

But when he realised that he was in a real grave, he was overcome by panic—he, who knew better than anyone that panic was the one thing to be avoided at all costs. Among the most important of his training exercises were those ensuring mental control under stress. In life and death situations, only keeping calm conserves air and allows the body to function efficiently. Mechanically he began to dig himself out, but felt his strength failing. He tried to shout, but his mouth filled with earth. Finally he managed to burrow his way out. He never tried this stunt again. He had typed some notes for a buried packing-case escape. Underneath them he added in pencil:

"I tried out 'Buried Alive' in Hollywood, and nearly(?) did it. Very dangerous; the weight of the earth is killing."

He thus enacted, and very nearly succumbed to, the nightmare which prompted, in the nineteenth century—that era of body-snatchers and Gothick imaginings—the creation of a Society for the Prevention of Premature Burial, whose members were promised the reassurance of a stab through the heart before the coffin was closed. Indeed, the nineteenth century, both Gothick and Decadent, was rife with such fantasies. Pictorially they are most notoriously represented by Millais's Ophelia and the famous photograph of the young Sarah Bernhardt elaborately laid out in her coffin; in literature, by *Dracula* and the stories of Edgar Allan Poe. Bernhardt with her infinite variety of death scenes, Bram Stoker's story of the Undead, Poe's imaginations of what it feels like to be dying—to be at the moment of death; to be dead—all explore that threshold, that point of elision between life and death, which was Houdini's overriding preoccupation. Houdini recognised this affinity. Not only did he know Poe's tales: one of his prized possessions was Poe's writing desk.

Poe, inevitably, himself imagined a Premature Burial. His protagonist, who is prone to cataleptic fits, has taken all possible precautions against such an eventuality—but it seems nonetheless to have arrived:

Despair—such as no other species of wretchedness ever calls into being—despair alone urged me, after long irresolution, to uplift the heavy lids of my eyes. I uplifted them. It was dark—all dark . . . the intense and utter raylessness of the Night that endureth for evermore.

I endeavoured to shriek; and my lips and my parched tongue moved convulsively together in the attempt—but no voice issued from the cavernous lungs, which, oppressed as if by the weight of some incumbent mountain, gasped and palpitated . . . The movement of the jaws, in this effort to cry aloud, showed me that they were bound up, as is usual with the dead. I felt, too, that I lay upon some hard substance; and by something similar my sides were, also, closely compressed . . . I could no longer doubt that I reposed within a coffin at last.

The therapeutic qualities of sublimation—of being able to order one's terrifying imaginings, then to express them as art—are a psychological commonplace. In the process, such fantasies are often transmuted. But both Poe and Houdini expressed theirs with remarkable directness. And those fantasies are very similar. They are claustrophobic; they are about the myriad guises of approaching death; they pursue the theme of consciousness after death. But in the end Poe and Houdini are not alike—indeed, they are almost opposites. Poe embodies horror and hopelessness. His stories express the tortures of the damned: they are written by *one of* the damned. The fact of Poe's death in destitution and despair comes as no surprise: overwhelmed by such horrors as he recounts, how could he fail to succumb? But this is not the case with Houdini. Despite all the morbid imagery, his is essentially a hopeful figure. Houdini had no intention of succumbing. On the contrary. He was single-mindedly dedicated to winning the daily battles which constituted his life. Diving into the maelstrom, he knew exactly how he was going to emerge from it: under the same circumstances, Poe's concern was with what, precisely, it feels like to face certain death. The same set of symbols may signify very different things. The act of drinking blood, in Count Dracula's hands—or fangs—is murderous. He sucks life out of his victim. But the Christian communicant, drinking Christ's blood in the sacramental wine, feels nothing sinister in his beverage. For him, this is the pathway to salvation. Both are imbibing immortality, but to very different effect.

It is clear from his career between the years 1908 (the first Milk Can escape) and 1913, when everything changed yet again, that what Houdini was pursuing was proof of his own immortality. He showed, time after time and in increasingly hair-raising ways, that death had no more power over him than the mere shackles which he regularly threw off within minutes if not seconds. Not that he did not fear death. The opposite was true. He was so haunted by it, the consciousness of it filled his thoughts so entirely, that his life was tolerable only if he could assure himself, time after time, that he could defeat it. If he was not to lapse into breakdown, he had to force himself to confront this terror. This is the essential Gothick situation: one in which the protagonist is faced by some nameless terror, which is in fact death, and which may be overcome by confronting it. The bonds with which he began his career had been, like all those gloomy castles and dark labyrinths, a mere symbol, a precursor, of the real, underlying thing.

He demonstrated his immortality in a variety of water- , milk- and beer-filled containers: nothing could hold him. In 1908 he saw an irresistible new possibility. Five years earlier, in 1903, the Wright Brothers had made the first powered flight. In 1908 he offered $5,000 for the use of a Wright Brothers plane. He planned to be flown over the West End of London where, handcuffed, he would parachute down, escaping from his manacles on the way, to land in Piccadilly Circus. This sensation, however, was not to be: "technical difficulties" intervened. But he did not forget about flying.

His opportunity came the next year, in Germany. He was playing at the Hansa Theatre in Hamburg when it was announced that an aviator named Grade would be demonstrating a new French biplane, the Voisin, at a nearby field. The Voisin was the latest thing in aviation technology. A similar machine had stayed in the air for an hour and twenty minutes near Rheims. Houdini watched the flight and was enthralled. He cornered the aviator and demanded to know where he could get such a plane and what it cost. There were at that time only about two dozen aviators in the entire world: there were certainly no flying schools. This did not deter Houdini. A week later, for $5,000, he owned a Voisin and had hired a French mechanic, Brassac, to teach him how to fly it. If Brassac's name has not survived along with those of the pioneers of flying machines, this shows merely how arbitrary is fame. He taught Bleriot to fly and actually built the monoplane which first crossed the English Channel. But for the next year he devoted himself entirely to Houdini.

Houdini persuaded German Army officials to let him do his learning at the nearby Hufaren exercise field, and they agreed on condition that he teach their officers how to fly. (When World War I came, he characteristically berated himself for having been the means of putting countless enemy aviators into the air for the first time—"I taught those fellows to fly and they may have killed Americans!" he mourned to Bess.) Every night he made his escapes at the Hansa; every morning before the cold November dawn, he and Brassac made their way to Hufaren. The weather was freezing cold, windy and snowy, so that, more often than not, flying was out of the question. Every morning he sat with Brassac in the cockpit learning what he would have to do when, finally, he could fly.

At length the weather cleared. Houdini took his place at the controls: Brassac swung the propeller. He was airborne—but not for long. "I smashed the machine. Broke propeller all to hell," he noted in his diary. The damage, however, was not fatal, and Brassac soon got new parts and repaired it. On 26 November 1909, Houdini made his first successful flight at Hufaren. After that he went flying every day.

Was it what he had hoped for? The ultimate escape, the genuine assumption—for real, at last—of superhuman power? If anyone could approach the sensations of Superman, that man was surely the pilot of one of the early flying machines. So light, so flimsy, constructed of wooden struts and sized canvas: a powered box kite. The pilot sat at the front; behind him was the engine—an eighty-horsepower Enfield—and behind that the wooden propeller. There was literally nothing between him and the empty air. But he could not stay aloft forever. Ten or twelve minutes was the maximum the engine's fuel capacity would allow. After that there was always the bumpy return to earth.

The Hamburg engagement finished at the end of December, and Houdini's next engagement was at the other side of the world. He was booked to go to Melbourne, Australia. Still obsessed by flying, he arranged to take Brassac and the Voisin on the trip with him. He would be the first person to make a flight on the Australian continent. He was not, however, the only one with this idea. Ralph C. Banks, the owner of the Melbourne Motor Garage, was importing a Wright aircraft with the same purpose in mind. When the ship finally reached Melbourne, the crated plane caused a certain amount of trouble with Customs. "They charge you 35% duty or you can bring it in . . . in bond. The Wright machine that is here is under 800 pounds bond. My machine is not quite that much, but by the time I am ready to leave Australia, it will cost that much." In fact he decided to bring the Voisin through, and ended up paying only £154 deposit.

The voyage had been a trying one for Houdini, who had lost twenty-eight pounds on account of seasickness. (The pain was slightly alleviated by the consciousness that the eager Australian management was paying him his weekly salary for the three-week duration of the voyage.) In the interviews he gave on his arrival at Melbourne he talked about his fear of sharks interfering with his dives, his impending retirement (after he had completed the eighteen months' work for which he was already contracted) and his superhuman toughness. He did not, however, mention his main concern, which was his aeroplane.

The airfield was at Digger's Rest, about twenty miles from Melbourne. He learned to drive a motor car in order to get there early in the morning, but he was an impossibly distracted driver and nobody except Brassac (for whom, one can only assume, anything actually in contact with the ground seemed safe) would drive with him. Once again Houdini and Brassac began the apparently endless business of waiting upon the weather. It remained stubbornly unsuitable. Houdini fretted. He saw the precious days passing and the record passing with them, out of his reach. Finally, on 18 March, he made his attempt. It was a success, and he was able to claim his trophy and a certificate signed by Brassac, his frustrated rival Banks, Franz Kukol and several others to the effect that "We, the undersigned, do hereby testify to the fact that on the above date, about 8 o'clock a.m., we witnessed Harry Houdini in a Voisin Biplane (a French heavier-than-air machine) make three successful flights of from one minute to three and a half minutes. The last flight being of the last mentioned duration. In his various flights he reached an altitude of 100 feet, and in his longest flight traversed a distance of over two miles." Houdini noted in his diary: "Never in any fear and never in any danger. It is a wonderful thing."

In fact it had not been quite as uncomplicated as that. During his longest flight Houdini had risen to two hundred feet at forty miles per hour, then turned and met the wind full on. The engines quit, and the machine fell towards the ground. "But when only a few feet from the ground the plucky aviator managed to start his engine again, and the plane rose once more." He was always very keyed up before a flight, as well he might have been considering the real dangers and the absence of possible precautions. But, he told the *Sydney Herald,* "As soon as I was aloft all the tension and strain left me. When I was rolling every muscle of me was taut. When she cants over at the turns—you know how she goes when she's rolling—I'm always afraid the wing will break in the air. It was different as soon as I was up. All my muscles relaxed, and I sat back feeling a sense of ease, freedom and exhilaration. That's what it is. Oh, she's great. I know what it is to fly in real earnest. She's like a swan. She's dandy. I can fly now." He wrote to a friend: "I have been very bisy trying to win the Australian Prize, and I'm pleased to inform you the trophy is MINE!!! But it was hard work, my engine seemed to go wrong, and though I had five men working on it for seven days and nights it refused to pull the amount required, and I almost gave up in despair. Finally last Sunday it awoke to the fact that I had no more days left, and I made the flight of my life. The wind was very strong, but though it carried me about like a feather, I managed to make a grand flight." He added: "I have had the Grave of Wm. H. H. Davenport all fixed up, and will send you a picture of it as it looks today."

His challenge to the air was over. He had won. Flying held no more interest for him. "It is time I had the biplane packed, or it would have given me nervous prostration," he noted. "Have not had much sleep for two months and now I seem to have lost the habit." The following year he read that an aviator named Moisant had crashed his Voisin, and sent a letter by wire, reply prepaid, "in which I offered you GRATIS my entire Bi-plane, propeller, and any spare parts you might have been able to make use of." This act of conspicuous generosity did not go unpublicised—why pass up a good opportunity? The letter was sent via the *Daily Mirror*. But to Houdini's indignation Moisant, possibly unable to believe that this princely offer was really what it seemed, failed to reply.

Houdini recognised the important part death played in his act—to a certain extent. He said: "I knew, as everyone knows, that the easiest way to attract a crowd is to let it be known that at a given time and a given place some one is going to attempt something that in the event of failure will mean sudden death. That's what attracts us to the man who paints the flagstaff on the tall building, or to the 'human fly' who scales the walls of the same building." His friend of later life, Sir Arthur Conan Doyle, said of him: "He had the essential masculine quality of courage to a supreme degree. Nobody has ever done, and nobody in all human probability will ever do, such reckless feats of daring. His whole life was one long succession of them."

In fact no man was ever less reckless. He had by now acquired a specialist team who travelled with him and helped with the preparations. Franz Kukol dealt with bureaucrats and arranged the music. Bess was in charge of the wardrobe and maintained sanity. Houdini thought out the stunts; and, in 1908, the year of the Milk Can, he hired someone who was able to embody his wildest ideas in solid form. This was Jim Collins, a Londoner, a master mechanic and cabinetmaker, who had the advantage of being utterly inconspicuous—the man you would not pick out in a crowd: an almost invisible accomplice. Houdini always insisted that he had picked Collins at sight and on instinct, much as he had picked Bess. There were also two other assistants, Jim Vickery and (in Europe) George Brooks. All these, and anyone who sold Houdini an illusion, had to sign an oath which inducted them into the dark melodrama of Houdiniland:

> I the *undersigned* do solemnly swear on my sacred honor as a man
> that as long as I live I shall never divulge the secret or secrets of
> Harry Houdini, or any thing I may make for him and the secret of
> the can I further swear never to betray Houdini . . . So help me
> God almighty and may he keep me steadfast

In those spacious times, they travelled in two railroad cars, one for the personnel, the other for baggage, props and Houdini's travelling library (built for him by Jim Collins) which would hold a hundred books. "I carry 40 pieces of baggage," he wrote in 1912. "And my chief assistant wears a uniform costs over $1000 in GOLD." The act occupied three dressing rooms—one for Houdini, one for the team, one for the apparatus, "the shop." Here new parts were constructed, keys cut, and any special tools needed to escape from challenges kept in readiness. While the act was on, the stage was always blocked off with special screens, so that no curious stagehands could penetrate Houdini's secrets. At the end of the week, to show that this was simply a professional requirement and not a sign of stand-offishness, trestles would be laid across the stage and all the other acts, the orchestra and the stagehands would be treated to beer and sandwiches. Meanwhile, at home on 113th Street, John W.

Sargent, a veteran magician, looked after the collection. Houdini had been in the habit of giving Sargent, an old friend, various secretarial tasks as his magical career thinned out and money got scarce. Finally Sargent moved full-time into Houdini's employ.

To be a member of Houdini's team was to have your life entirely subsumed in his. This was the return he demanded for what was, for him, the hardest thing in the world: the bestowing of his entire confidence. The team alone were privy to his "secrets." Only Bess was as intimate with him. In a way she was simply the longest-serving team member, the only difference being that he couldn't sack her. He would frequently lose his temper and dismiss the others: they learned to disregard these outbursts, which would be forgotten the next day. No one would have been more shocked than Houdini had they been acted upon.

The team supported Houdini in all aspects of his life. "Laying off to have Bess celebrate her birthday," reads one diary entry. "Came from Philadelphia. Even had fine menu cards printed, though at first she didn't wish them. Bess originally invited thirty-six guests, but lo and behold, sixty-five arrived. Bess was equal to the occasion, though somewhat flurried, and my assistants, Franz, Collins and Jim Vickery, helped in the kitchen." When Houdini died and left his act to Hardeen, Collins and Vickery went with it. They were part of the act.

Of course jumping off the Golden Gate Bridge while wearing leg-irons must always remain a dangerous activity. But it was possible to minimise the danger. "In the first place," Houdini advised,

it is absolutely necessary that the aspirant be a good swimmer, well versed in treading water, floating, and all methods of keeping afloat without the use of hands. This is not as difficult as it at first appears . . . It is also necessary to acquire the art of swimming with a forward and back motion of the feet, in place of the old scissors stroke, and once having mastered this method the body can be kept afloat as easily as by the old style. The necessity for the above is apparent when we consider that the hands must be used on the knots continuously. Bear in mind that the release must be accomplished rapidly, not only on account of the necessity of breathing, but because the ropes shrink when they become watersoaked, although this is not rapid enough to seriously interfere with your work . . . Deep breathing in order to strengthen the lungs and increase their capacity must also be practised, for it will be necessary to hold the breath for a considerable time, and as the escape is bound to require rather violent struggles, this is no child's play . . . This is dangerous business at best, and two of my imitators have been drowned when thrown overboard in manacles. If you are not an absolutely fearless swimmer, I warn you to keep away from ropes under water, and unless you are an expert of the highest order, never substitute handcuffs unless you resort to fixed cuffs, which require only a pull to open, and even these might go wrong with disastrous results. I have never used fixed manacles in any of my stunts, always allowing stage cuffs to be affixed. When I did use my own it was only to lend extra weight, so that I might sink quickly to the bottom and out of sight of my audience, so that they might not inspect my method of releasing myself.

To this end, holes were bored in his boxes and extra weights were attached to them. And as he supervised the immersion of the box, Jim Collins invariably waited for the signal from within telling him that Houdini was free of his bonds and shackles before he gave the signal to lower away. To the watching crowd, of course, Collins was effectively invisible, and Houdini remained a lone hero.

But out of doors, even with the most careful preparations, something might always go wrong since the environment could never be wholly predictable. The most spectacular stage stunt was, by comparison, relatively safe—though nothing was entirely foolproof. The world of magic was shocked when William Robinson, aka Chung Ling Soo, an old acquaintance of Houdini's, was killed during his famous bullet-catching act—an act which he had performed countless times. All sorts of rumours about murder and suicide floated about. In fact what happened was an accident. In this act, a real bullet was placed in the gun barrel, presumably onstage. But there was already a blank charge in the ramrod tube. The mechanism of the gun had been altered so that only the blank ignited when the trigger was pulled. But the thread of the breech block in Soo's gun had worked loose from being constantly unscrewed, and on this fatal occasion the very fine powder he used worked its way down so that not only the blank charge in the ramrod tube but the real charge in the barrel was ignited. Houdini would never do this trick. His friend Harry Kellar, the doyen of American magicians and the one father figure with whom Houdini never fell out, had advised him not to in the most emphatic terms: "No matter what precautions are taken with the bullet-catching trick, it's a damn-fool trick, and the chances for an accident or a 'job' are always present. Now, my dear boy, this is advice from the heart. *Don't try the bullet-catching trick.* There is always the biggest kind of risk that some dog will 'job' you . . . Harry, listen to your friend Kellar, who loves you as his own son. DON'T DO IT!" Houdini needed no telling: he had himself warned of the act's dangers in the *Conjurer's Magazine.*

His own most famous stage stunt was far less risky. It was built for him by Collins, and known as the "Chinese Water-Torture Cell." Houdini always referred to it as "the old Upside-Down" or "U.S.D." In it, a glass-fronted tank was brought onstage and filled with water. Houdini, his ankles clamped in stout wooden stocks, was lowered into it head-first, and the top was secured by a metal grille. Kukol, armed with his fire-axe, was always ostentatiously at hand in case the escape could not be effected. The inside of the tank was fitted with horizontal iron bars, ostensibly so that no injury would result should the glass need to be broken. The function of the bars was actually to allow Houdini to "walk" his head and shoulders to the top of the tank, where, doubled up, he released the catch holding the stocks. The back of these then pulled out like a drawer, allowing enough space for Houdini to scramble out. In a later design there were no bars: the catch was probably activated when the water in the tank reached a certain level after Houdini's immersion.

·   ·   ·

The persona Houdini now presented was no longer that of a mere escape king, but of an invulnerable hero. Invulnerability may be judged in absolute terms; but also in comparative ones. "The moment of *survival* is the moment of power," writes Canetti, and adds: "The moment of confronting the man he has killed fills the survivor with a special kind of strength. There is nothing that can be compared with it." In the cemeteries, the knowledge that he was alive when all the great names he revered were underground had strengthened Houdini's hold on life. Now, however, there were keener pleasures to be had. He was not in the business of killing his rivals. But he took an unmistakable delight in recording the details of how they killed themselves. A swimmer in Pittsburg jumped, bound, from a bridge: his body was retrieved ten minutes later, when it was found that his knots had failed to slip as intended. A Human Fly fell to his death. Houdini noted these happenings with some satisfaction. Everyone who died in this way contributed not only to his legend, but to his immortality.

Invulnerability was both a psychological and a physical affair. From his earliest youth, Houdini had been preparing himself not merely to remain calm but to meet any physical eventuality. He cultivated his body fanatically. Absolute fitness was essential to his job. The knowledge that he could always rely on his body was essential to the control of his mind.

But there was more to it than that. Which came first, the chicken or the egg? The mind or the body, or the body or the mind?

Yukio Mishima, the Japanese novelist, shared many of Houdini's preoccupations with death and the cult of the body. Mishima, who ended his life with a public ritual suicide, wrote a novel, *Kyoko's House*, in which one of the main characters is an actor–body-builder. The question he asks himself is, "Do I really exist or not?"

"On the one hand," says Robert Jay Lifton, discussing Mishima as he speaks through the actor, "in rendering his body beautiful, agile, and capable of disciplined violence, he could find in it a constant source of transcendence—of what he called the ' "ultimate sensation" that lies a hairsbreadth beyond the reach of the senses.' And . . . he goes on to say, 'My solace lay more than anywhere—indeed lay solely—in the small rebirths that occurred immediately after exercise . . . By now . . . it was not words that endorsed my existence . . . but something different. That 'something different' was muscle.' "

Mishima's addiction existed, as addictions do, on two levels. One was psychological. Like Houdini, who was always inviting people to feel his iron-hard body, he conceived of himself narcissistically in terms of muscle and what he was able to do with it. For Mishima, as for Houdini, this narcissism was to play a part in his death—in Mishima's case directly, in Houdini's, indirectly. But the addiction was also physiological, in those "small rebirths."

In one way this may have been fairly straightforward. It is well-known that intensive exercise stimulates the production of endorphins and produces a high, so that stopping the regime may bring on withdrawal symptoms. It is very probable that this was true of Mishima and also of Houdini: he had to get his fix of urgent struggle. "Sometimes I think that these stunts hold far greater thrills for me than they have even for the spectators," he wrote revealingly.

But there was more than a simple high to these extreme occasions, so often repeated. Mishima's "ultimate sensation" recalls that state of mental transcendence achieved by masters of Zen and some of the martial arts. Such a state may of course be attained in many other ways. "The list," says Lifton, "suggests a continuum from extraordinary Dionysian 'excess' (sexual orgy or absolute union with God) to relatively 'ordinary excess' (sexual intercourse, athletics) to much quieter, indeed, Apollonian moments (contemplation of the past or any kind of beauty.) The crucial requirement for feeling ecstatic—'outside of oneself'—would seem to be not so much excess per se as the breakout from prosaic psychic complexities into a state of pure focus, of inner unity and harmony."

There are probably as many routes to ecstasy as there are people. Some people take drugs to attain it. A great many religious rituals—the whirling of dervishes, yoga, speaking in tongues—are designed to induce it. But religion has no monopoly on it. It seems to me almost certain that Houdini experienced transcendence in the course of his exploits. He said to Conan Doyle: "It all comes as easy as stepping off a log, but I have to wait for the voice. You stand there before a jump, swallowing the yellow stuff that every man has in him. Then at last you hear the voice and you jump. Once I jumped on my own and I nearly broke my neck." Conan Doyle took this to mean that Houdini had to admit, in spite of himself, to having had "psychic experiences"—i.e., having been in touch with another world. But I think he was simply explaining how, like a kendo master, he had to attain a "pure state" permitting effortless concentration before he embarked on action. He was certainly aware of the effects of concentration. In 1922 he wrote, apropos crystal-gazing: "The practice induces calmness which is very helpful for people of nervous temperament, and of great assistance in the practice of collecting one's thoughts at a crucial moment . . . Concentration constitutes a powerful magnet that enthralls an audience spontaneously." He thought that sufficient concentration would induce self-hypnotism and trance, leading (in this case) to hallucinating images in the crystal. "Keep on trying and eventually you WILL SUCCEED," he added with the certainty of personal experience. Action, at that point, was exquisite in its perfect control.

There were other possible delights. It seems probable that Houdini took a sexual pleasure in bondage. And near-asphyxiation can reputedly induce exquisite pleasure. Did he also experience it in the state of surrendering himself to danger? In French, those moments at the extreme boundaries of consciousness which include drunkenness, vertigo, fits and also orgasm are given the generic name of *petites morts*. One might add to the list the instant of complete absorption in mass violence. All these routes lead to the same point: the overwhelming present, when conscious thought ceases.

· · ·

Picture the scene as Houdini performs one of his bridge jumps, so often described with such unvarying excitement. The excited crowd, several thousand strong, jostles around. Houdini and his team arrive. A silence falls. Houdini strips to his bathing suit and climbs onto the parapet. The attention of all these thousands of people is focused upon him—a small man, slightly bow-legged, very muscular. The local chief of police comes forward carrying hand-cuffs, often two sets; leg-irons. Houdini allows himself to be mana-cled. He stands there, waiting until he "hears the voice." Then he jumps. The crowd surges forward. It is waiting for—what? What it sees, in a minute or so, is Houdini, swimming strongly for the bank or the boat, brandishing the irons in one hand. It is slightly disap-pointed, but also satisfied. Death has been defeated once more.

Occasionally, circumstance interrupted the lone dignity of the performer. In Australia, a jump into the muddy Yarra River dis-lodged a corpse which floated to the surface alongside an appalled Houdini. He was so shocked that he was unable to swim away and had to be hauled aboard a boat. But generally the ritual was undis-turbed. For ritual it surely was. What does the scene recall so much as an ancient ceremony of human sacrifice, death and rebirth? The old year's king killed in the sacred grove, the living hearts offered to the Aztec gods, the sacrificial figure central to all mythologies in which death is followed by resurrection, as spring follows winter? *"Come forth, Lazarus! And he came fifth and lost the job."*

The specific functions of these sacrificial figures vary according to mythology. But one role is common to them all. They are the surro-gates detailed to investigate, experience and if possible exorcise, on behalf of the rest of us, the great mystery: Death, the consciousness of which differentiates man from other animals. We may refuse to think about it. Dr. Johnson considered that "it matters not how a man dies, but how he lives. The act of dying is not of importance, it lasts so short a time." But even Dr. Johnson could not escape the reluctant consciousness that life is finite. And *what happens then?*

That, as they say, is the question. It dominates many lives: it dominated Houdini's. People yearn for an answer. And the disadvantages of a sacrificial victim when it comes to supplying one are evident. He is dead, and communicating with the dead is problematical.

So another way of probing the great mystery evolved. People came forward who would, so to speak, dip their toe in the water; who would take on death in the hope of coming out the other side imbued with wisdom.

These people, shamans, are a feature of most primitive societies. They are figures of great power. They can intercede with the powers of darkness because their life experience has been in some way extreme. Everyone has to cope with life's crises, starting with the separation of birth. The potential shaman has for some reason experienced these more intensely, and has had to evolve special ways of dealing with the intensity of his or her experience. All Houdini's brothers had to cope with the same difficult circumstances; only he had to work out a special route to survival.

Shamans derive from the extremity of their experience a knowledge which is denied to most other people. They have journeyed from horror and madness through countless dangers to rebirth and joy. They are healers, psychologists, repositories of ancient wisdom; they are feared and honoured; they are outside society. They operate through performance—elaborate dramatic ceremonies during which they not only speak with spirits in their own languages but become them. A shaman performs miraculous feats. In his own body, he descends to the underworld and returns unharmed. Siberian shamans enact this by diving through a hole in the ice and then resurfacing through it: a scene with which Houdini enthusiasts will be familiar. The shaman may ascend to the sky as a bird or travel to the depths as a marine creature: he (or she) is a master of transformation. In short, the shaman is a magician. Or rather, he is magic: a mage. The connotations of magic have always been religious. It is a very ancient word. In Akkadian, "imga" meant priest; this was transposed by the Assyrians to "maga" and Latinised to "magus"—a man of power. For some, even in the modern West, magic is still a religion: and the knowledge and mastery of death is still the centre of its mysteries.

The most common term for the art of magic—conjuring—was in its earlier meanings associated with devils, spirits and the unholy powers. In his performance, the shaman's body is inhabited by these powers, and they are defeated by him. He acts out the innermost fears of his society—fears of madness, sorcery, disease: above all, the fear of death. He undergoes these experiences on behalf of the assembled watchers. He is a mythic figure.

For Houdini, his performance was as grave an affair as any religious ritual. Any attempt to introduce a lighthearted note was met with a fury few could comprehend. When the comedian Loney Haskell, during a benefit performance, cracked some jokes about how Houdini, who lay tied in a straitjacket on the other side of the stage, could not escape from the traffic jam at Forty-second Street and Broadway, he was stopped by a tremendous kick in the shins. Houdini, still tied, had wriggled right across the stage to administer it. He was red with anger. "No, no," he whispered. "No comedy, Lon. I just can't stand comedy." In this ritual and symbolic role, all his peculiarities and obsessions fell into place: the lack of detachment and irony, the absolute seriousness, the compulsion to perform, in public and in private, the ceremonies of his personal drama, which was at the same time so absolutely universal.

It was perhaps at this moment, when he assumed the symbolic role for which his whole life had been an unconscious preparation, that Houdini stepped over the boundary between magical performance and real magic. The relations between the two have always been close; but they are not the same thing. When Hero of Alexandria used newly discovered physical laws relating to water vapour and air pressure to make temple idols move and pour libations, the awe this inspired was occasioned very largely by its setting. In a fairground booth, the effect would have been quite different. Magic is not contained in conjuring tricks, although these may enhance it. Real magic is what goes on in people's minds when, for instance, they receive the sacraments. The wine does not have to change physically into blood for that to occur.

Houdini's performance differed from that of a shaman on two counts. One was that he was not conscious of the resonances of his performance. He did not, for example, know *why* comedy was so inappropriate to it, only that he couldn't bear it. The second was that his performance was an essentially egotistical affair. He was doing what he did in order to save himself, not on behalf of society. The shaman's role is always a lonely one. When its social context is not recognised, it becomes uniquely narcissistic.

The remains of shamanism in Western society can be traced to various groups which operate essentially outside that society, on its boundaries and outskirts. It is an appropriate place for them, since the shaman deals essentially with those transitional moments for which civilisation has little to offer: the moves from childhood to adulthood, from life to death; the occasions for rites of passage. The shaman is essentially a liminal figure, on the threshold between this world and the next; sometimes, between one sex and another. His performance is a drama, and includes tricks and miracles. Where he is still truly a powerful figure, these are peripheral to the main religious and healing purpose of the performance. As that power wanes they assume a greater importance in attracting and holding the audience. Finally, as with the commedia dell'arte, they constitute the whole show, a tradition handed down from player to player in those groups whose existence is barely tolerated by the authorities but which—because of their popular appeal—have never really been suppressed, popping up in fairs, on holidays, wherever a crowd gathers. They are the travelling players, the fairground magicians and fortune tellers, the medicine shows, the freaks, the dime-museum players . . . They are the actors and singers who, once again today,

wield huge popular power because they speak to those dimly perceived needs which society has attempted to rationalise and educate
out of existence.

This is not the high-art performance favoured by authority where
the approved text is played upon a stage and watched with respect in
a theatre, a concert-hall, a church. On the contrary: here the audience is a part of the show: it makes a vital contribution. Engagement
is total. If a ritual may be seen as an "organization of mythological
symbols," the participation enables the audience to experience the
living myth: arguably, the true religious experience. So the scream-
ing, fainting audience is as much an essential part of the show as the
rock star. And the crowd tensely waiting to see if he would emerge
once more from the jaws of death, the invulnerable hero, the quasi-
supernatural figure, was as important to Houdini's performance as
the feat itself.

The performer's needs speak to those of the audience. Together,
they experience catharsis. In this sense, charisma is the antithesis of
civilisation. Civilisation is about control, of both the individual and
the crowd; cathartic release is about the abandonment of that control. The shaman's crowd is uncivilised. So civilisation views the
charismatic figure, rightly, as its enemy.

The year 1912 was the high point of Houdini's vaudeville career.
That summer he was offered eight weeks at Hammerstein's Roof
Garden at $1,000 a week. He determined that, this time, he would
conquer the New York press, which alone still resisted him. Hitherto, the bridge jumps and the container escapes had been two quite
separate acts. The handcuffs and leg-irons were now no more than
an accessory—an essential accessory, but an accessory nonetheless.
They magnified the drama; they were no longer the drama itself.

Now, early in the morning at the Municipal Swimming Pool on
Eightieth Street and the East River, Houdini and his team began to
practise a new stunt. He would be lowered into the river, manacled,
in a formidable iron-weighted box specially constructed by Jim Col-

lins. The box would defy the closest inspection. It was solid in every respect; only the team knew that one of its boards was attached by those short screws which Houdini had so bitterly denounced in his rival's coffin.

The stunt was announced for the day he was due to open at Hammerstein's. The press was notified and turned out in force at the East River pier. Mrs. Weiss was present to watch her son in his supreme moment. Crowds filled the docks. Then at the last moment the police showed up and forbade the stunt. Jumping off piers in New York was forbidden. But by prescience or good fortune, a tugboat just happened to be on hand. Houdini jumped in, his packing case was loaded aboard, and the pressmen followed. Once out in the harbour he had them inspect the handcuffs and leg-irons and lock them in position. Then he was helped into the box, the top was nailed in place, and Jim Collins supervised its lowering into the water. The pressmen took out their watches.

They waited, counting, for fifty-seven long seconds. Then Houdini appeared. The most cynical news corps in the world burst into cheers. The box was hauled up. It was tightly closed: inside were the cuffs and irons. The evening's headlines were secure. That evening he repeated the stunt in the large pool which was one of the features of Hammerstein's Roof Garden. Houdini had conquered New York.

It was at the end of this week that he demanded his first thousand dollars' salary in gold, so that he could pour it into his mother's lap. This scene is of course familiar to us all from fairytales. The poor boy leaves home and accomplishes the ten impossible tasks that will make him rich, marry him to the beautiful princess and give his parents a secure old age. In the fairytale, however, all is rarely what it seems. As often as not the gold turns back into dead leaves or stones. But in this case that did not happen. Mrs. Weiss held out her apron and it really was filled with real gold: an archetypal fulfilment, as was only fitting for an archetypal personage.

12

THE LADY VANISHES

The power to vanish—or to make someone else vanish—is one of the classic magical attributes. Invisibility, in the old tales, is a gift from the gods or the fairies. It is a protective device bestowed upon their favourites to render them invincible and untouchable. Vanishing other people is an altogether different matter. It is often an aggressive measure, the prerogative of witches and wizards, who are also apt to materialise suddenly out of nowhere, usually with the worst of intentions.

Where do they come from, where do they go to, all these invisible people?

If you are merely protected by the cloak or ring of invisibility, the answer is simple. You don't go anywhere: you are there all the time. You can't be seen, but you can be felt, and you can make yourself felt: a circumstance upon which more than one story has pivoted. But the matter is more complicated if you are vanished (or if you materialise). The understanding under those circumstances appears to be that the invisible one arrives from a kind of limbo, an incorporeal state symbolised by the traditional puff of green smoke which marks the appearances and disappearances of the Demon King in the pantomime.

The puff of smoke fulfils not merely a dramatic but a practical purpose: it distracts attention from the mechanics of what is going on. For it is not only wizards in fairytales who can make people vanish at will.

As with most famous illusions, there are many different ways in which the effect may be achieved. For example, the vanishing lady may assume the cloak of invisibility. This happened in an illusion called "Gone!," which was invented by W. E. Robinson, who later performed as Chung Ling Soo (and died, it will be recalled, when his bullet-catching act went wrong). In this illusion a girl sits on a chair and is hoisted six or seven feet into the air. The magician fires a pistol at her, she screams, the pieces of the chair fall to the ground, and she is—gone!

"Gone!" is performed against a black backcloth. The chair is hoisted by a winch mounted on a scaffold framework. In the top bar of the frame are two pulleys through which the ropes pass to the winch. In the middle of the frame is another bar, apparently to strengthen the framework, but important to the trick. Behind this bar is a kind of roller blind, connected to the top bar by powerful springs. When the catch is released, the blind—black to match the backcloth—shoots up to the top bar. The girl is sitting on a loose seat hooked to the ropes. By pressing a catch on this, she disengages the collapsible chair, which falls onto the stage in pieces.

Or it may all be done with mirrors. An angled mirror will reflect the backcloth in such a way that the mirror itself is invisible to the audience, although it is of course opaque and will conceal whatever needs to be hidden. This property is the basis of a great many illusions (for instance, disembodied talking heads) and may be used in a variety of ways to effect a successful vanish.

A third method is to use a collapsible framework. This is the secret of those illusions where the magician throws a cover over the lady, claps his hands or waves his wand or fires a pistol, and whips off the cover (and the framework) to reveal—nothing at all. What has happened is that the lady has been lowered off the stage through a trapdoor while the framework holds the cover in place. This was the method used in some very famous illusions, notably David Devant's "Mascot Moth" and Buatier de Kolta's "Vanishing Lady" (which was later acquired by Houdini).

One thing all these tricks have in common is, of course, that the lady later reappears. Here magic has it over reality. For in the final disappearing act of all, there is no return.

After his triumph at Hammerstein's Roof Garden in 1912, Houdini returned to Europe. But he agreed to return to Hammerstein's in 1913 for a two-week engagement in spite of the fact that the round trip would last almost as long as the engagement. His mother was by now seventy-two; she was getting frail, and he would not have another chance to see her that year. She sat in the front row and beamed while he escaped from straitjackets and the Water Torture Cell, which was here presented for the first time. "It is his act and practically his act alone, which gives the present bill its one gleam of intense interest and originality," noted *The New York Times*. "Owing to this man's wonderful flubdub and personality, one follows his entrances and exits as breath-batedly as if he were pushing himself through the small and hindermost entrance of a Yale lock. And he would get himself out of there—that's the wonder of the man."

On 7 July Houdini had dinner with some magician friends, including Ching Ling Foo, who (unlike Chung Ling Soo) was genuinely Chinese and who was taking over his spot at the Hippodrome. Next day he sailed for Europe and an engagement in Copenhagen. Hardeen, meanwhile, was engaged to perform in Asbury Park, New Jersey, from 14 July, and invited Mrs. Weiss to take a holiday and accompany him down there. She was to stay at the Imperial Hotel while he leaped, manacled, from the end of the pier, and performed straitjacket releases, handcuff escapes, the Milk Can act and other items from the old Houdini repertory at the Lyric Theater. On the night of the 14th Mrs. Weiss suffered a stroke which left her paralysed. Theo called his sister Gladys in New York: she arrived next day. Mrs. Weiss's condition was critical. On 16 July Hardeen performed his act as usual, then rushed to his mother's bedside. She seemed to be trying to say something. Then she fell asleep, never to wake again.

Houdini, meanwhile, had opened at the Cirkus Beketow in Copenhagen. Two members of the Danish royal family, Prince Aage and Prince Axel, were in the audience. He had memorised his patter in Danish, according to his principle of addressing audiences in their own language. ("I am doing my entire act in Danish," he told Nelson Downs as early as 1901. "It is 100 percent better than my German, I mean worse, but it is very funny and I make a hit with my introduction.")

This trick, along with all the others, worked like a charm. The audience went wild with enthusiasm. Next day at noon, Houdini joyfully met the press in the circus vestibule. He wanted to thank everyone for his wonderful reception the previous evening. As he talked, he was handed a cable. He opened it, read it and fell unconscious to the floor. When he came to, he was sobbing, "Mama—my dear little mother—poor little mama." The pressmen quietly left.

Houdini did not perform that night. Next day a Danish doctor diagnosed shock followed by a recurrence of chronic kidney trouble. In 1911 he had suffered a ruptured blood vessel in his kidney brought on by too many strenuous straitjacket escapes. The doctor then had prescribed three months' rest and no more straitjacket escapes or other such exhausting stunts. Houdini was unable to contemplate such a thing. His aura of invincibility was as essential to his self-image as to his public image. Not only could nothing contain him, not only was he immune to deathly dangers, but disease could not be allowed to touch him as it might any ordinary mortal. He went on playing for the next three nights in great pain, then rested for a fortnight. "Think I started work too soon," he confided to his diary. "Wish I had laid off another week." The kidney never really healed. It gave him intermittent trouble from then on. He had to sleep with a cushion under the affected side; it was after this that he took to wearing a black silk eye-mask in bed, since the least ray of light would wake him from his troubled sleep. Now mortality was reaching out: it had claimed his mother; he could feel its fingers on his own body.

Distraught, he cabled Hardeen to delay the funeral. He was coming home at once. He and Bess managed to get berths on the same ship that had brought them to Bremen. Bizarrely, or appropriately, it was named the *Kronprinzessin Cecilie*. They landed in New York on 29 July, in time for Houdini to see his mother in her coffin. On 30 July the funeral took place. "This day Cecilia Weiss, *geboren* Steiner, my darling Mother, was laid to rest alongside of her husband and my father. (As we stood on the deck, July 8, Mother asked me to bring back a pair of the warm woollen house slippers and she said, *"Nicht verges' nummer 6."* In Bremen I bought the slippers on our return journey and they were placed with her when she was laid to rest.)"

For a month afterwards he could think about nothing but the freshly dug grave. He visited it every day, throwing himself upon the mound of earth as if physical proximity might restore contact with his mother. Bess said that a certain youthful joyousness disappeared from him then, never to return.

Why was Houdini so obsessed by his mother? Why just him, and none of his several brothers? That he was so can hardly be in doubt. Erich Fromm's description of the mother-fixated man might have been written with Houdini in mind:

Mother-fixated men . . . are usually quite affectionate and in a qualified sense "loving," but they are also quite narcissistic. The feeling that they are more important to mother than father is makes them feel that they are "wonderful," and since they are already "father," they are already grown up and need not do anything in reality to establish their greatness; they are great because—and as long as—mother (or her substitute) loves them exclusively and unconditionally. As a result they tend to be extremely jealous—they must keep their unique position—and they are simultaneously insecure and anxious whenever they have to perform a real task; while they might not fail, their actual performance can never really equal their narcissistic conviction of superiority over any man (while having at the same time a nagging, unconscious feeling of inferiority to all).

Clearly Mrs. Weiss's Ehrich could not offer her or receive from her the sexual and emotional fulfilment which she had enjoyed with his father, and to which their numerous children and her sadness at Rabbi Weiss's death bore testimony. So he looked elsewhere—to the world of make-believe. The happiest moments of Houdini's life had been those when, together, he and his mother had shared the fulfilment of some fairytale fantasy. There was the time when he had dressed her in the Queen's dress and thrown a royal reception for her in Budapest. There was the occasion when, as a young boy, he had brought home the rent ("Shake me, I'm magic!"); and the not dissimilar occasion when he had emptied his shower of gold into her apron: both characterised as "the happiest day of my life."

Now it was as if that life had lost its mainspring. Houdini's real life was in his act. And that act and the fascinating power which lay behind it were intimately related to his mother fixation.

There is general agreement among the many psychologists who have discussed Houdini that inside this conspicuously brave man was a conspicuously frightened man. In order to face life at all he had to prove to himself again and again that he could overcome his deepest fear: the fear of being separated from his mother, as he had been so brutally when he was born. This fear must, logically, have been the background to his entire life. At least one school of psychoanalytic thought sees birth, that earliest of all separations, as the causation of all the neuroses.

Houdini, characteristically, was especially direct in the expression of his neuroses. His dearest wish was to return to the safety and security of life with his mother, and above all, to the safest and securest place of all: right inside her. He always particularly enjoyed laying his head upon her breast "in order to hear her heart beat. Just [one of the] little peculiarities that mean so much to a mother and son when they love one another as we did." The mother's heartbeat is of course the pervading sound heard by the foetus in the womb: recordings of it have a soothing effect upon young babies.

His act was a constant evocation of this ideal spot. Womblike containers filled with water were at its centre. Shut inside them, with no exit apparent, he reenacted again and again the moment of his birth. The trauma of his entry into life constituted, paradoxically, his drama of death. He clipped a report about three American murderers "Sealed up for Life in a Mexican dungeon . . . A bottle-shaped cell, about ten feet in diameter at the bottom and twenty feet high, has been cleared of the accumulated rubbish of years for [their] reception." What was that but some enormous womb, the prison of his dreams?

Birth is just the first of many separations which must be endured and accommodated on the path to adult life. Houdini, in this sense, fell at the first fence. His precarious equilibrium needed constant reinforcement. The repeated reenactment and overcoming of his besetting fear—that he would not survive separation from his mother—the almost daily demonstrations that he was literally a superman, immune to all the bonds and physical limitations which generally restrict mere humans—these barely sufficed to reassure him. Everyone who lived or worked with him knew how easily he was upset. He was always certain that any joke, even the mildest, was part of some plot to make him look a fool. Towards the end of his life, when his position was unassailable, when he was rich, famous and on visiting terms with the president of the United States, he agreed to edit a weekly supplement to a Brooklyn paper which would be called *Red Magic* (it was soon abandoned). Since he was extremely busy it was clear that he would do little more than lend his name to this: the real work would have to be done by others. There happened at that time to be a young man working for the paper by the name of Hugh Deeny. The editor, thinking Houdini might appreciate the joke, sent young Deeny along to offer what help he could. But when he arrived at the Houdini house and announced himself, the great man's first reaction was to throw him out and shut the door in his face. It was only after repeated and prolonged pleadings that he accepted that this was the young man's real name, not some malicious practical joke, and agreed to let him do the work he had been assigned to. But he could never bear to call him anything but Murphy.

His team knew that his angry outbursts must be ignored, for their sake and for his, since next day they would be forgotten. But in other circumstances his anger was not so quick to vanish. He was always ready to pick a quarrel with anyone he saw as infringing upon his copyright. He saw insults everywhere and remembered them indefinitely. For years he nursed a bitter grudge against Dr. A. M. Wilson, editor of *The Sphinx,* a magical magazine. Acquaintances had to choose between them. "Some time ago I wrote you that a certain Dr. Wilson was a bitter enemy of mine and that if you wished to take your choice, as to which one you wanted as friend, you had that right," he informed a fellow magician, Ottokar Fischer. "As you have seen fit to accept his friendship by writing for his paper, which it still is, although you try to tell me different, you can consider our years of friendship at an end and I trust you will have the good sense NEVER TO WRITE TO ME OR APPROACH ME IN CASE I PLAY YOUR CITY NEXT SEASON." Fischer was an old friend who had been "the very able Viennese correspondent" of the *Conjurer's Magazine.* But he was a friend no longer. In 1915

Houdini and Dr. Wilson were reconciled (by Martinka, who engineered a meeting in his famous New York magic shop, a point of call for all magicians). They liked each other enormously and much regretted the lost years of what could have been friendship. The origin of the quarrel was lost in the mists of time. Nevertheless, Houdini continued to bear his grudge against Ottokar Fischer: it lasted for the rest of his life. In 1925 he was still seeing slights in every mention Fischer made of him. "Have no desire to write to him, he having elected to slight me years ago and an explanation in order from him for that incident," he wrote indignantly to Harry Price. These things, for Houdini, were not open to reason. They came from somewhere much deeper and darker than that.

For several months following her death, Houdini could think of nothing but his mother. It was now that he adopted the birthday she had preferred for him—6 April—rather than his real birthday, 24 March: "It hurts me to think I cant talk it over with Darling Mother and as SHE always wrote me on 6 April, that will be my adopted birthday." He visited her grave daily. He had her letters, which he had saved since 1900, transcribed into good German and typed up so that he could read them more easily. He had the clock which he had given her stopped at the hour of her death. He had cards printed with her photo and the legend "If God ever permitted an Angel to walk the earth in human form, it was my Mother." He referred to these as his "mother cards," and sent them to friends whose own mothers were unwell or had died. He ordered new writing paper, thickly bordered with black—"This is my new letterhead, and it was not with gladness that I ordered same."

He became apathetic about everything unconnected with his mother. For the first time in his life he, who had always been such a compulsive worker, lost interest in his act. "I never knew what it was to shirk work, until one morning I awoke July 17th and (1913) found that my Mother had departed . . . since then I 'loaf' in some of my work." To Dash he wrote: "Dash, I knew that I loved

Mother, but that my very existence seems to have expired with HER, is simply writing my innermost thoughts . . . With all my efforts, I try and still my lounging, as I know positively that Mother would not like the way she Passing Away has effected me, but what can I do." He brooded endlessly upon her last moments—those last moments which he had not been there to witness. She had tried to say something at the end. What could it have been? Dash seemed to think that it had been "Forgive . . ." What or who was there that needed forgiving? Houdini himself, perhaps: he had been far away performing when his mother needed him most. But this was not a thought it was possible to entertain.

"Time heals all Wounds, but a long time will have to pass before it will heal the terrible blow which MOTHER tried to save me from knowing," he wrote Dash that November. The nature of this blow remains unclear. But it seems to have to do with a marital muddle which enabled Houdini finally to assign elsewhere the unbearable burden of responsibility for his mother's death.

This was eventually saddled upon his youngest brother, Leopold, who was always known as Dr. Weiss but who was in fact a radiologist. Leopold was living with Sadie Weiss, the estranged wife of his brother Nathan, the second eldest of Cecilia's children. Nat was a rather unsuccessful businessman. If his diary is anything to go by, Houdini never had much time for him, although he had been fond of Sadie, while he and Leopold were very good friends. Leopold's consulting rooms were located, at least until 1913, in Houdini's house at 278 W. 113th Street. And in fact it seems that for some considerable time after 1913 they remained good friends. On 16 July 1915, two years after Cecilia's death, Leopold joined Houdini and Dash on a trip to Asbury Park to visit the scene of the tragedy. Nor did Houdini apparently disapprove of Sadie's behaviour: Nat had found another girlfriend, and, writing about the situation to Dash, Houdini remarked (in January 1914), "I hope [Nat] gets divorced." Eventually he did; and Sadie and Leopold took advantage of the event to marry.

It was at this point, in 1917, that Houdini's wrath descended upon Leopold. Apparently arbitrarily—for their behaviour was no worse, and arguably more acceptable than it had been hitherto— both Sadie and Leopold were dismissed to outer darkness. There was an old family photograph, taken in 1909, commemorating a trip Mrs. Weiss and Bess's mother Mrs. Rahner had made together to Europe, to visit Bess and Houdini who were playing there. Leopold was also in London at that time, and the photo showed all five of them. Now Houdini took the photograph and, with a pair of scissors, cut off his brother's head. On the back he wrote: "This is the picture from which Houdini later cut off his brother's picture, because he thot that an act of the brother had hastened his mother's death." The picture has been frequently reproduced: the mutilated figure of Leopold is invariably airbrushed out.

Like Ottokar Fischer, Leopold was never forgiven. But blood was thicker than water, or at any rate family blood was thicker than the unrelated product. In his will (dated 20 July 1924) Houdini made his feelings quite clear: "It is my express desire, intention and direction that no part of either the principal or income of my Estate shall ever directly or indirectly go to Sadie Glantz Weiss, the divorced wife of my brother Nathan Joseph Weiss and the present wife of my brother Doctor Leopold David Weiss." Nor was Leopold to receive anything "unless his present wife, the divorced wife of my brother Nathan . . . shall have died." Even should that occur, Leopold was excluded from the ultimate benefit in Houdini's gift. His name did not appear upon the list of those entitled to be buried in the family plot at Machpelah Cemetery. As to the nature of the original crime, that was lost in the mists of Houdini's fantasy—where it had originally taken shape. Perhaps the crime was Sadie's, in preferring Leopold to Harry when she left the disreputable Nat. It seems improbable that it was ever formulated with any distinctness.

Life, however, had to go on. As Houdini was constantly aware, his income depended on his continuing to work. By September 1913 he was back in Germany. Early in 1914 he wrote: "From what I can find out we will with the Will of God return to America June 17th possibly on the Imperator. Hope to be able to get a few contracts so that I can work America though it does not seem so important to me now as it did before God called for Ma."

The *Imperator* trip in fact provided one of the few highlights of this period of his life. Among the other passengers was Theodore Roosevelt, whose acquaintance Houdini determined to make. He succeeded in doing so by a spectacular coup which delighted and mystified the great man. On the second day out Houdini was asked to act as spirit medium and answer questions from the passengers. His "control" was W. T. Stead, the famous journalist and enthusiast for spiritualism, who had recently been lost on the *Titanic*. Colonel Roosevelt, who was returning from an exploring trip to South America, asked "Stead" to trace on a sheet of paper the path of his journey—about which nothing had as yet been published. Using a slate, "Stead" reproduced the exact map of the travels in question. Roosevelt was understandably astounded. He told Houdini it was the most amazing thing he had ever seen. They were photographed together on deck, together with several other passengers. Houdini later had the photograph reproduced with the other passengers airbrushed out.

In an article, Houdini revealed how he had done this trick, which he described as "really nothing more or less than a case of practical forehandedness on my part."

I was about to sail from London for America, and learned at the ticket office that Colonel Roosevelt was to be a fellow-passenger, although no public announcement had been made of the fact. Figuring things out in advance, I foresaw the customary request from an entertainment committee of passengers for a performance from me on board ship, and I also realized that Colonel Roosevelt would be the dominating presence in the audience. I therefore resolved to work up something which would involve some recent activity of his.

1. The lone figure of Houdini leaps, manacled, from the Charles River Bridge in Boston.

2. Ehrich Weiss, aged 15 or 16.
The model necktie-cutter.

3, 4. The budding athlete, aged 16 or 17. He already prefers to strip to be photographed.

5. The earliest professional pictures of Harry and Bess. He was 20, she was 18. She is wearing the tights that caused so much heart-searching.

6. Mysterious Harry and La Petite Bessie try to take their act on tour.

7. The Welsh Bros. Circus, c. 1895. The Houdinis are at the right of the front row.

8. Houdini's father, Rabbi Weiss.

9. Mrs. Weiss, Harry and Bess in perfect harmony.

10. The Weiss Brothers: (*l to r*) Leopold, Nat, Dash, Wilhelm, Ehrich.

my first book. Houdini

Mysterious
HARRY HOUDINI.

Signed may 29/192?

Published so near so soon remember

about 1894   H. Houdini 1894

TRICKS.
Requiring no practice or special apparatus.
Price 25 Cents.

Printed in Chicago. Ill

11. Houdini the collector annotates his first book 25 years after it was published.

12. An early beefcake shot. Even the singlet is now abandoned.

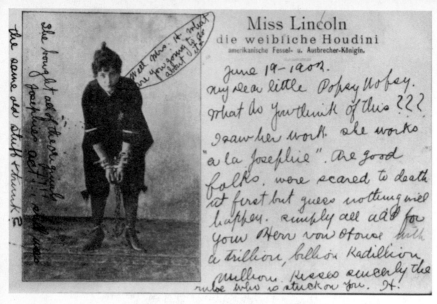

13. Postcard to Bess, "My dear little Popsy Wopsy," during Houdini's first great success in Germany. This was one of his many imitators.

14. Russian poster, 1903.

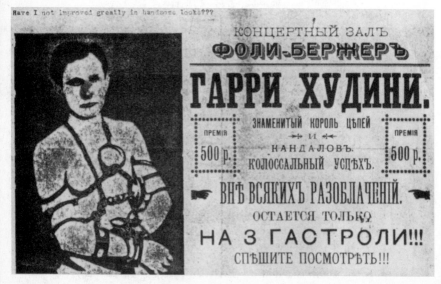

15. A typically over-the-top publicity display.

16. A publicity procession marches through town.

17. Houdini's first flight, Hufaren, Germany, November 1909.

18. Scenes from the record-breaking Australian aviation venture, March 1910.

19. Houdini caged. The bars of the cage are actually drawn on, as are the trunks.

20. Another pose for the same pre-Freudian series.

21, 22, 23, 24. At the graves of old
magicians: Lafayette, Bosco, Heller,
and John Anderson.

25. After Houdini's mother's death, his brother Leopold
was cut out of the family photograph.

26. The same photo as later reproduced.
Leopold has now been airbrushed out.

Taken on Board the
Hamburg American Liner "IMPERATOR"
In Mid Ocean June 23.1914.

27, 28. Two versions of
Houdini with Teddy
Roosevelt. In photographs,
but not in life, unwelcome
intruders could simply be
airbrushed out.

29. Jim Collins awaits the signal that Houdini is ready to be lowered.

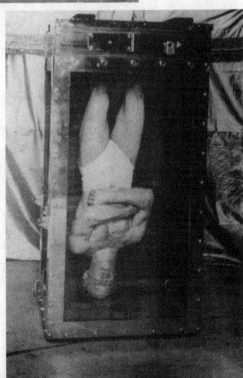

30. The "old upside down": Houdini in his Chinese Water Torture Cell.

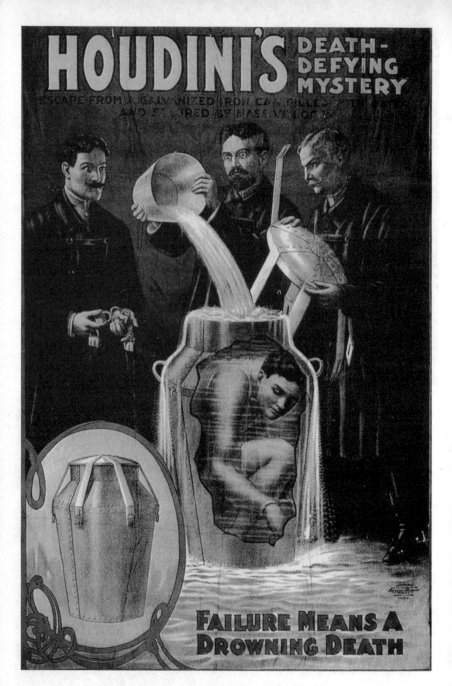

31. Back to the womb: the Milk Can act.

32. What the crowd saw: Houdini, hanging from the top of a skyscraper, escapes from yet another straitjacket.

33. What Houdini saw: a sea of hats and marooned tramcars as he stops the traffic.

34. Houdini performs a particularly gymnastic screen rescue.

A Man Entombed in a Massive Casket of Ice 100 Years Comes Back to Life

HOUDINI in The Man from Beyond

The Weirdest and Most Sensational Love Story Ever Screened

THE HOUDINI HISTORICAL CENTER

AND HOUDINI HIMSELF IN 30 MINUTES OF MYSTERY FEATS

TIMES SQUARE THEATF 42nd nr. B | Commencing **SUNDAY** EVENING | **Apr. 2** | Daily Twice Thereafter

35. Houdini emerges from his block of ice in *The Man from Beyond*.

36. Houdini with Sir Arthur Conan Doyle.

37. With Sarah Bernhardt, 1917, after Houdini had failed to restore her leg by magical means.

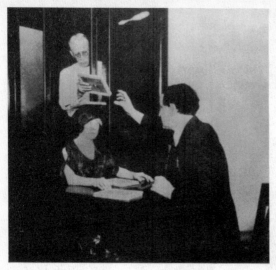

38. Houdini, Bess, and Jim Collins show how the slate-writing substitution trick works.

39. Houdini in his medium-trapping disguise.

40. Houdini meets the ghost of Abraham Lincoln in a demonstration of spirit photography.

41. The face that captivated a thousand professors: Mrs. Mina Crandon, aka "Margery," the medium.

42. "Ectoplasm" emerges from Margery's nose and/or mouth. This variety bears a strong resemblance to crumpled fabric.

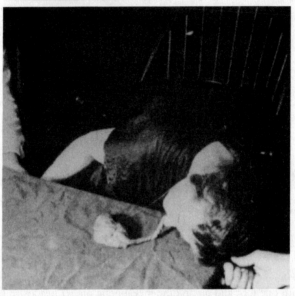

43, 44. Margery and her spirit pseudopods (made of liver and lights).

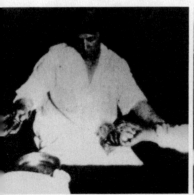

45. Houdini's view of how Margery produced her effects
(and how he detected her methods):

She works the bell-box by inclining her leg toward it.

She gives the impression that both her feet are "controlled" while overturning the
screen with one foot and placing the megaphone on her head with her free hand,
preparatory to throwing it wherever requested.

She uses her head to "levitate" the table while her hands and feet are all "controlled."

46. 278 West 113th Street, Houdini's New York house.

47. Houdini in his library. Note the picture of Cagliostro in the background.

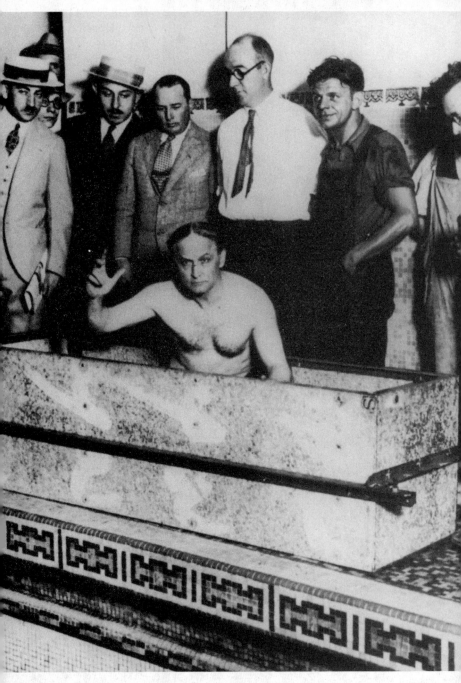

48. Houdini in his coffin before the swimming-pool underwater test, 1924.
The years are beginning to tell.

49. Houdini supervises the construction of the family tomb after his mother's death.

50. Houdini poses with the bust destined for his tomb.

51. Hardeen and Bess at Houdini's grave, finally complete with bust and plaque to mark his presidency of the Society of American Magicians.

It so happened that he was returning at that time from his trip of exploration in South America with the announcement of the discovery of the River of Doubt. He had given—privately—a map of his explorations to a famous London newspaper and it was to be published three days after the steamer had sailed. No one, with the exception of Colonel Roosevelt and one or two others, knew the details of the map. I, therefore, determined to get a copy.

I will not tell you how I managed to secure this copy, but I can say that it is always easy to get people to assist one in a trick. They feel that they are being "let in on the ground floor," and will practice all kinds of deceits to which they are unaccustomed by nature, simply for the sake of being one of the few in a large crowd who are "in" on the thing. It is a human failing which I have seldom been unable to make use of . . . So it was that I got a copy of Colonel Roosevelt's map.

It remained to manoeuvre Roosevelt into asking his question. This again was a matter of psychology. All that was really needed was to engineer a situation where the audience put up questions for Houdini to answer. Roosevelt would certainly be one of those who did so; and this, or something related to it, would almost certainly be the question he would ask.

Back in New York, Houdini found it impossible to take up the threads of his old life. He could not bear to live on West 113th Street, where everything was associated with his mother. On 25 August he announced that he and Bess were moving to Dash's house in Flatbush. It is not known what Dash thought of this arrangement. He had a wife and two children of his own, and even allowing for Houdini's frequent absences, the move can hardly have been very convenient for them. But Dash had always been ruled by Houdini—not surprisingly, since his livelihood consisted of imitating him slavishly. No doubt Houdini did not hesitate to remind Dash of this if the need ever arose. So the Houdinis and their voluminous baggage stayed in Flatbush for three and a half years, until, in February 1918, he moved back: it was reported that Harry Houdini had bought a

Manhattan home at 278 West 113th Street and that the move from Flatbush had required two vans to transport his magic curios, automata and other conjuring paraphernalia, plus four more for his library and collection of rare manuscripts.

This Flatbush interlude was for Houdini a period of half-life. It was as if he considered himself in all important respects already dead. He knew exactly what his grave—or its tombstone—would be like, because he was busy having it made. The plot at the Machpelah Cemetery which now housed the bones of his mother, father and brother Herman was intended for the whole family, but—literally above all—himself. Jewish tradition dictates that a tombstone is erected on the grave a year after the funeral. I do not know what memorial if any had been erected to Rabbi Weiss or his son, but once Cecilia had joined them, Houdini commissioned a design which exceeded the statutory year as greatly as it exceeded the average family tomb. In 1916 it was reported that a sculptor had been toiling for a year to produce "last resting places for Houdini's father and mother . . . It has taken over two years of constant work to construct and place the Exedra in position and there is yet six months to a year's work ahead to complete it. The Exedra weighs more than 50,000 pounds and 1,000 tons of Berry Vermont granite were used in the setting and building. Each piece is cut from solid stone. Of the original block of fifteen tons required for the seat only eight remain in the finished product. The check stones each were ten tons in the block but only five remain. So a great deal of granite was hewn away to make this odd Exedra."

The Exedra is a sort of semicircular granite wall with a step or bench against which (in strict defiance of the Jewish custom forbidding statuary) kneels a weeping stone female figure. In the centre is a block reading WEISS in large letters. This was finally unveiled in October 1916. After Houdini's death a central pillar was added, completing the design, topped with a large portrait bust with HOUDINI inscribed on its base in even larger letters.

Houdini took a good deal of pleasure in controlling the dispositions of this final home in which he so vividly pictured himself. He ruthlessly dictated who was and who was not to be buried there. Leopold and Sadie, the guilty couple, were out. The rest of his brothers and sisters would be welcome, but none of their husbands, wives or offspring. The only exception was made for Bess.

It is clear that this extraordinary construction and the arrangements concerning it were a form of therapy for Houdini in his desperation. One function of any tomb is to comfort survivors. Elaborate tombs help them bear their loss by letting them make various expenditures and symbolic substitutions which compensate for that loss. Nothing less than this palace among tombs would have sufficed for Houdini's mother. Moreover, its design and construction placed him in the delightful situation of being able to preside over his own obsequies even though he was still nominally alive. He could thus ensure that his own tomb would be grandiose enough to satisfy even himself.

The death of his mother, not surprisingly, raised tricky questions regarding his relations with Bess. Still with his mind firmly ensconced in the grave beside his mother, he set out elaborate arrangements regarding Bess's conduct in the event of his death, evidently determined to control her life as firmly after his decease as he did in the flesh:

January First 1916
First letter this year

My Darling Sweetheart,
    Just a few important instructions, after our conversation, in case I die first.
    If it enters your mind to once again enter the "bonds" of wedlock, I want you to be able to protect yourself from any one who may marry you simply for the money that is left to you.
    Make whoever it is *sign away his marriage right in everything, otherwise do not marry him.*

If he will give you as an argument that you do not trust him, it is evident that he does not deserve to be trusted.

Under no circumstances what so ever, marry any one who will not sign away the marriage potion, as they will have half of everything I worked and slaved for, suffered and went hungry and sleepless nights to earn.

. . . I ask you from my tomb *to protect yourself,* then I will be able to sleep easy and know that I have succeeded in helping you to a restful and happy old age. I know you will miss me, but sweetheart never grieve for me, for I am through, my ascent is settled, and if you will only enjoy life that is my request.

Save this letter and read it when anyone comes to you for any of the above motives.

I am wishing you a Happy New Year, for I am herewith in a position to do so.

Who was this letter intended to benefit? A Houdini enthusiast I discussed it with feels it shows a tender regard for Bess and her welfare. But it doesn't strike me that way. Houdini is the only person whose interests are consulted here. He wants to make quite sure that "everything I worked and slaved for" doesn't end up in the hands of some unworthy fellow. He wants to be certain that Bess, after his death, will continue to play the role he has allotted her in the strange drama she entered when she married him. He evidently regarded this letter as particularly important and satisfactory. He frequently re-read it and countersigned it: "Have re-read this June 2 1918 and found it to my desire. Re-read Feb 26 1921. Re-read May 1926."

But he was not yet dead; and his mother's death meant he had to rethink his relations with those living women who were close to him. These were the kinds of questions he had tried to preempt with that abrupt marriage twenty years before. He tried to work out his feelings in a curious letter centred, like almost everything he did or wrote at this time, upon two deaths—his mother's and his own:

Monday Feb 15 1915   11.30 a.m.

It is my wish that all of my Darling Beloved Mothers letters also the 2 enclosed letters, shall be placed in a sort of black bag, and used as a pillow for my head in my coffin, and all to be buried with me.

The two letters, one that I wrote to Ma before my marriage and the love letter from my dearest wife, all can be buried with me, and they are of no use to anyone. My wife may read the letters if she desires, and then let her place them under my head.

I have loved two women in my time, my MOTHER God bless her memory and my wife.

My sister I love, so when I mention two women she need not think that I do not love her [added later:] I love her as very darling sister. My actions in the past has proven that I hope.

With the jewelry found Bess should keep it a year and then do what she likes with same [added:] the big jewel I bot in England, give to my sister Gladys. June 13 1915 (All attended to re this as you Bess gave it to Gladys. HH)

Harry Houdini
Ehrich Weiss
also Sept 27 1916
OK HH Feb 26 1921

Bess herself was merely a bit player in this welter of brooding and grieving. How can she have felt? Presumably she was by now used to Houdini's curiously impersonal style when he was supposedly addressing her on the most intimate matters. Had he ever achieved anything more relaxed in the course of day-to-day communication over twenty years?

Mrs. Weiss's death had removed Bess's chief rival for Houdini's affections—although there must have been moments, during his violent and prolonged mourning, when she felt that it had also claimed her husband, totally and irretrievably. Who can compete with a memory? Nevertheless, it was at this point that he began writing Bess daily love letters, a practice he kept up until his own death. He would leave them around the house for her to find:

"Good morning, my *handsome* sweet wife—Houdini [this was a very ornate signature]—the rare signature only found on his cheek and his heart letters to his *wife*."

As usual, these notes, with their curiously public style (as if they had been written to be read aloud in his defence, perhaps on the occasion of the Last Judgment), catered to Houdini's needs rather than Bess's. What they conveyed was Houdini's total emotional dependence upon Bess now that his mother had gone. He had to be sure that she would always be there to supply the uncritical support he craved—a need which extended to the grave and beyond.

These letters from the dead—these notes, as it were, from underground—resemble nothing so much as the kind of letters which are often written by intending suicides. In November 1913 he noted in his diary (he was then playing the Alhambra, Paris): "Am doing needle trick and U.S.D. Doing very big. Am very melancholy." Suicide was much on his mind. In December he took Bess to Monte Carlo. He needed a rest, and gambling had always diverted him. He felt like losing some money. Instead, he won: five hundred francs on his first visit to the casino, fifteen hundred the second time. So he abandoned the casino and spent most of the rest of his time in the place that most answered his mood—the suicides' graveyard. It was the only part of the trip he described in detail. He took his usual lively technical interest in details relating to death and burial:

> Dismal day. Visited graveyard where all suicides are buried. Persons who had lost their money and then committed suicide. A terrible feeling pervades the first time one sees the graves, and thinks of the human beings who finish their lives in this manner.
>
> More suicides in winter than in summer. Casino now pays return fares to losers, makes them sign papers, etc., and even ships bodies to their home towns to keep things quiet. When a body is found, money is stuffed in the pockets to cause the belief that money affairs did not cause the deed.

Suicides are buried for seven years, then dug up, placed in boxes
and saved in this manner for future reference in case relatives wish
to take bodies away . . . Saw grave of man and wife who committed
suicide together.

The first crisis passed, but two years later, death and his mother
were still uppermost in his mind. "When you say your Mother's
word is sacred, I envy you still having your Mother, for I lost mine
23 months ago, and Time has NOT healed the terrible wound, in
fact it has caused my hair to turn white . . . I take the liberty of
enclosing one of my Mother cards. Never forget her birthday or the
holidays, for Time will call some time when you least expect it . . . I
only work six months a year since I lost my Mother, and that is all I
ever expect to do for some time to come."

Why, feeling like this, did Houdini not actually commit suicide?
Death was an old prepossession, almost an old acquaintance. The
temptation—given his opportunities—must have been very great.

Sublimation is one partial answer. Artists are able to deal with
destructive and self-destructive feelings by diverting them into their
art; and Houdini was an artist of death. But this does not prevent
them from eventually committing suicide just the same. Edgar Allan
Poe and Yukio Mishima both shared Houdini's imaginative preoccupations, and both expressed them through their art to overwhelming effect. But this successful sublimation of their terrors did
not prevent them from killing themselves in reality as well as the
imagination. Poe drank himself to death, which may be seen as a
particularly protracted and painful form of self-destruction. For
Mishima, his suicide was—or was intended to be, for it was terribly
botched—the culmination of his life and art.

But their dramas were centred only upon death. Resurrection had
no place in them. For Houdini, however, it had always been the
central thing. He could not kill himself because he was too used to
saving himself. The reflex had become so strong that it was in the

end impossible to resist. In a sense, he committed suicide thousands of times. Louis J. Bragman, one of the earliest of Houdini's psychological devotees, remarks that "almost every stunt staged by Houdini represented a form of pseudo-suicide." But the whole point was that Houdini's suicides did not end in his death, but in his miraculous survival.

Nevertheless, after his mother's death, his stunt-dramas, which had always been fairly dangerous, became truly terrifying. The last limits seemed to have been kicked away. It appeared that there was nothing he would not risk, nominally in order to get publicity, but in fact to act out his own despair. It was now that he began to do straitjacket escapes while hung by his ankles from the top of skyscrapers. Although this position facilitated the escape, the stunt held a number of dangers apart from that of falling head-first to the ground. "A number of times his body, held taut by the strait-jacket, was swung towards the building by the wind, while a murmur of fear arose from the crowd," ran one account. "A minute, two minutes passed, and the crowd roared. Houdini's body, held rigid by the strait-jacket, was beginning to move. Slowly, but surely, the man who has startled the entire world by his feats and by his magic, began to work himself free from the instrument of torture. The wind continued to swing his body back and forth as it hung suspended by the feet in mid-air. Again the wind swung him towards the building, but once more he narrowly escaped being dashed against the brick wall. A roar from the crowd and the strait-jacket slowly floated to the ground!! He was free!!! Houdini waved his hands to the cheering crowd as he was lowered to the street again. Although the temperature was rather low, he was perspiring freely when he was released from the ropes that bound his ankles."

The routine was that he would seek out the leading newspaper of whatever city he happened to be playing and arrange to do the stunt from their building. This ensured that his picture would make the front pages and his name would be on the lips of the entire population, a large proportion of which would flock to his show.

In Pittsburgh, the crowd "not only packed the streets but filled every window and rooftop within view of the scene," reported the *Sun*.

. . . Urbane, smiling, the elusive Houdini appeared in the office . . . at 12 o'clock. The two attendants from Mayview [insane hospital] awaited him, and with them the straitjacket, in a satchel. Houdini shook hands with both men, speaking humorously of his position as substitute for the deranged persons the two Attendants ordinarily handle . . . "Treat me," he advised, smiling, "as you would the most dangerous of the criminal insane."

. . . It was almost 12:30 o'clock. Houdini glanced out of the window, and again his characteristic, quiet smile came to his face as he saw Wood street and Liberty avenue congested from wall to wall . . .

Then, a white-clad attendant on each side, he went downstairs to the street to be bound. A suppressed shout came from the crowd as he appeared in the doorway of the Sun building . . . Above him, like a gallows, a single beam projected from a window at the top story of the building, and a rope swung clear, coiling in sinister fashion at his feet. Houdini had removed the outer clothing from the upper part of his body. "Ready," he said.

The two attendants pressed close. His arms were inserted in the long, closed sleeves of the straitjacket. One of the attendants clasped him about the body, as if fearing he would make some mad effort to escape. The other standing behind him, fastened strap after strap . . . "Make it tight," came the quiet word from the prisoner.

The man's knees went up for purchase in the small of Houdini's back. Using apparently every ounce of strength in his broad-shouldered six-foot body, the attendant drew the big strap through the buckle until it would not yield even a sixteenth of an inch more. He caught it there and made it fast.

Then the arms of the prisoner were crossed over his body, and the ends of those closed sleeves were brought around in back. Again the knee was brought into use. Again the strap was pulled to its highest tension . . . Then Houdini's ankles were fastened to the rope, by a special appliance that prevented injury, but insured safety.

A word was spoken. The two attendants seized the bound man's body. Workmen drew the rope steadily through the pulleys. Houdini's feet went up, and as his body cleared the platform it was released. The handcuff king dangled head downward. Each

moment he was drawn higher, swaying slightly, spinning dizzily . . .
Then he hung still.

Only for a second. While watchers gleamed in the crowd below,
the handcuff king was seen to struggle, not frantically, but with a
steady systematic swelling and contracting of muscles, and almost
imperceptible lithe wrigglings of the torso. The struggle went on.
One minute—two—then three—

Would he do it? . . . From above came an inarticulate shout. The
muffled arms writhed one after another over Houdini's head. His
hand, still encased in the sleeves of the straitjacket, fumbled quickly
and effectively with the buckles at his back. Another contortion and
the straitjacket slipped down over his chest, over his head and was
flung from his arms to the street, in a crumpled heap.

Once again he had succeeded. Once again he had failed. That was
November 1916. The tour was to continue until the following
March. In September 1915, "the greatest street throng in the history of Los Angeles"—20–25,000 people—had seen him swing
from the Los Angeles *Tribune* building. The same month, 5,000
saw him in Kansas City, where the tie-in was with the Kansas City
Post. The following April 50,000 watched him in Baltimore; the
same month, he repeated the stunt in Washington, D.C. In San
Antonio, Texas, 12,000 gathered to see him at the San Antonio
Express building. He gave an interview there in his dressing room in
the Majestic Theater. "I don't know how long this thing can last,"
he said. "I have given myself from one to eight years, and that's a
liberal estimate. I am now forty-two years of age. I feel like I am
fifty-two years, and some of the time much older—just as I do this
afternoon. I have been told that it is hardening of the arteries. Perhaps it is. Whatever it is I am getting old and yet I have no particular
regrets. Some time or another we all grow tired. I have been tired
for a long time."

13

$\mathcal{F}$ILM STAR

 Houdini knew exactly how he would go over Niagara Falls in a barrel. Or rather: how he would "go over Niagara Falls in a barrel"—a very different thing. People *have* gone over Niagara Falls in a barrel and lived—the first, incredibly enough, was a schoolmistress in her forties—but that was not what Houdini was proposing. "The idea," he wrote, "is to be nailed in a packing case, thrown over Niagara Falls, and eventually make an escape!"

> So that the crowd can see I am being nailed into the packing case, the nailing is done on a platform, into which I can slide after the box is nailed up.
>
> The best way would be to have the platform on a large wagon, which is drawn down to the landing place, where I get into the water according to opportunity.
>
> Or else get back into the box when placed on wagon, and be found there, having failed to escape (being "knocked out" coming over falls.)
>
> This can be worked into an extra good idea and needs doing some time.

The nearest he actually came to realising this "extra good idea" was on film. In *The Man from Beyond* the heroine, who is unwisely canoeing in the Niagara River, finds herself drifting helplessly towards the falls. She is rescued in the nick of time by Houdini, the eponymous Man from Beyond. This is one of the more effective scenes in the Houdini movies. As *Variety* put it, "It has a whale of a punch." In *The World*, Quincy Martin "quivered at the views of the couple battling in the rapids on the verge of the cataract and almost cheered when they made the crawl to safety." The *Tribune* asserted that: "There is no fake about this: Houdini actually does it."

Really? Movies are not about *live* suspense. Film suspense, as every Hitchcock devotee knows, is created in the cutting room. Cary Grant was never in any real danger from that aeroplane in *North by Northwest*. What would have been the point? What use to a film is a dead film-star, or even a disabled one?

Nevertheless, "It was said later," Milbourne Christopher reports in the tone of one who reveals a shameful secret, "that dummies had been used for some shots." And why ever not? Houdini and his director would have been out of their minds if they had not used dummies, or safety lines, for this scene. But of course the answer is obvious. The Houdini legend was founded upon live risk. To acknowledge anything else would fatally undermine it. And the Houdini legend was what was going to sell the movies. In other words, everything Houdini was about was in direct opposition to everything movie making was about. It was a fatal contradiction, and he never resolved it.

Houdini went into movies because it was clear that something new had to be pulled out of the bag. He was getting older. He could not spend the rest of his life hanging off tall buildings in straitjackets. No stunt has eternal drawing-power. The public quickly gets blasé and demands something even more spectacular. Imitators spring up. And although he still missed his mother terribly, time dulls the edge of even the keenest grief. He no longer felt so suicidal. By 1918 he could bear to move back into his own house. He had by now a large staff to support, as well as an ever-growing library to house and feed. All this cost money. Houdini was always one for the coming thing: and movies were the coming thing, just as vaudeville was quite obviously on its way out. In 1908 the Kinetograph, showing "Interesting and Humorous Motion Pictures"—an international cross-country run in England and a melodrama, *And the Villain Still Pursued Her,* with musical accompaniment—had followed Houdini, who had the next-to-last star spot, as just another vaudeville attraction in the Keith Theater circuit. In 1927, following the overwhelming success of Al Jolson in *The Jazz Singer,* the Keith-Orpheum circuit wound up its theatre interests and joined with the Radio Corporation to form the RKO film company.

The fact that films were potentially a far greater draw than vaudeville had been obvious to the future Hollywood moguls for years. Many of them had started in show business by opening vaudeville arcades "filled," as Jesse Lasky remembered, "with automatic fortune tellers, strength testers and other fascinating gadgets." The gadgets also included movie peep shows. And "a row of movie peep-box dispensers of thirty-second dramas was collecting the steadiest stream of coins." William Fox had a similar experience with the burlesque theatre he acquired in Williamsburg, Brooklyn, in 1906. Fox's theatre combined movies and vaudeville at popular prices—fifty cents for the most expensive seats, ten cents for the cheapest. In 1911 he decided to do some audience research and sent out ten thousand cards requesting his customers to say what part of the performance they liked best. "Fifty-five percent of the answers were in favor of moving pictures," he told an interviewer. "Interest in 'comedy scenes' and 'heart interest' photoplays seems to be about equally divided. Instructive pictures showing countries and their manufacturing industries are appreciated most in the poorer districts. But everywhere it is the pictures, more than the vaudeville acts, that hold the audiences. The only explanation I can find is that motion pictures, perhaps, realize the American idea of speed and activity."

The Jews were able to take over the moving picture industry because it was not respectable. Movies were "toys" or "peephole sensations," and old money, gentile money, would have nothing to do with them. At best they were a fad, at worst, a moral embarrassment. Respectable finance refused to touch them or to recognise that this was where new money was to be made. First-generation Jewish immigrants, however, suffered from no such inhibitions. They were alert to any new business opportunities. As a rule, the route led from the Lower East Side to the garment trade. Marcus Loew was in velveteen capes; Adolph Zukor made his pile in furs; Carl Laemmle was a clothing salesman in Oshkosh. The garment trade made them prosperous. They were looking for new outlets for their energies, and they saw that vaudeville arcades, moving picture theatres and burlesque theatres had enormous business potential. They quickly realised that the movie business was far more interesting than garments. Of his first venture into the new field, an arcade called Automatic Vaudeville which was never meant to be more than a sideline to the fur business, Zukor wrote: "Our fur offices were nearby in Twelfth Street and, though handling the main end there, I couldn't keep away from the arcade." They began by smartening up the theatres, in order to change the movies' sleazy image into something respectable the whole family could enjoy. Laemmle called his first theatre the White Front—the cleanest image he could conjure up. They financed all this themselves, bringing in friends and family when they wanted to expand. (Hence the famous Hollywood rhyme: "Uncle Carl Laemmle/Has a very big faemmle.") Then they went into distribution, supplying their own chains of movie theatres. Production was the last, logical link in the chain.

It was Zukor who realised that the barrier movies had to overcome was not artistic, but psychological. By 1908 he had perceived "that these short films, one-reelers or less, didn't give me the feeling that this was something that was going to be permanent." For something permanent, he needed to be able to attract a middle-class as well as a working-class audience: films would have to be weightier—longer, and better. "You couldn't head him," recalled his associate at the time, William Brady. "Presently he was in my office bubbling over with grandiose ideas about the future of the movie racket. Some sixth sense had convinced him that the day of mere shorts was drawing to a close and full-length features, like *The Great Train Robbery,* only far longer and far better, could be the coming thing . . . It didn't make sense to me then . . . Zukor was about the only living human being who could guess what would happen."

And soon it was happening. In 1913 F. E. Powell, a well-known magician and a good friend of Houdini's, reported from Cuba to the magical magazine *M.U.M.* regarding the writing plainly visible to him on the wall. The "movies," he said, "now almost monopolize the best houses to the exclusion of the legitimate. The moving picture business has extended to an amazing degree, and the increase of theatres in all parts of the island is marvelous."

And yet it did not seem that Houdini was finished as a stage star. The years of World War I, which were also his years of despair at Flatbush, saw him at the height of his fame. Never had he received more publicity.

Not all of it showed him in a good light. In 1915, in Los Angeles, he had a set-to with the world heavyweight champion, Jess Willard. Hearing that Willard was in the audience at the Los Angeles Orpheum, he invited the boxer to come up onstage as one of the audience committee. Willard declined. Houdini would not take no for an answer. He turned the occasion into a contest of wills between himself and Willard. Willard, who was famously sulky and aggressive, was on a hiding to nothing. Houdini knew all about controlling his audience and getting it on his side. And in a public contest of this sort, it was never enough merely to make his point. He would never rest until his opponent was entirely destroyed.

This destruction was accomplished by means of a bludgeon, not a rapier. That was Houdini's mode; and that is the reason Houdini was and is not universally admired among connoisseurs of magic. "I don't like his style," is the way one of them puts it. "I don't like the way he rapes the audience." Hearing the recording of his patter for the "Water-Torture" act, one is struck by this quality. There is nothing here of the silky charm or wit that is many magicians' stock-in-trade. Each phrase is punched out with shattering force.

But Willard, who was not a bright man (nor a particularly popular champion) was used to trading physical, not verbal blows. He continued to refuse Houdini's entreaties, and soon became insulting. The audience cheered Houdini's sallies and hissed Willard's furious replies. Houdini won. Willard finally slunk out of the theatre amid hisses from the audience. Next day the headlines were Houdini's: 2,000 HISS J. WILLARD, CHAMPION DRIVEN FROM THEATER BY HOOTS AND CALLS, reported the *Los Angeles Times;* and the next day it followed this up: WILLARD LEAVES TOWN, SNEAKS OUT OF TOWN AS INDIGNANT FANS ROAST HIS CONDUCT. Houdini was jubilant. "My Dear Sister Gladys," he wrote,

> Well, at last I manage to sit down and relate to you how I defeated the World Champion Heavyweight Pugilist Mr. Jess Willard, and why the newspapers gave me the decision over him, which makes me the Newspaper Champion of the World.
>
> As usual I called for my committee during the course of my performance, and only seven men responded, so I stepped to the footlights and made a neat little speech, which you know is one of my favourite pastimes. I said that I would be highly honoured, and I thought the audience would likewise, if instead of three men, one who was equal to three would come up. "I refer to Mr. Jess Willard, our champion, who is here in the house." . . . Willard glowered down upon me . . . "Hey, you, go on wid the show—but if you pay me what youn pay those seven men who are on the stage, I'll come down."
>
> The audience started to hiss and boo him.
>
> "All right," I said. "I accept your challenge. Come right down and I'll pay you what I pay these seven men. Don't crawfish. Kindly step right downstairs and come on stage."

Audience applauds.

Mr. Jess Willard half arose and was going to crush me forever, blurting out in his guttural voice, "Go on wid the show, you faker, you four-flusher. Everyone knows you're a four-flusher."

Hisses from the audience, and I walked right down to the footlights nearest his side . . . "Look here, you. I don't care how big you are or who you are. I paid you a compliment when I asked you to be one of the committee. You have the right to refuse, but you have no right to slur my reputation. Now that you have thrown down the gauntlet, I have the right to answer, and let me tell you one thing, and don't forget this, that I WILL BE HARRY HOUDINI WHEN YOU ARE NOT THE HEAVYWEIGHT CHAMPION OF THE WORLD."

. . . Nothing like this howling mob of refined ladies and gentlemen ever crossed my vision of success . . .

The next night Willard was to referee a boxing match, but he was not allowed to appear.

Honest, Gladys, I have received at least a million dollars' advertising space from this fray.

(Willard had the last laugh, however. When he appeared at Hammerstein's Victoria Vaudeville Theater he was paid $4,000 a week to Houdini's $2,000. Evelyn Nesbit Thaw, presumably performing at the height of the Harry Thaw trial scandal [when her husband was arraigned for shooting her lover, Stanford White] received $3,500.)

In some ways, this might not have seemed the kind of publicity Houdini should be seeking. In his book *Handcuff Secrets* he was emphatic as to the importance of stage manners. "Nothing is more offensive to an audience than a performer to appear surly and bad tempered. He is there to please the public, and to do so he must be on the best of terms with himself and, I may add, in the best of humour."

But that had been written some years earlier; and with every year that passed Houdini was gaining confidence in his ability to control an audience. By now he had this down to a fine art. Audiences were an instrument which he had learned to play just as he wished. If misdirection was to succeed, nothing was more essential than complete mastery in this department:

> Suppose I want to use a short flight of steps from the stage down to the audience. I never have a carpet on them, because while I am transferring a watch or producing an egg from a hat I tramp heavily, and so draw your attention to my feet. If I think the audience is watching me too closely, I signal my assistant to drop something, or to make some sudden movement. If I want a chair, table, or basket brought on the stage, and don't want you to see it, I simply walk to the opposite side of the stage . . . All magicians know that the average person never raises or lowers his eyes very much. Most people just look on a straight level. Therefore, whenever we use tables fitted up with magic devices, we always raise them slightly above the level of the eye, so that when you think you are looking at the top of the table you are not. Really to see the top you would have to raise your eyes; and as this would be an effort you just don't do it.

Two years later, another free publicity opportunity presented itself. Sarah Bernhardt, then touring the States, was to be honoured by the American acting profession. They gave her a grand reception at the Metropolitan Opera House, New York, and presented her with a bronze statuette which they had had especially designed and made for the occasion. Unfortunately nobody had thought to pay for the statuette; and its maker, having failed elsewhere, sent the bill—for $350—to Bernhardt. She, understandably, returned the object forthwith. Houdini, reading about this, immediately stepped in, paid the bill and saved the day. Within a fortnight he had received 3,756 newspaper clippings, all praising his action and linking his name with Bernhardt's. A newspaper columnist, estimating the advertising at the reading-matter rate of a dollar a line, worked out the sums. Houdini had received publicity worth $56,340 for an outlay of $350.

Bernhardt was nearing the end of her long and illustrious career.

She had recently had a leg amputated. This tour was by way of a proof (to herself and others) that she was nevertheless undiminished. But the proud façade which she maintained so stoically, with her family no less than with her audiences, cracked before Houdini. She had heard that he had magic powers. Could he not (she begged him) restore her leg?

> "Good heavens, Madame, certainly not; you cannot be serious. You know my powers are limited and you are actually asking me to do the impossible."
>
> "Yes," she said as she leaned closer to me, "but you do the impossible." . . .
>
> "Are you jesting?"
>
> *"Mais non, Houdini, j'ai jamais été plus sérieuse dans ma vie,"* she answered.

Alas poor Sarah! She had fallen for the line Houdini was always promoting, that "secret" of his that stood him, in the mind of the audience, on the very edge of real magic. "It is when you do the 'impossible' that people sit up and gasp," he wrote. "That is why I do a different sensational trick every year."

Now, when he was thinking about moving from escapes into conjuring proper, he came up with his two most famous such tricks.

The first was walking through a wall, first performed in 1913. The stage was covered with a seamless carpet. On to this was wheeled a steel framework which stood about two inches clear of the ground and was several feet high. A team of bricklayers came onstage and built a solid brick wall inside this framework. When this was finished, Houdini stood on one side of the wall. Screens were placed at either end, and the stage committee was strategically stationed to ensure that there would be no slipping round the back. Houdini would wave his hands over the screen on one side of the wall and shout, "Here I am!" A minute would elapse. Then his hands would be seen waving over the other side: "And here I am now!" The screens would be drawn away. And there he was on the other side of the wall.

When rumours spread in some quarters that Houdini was able to dematerialise, this was one of the feats that was cited to prove it. But the secret, as with many tricks, was childishly simple. The wall was built over a trapdoor in the stage. This was covered by the carpet. Although this was seamless, it had enough give to produce a hollow deep enough for Houdini to crawl through. Then the trapdoor would be shut and all was as before. The trick made a great sensation. But he never repeated it after its single season (handing it over to Hardeen, who took it to Europe), because there were squabbles over the trick's provenance and ownership, and the secret had begun to leak out.

His other great illusion was the "Vanishing Elephant."

"People are much more interested in seeing things disappear than seeing them appear," Houdini wrote at about this time. "When you make things appear they say, 'Oh, he had it on him all the time!' But when you make things disappear, they are amazed." Vanishing rabbits were literally child's play; vanishing ladies were a cliché. But a vanishing elephant was something else. A vanishing elephant was there for the headline value.

The elephant was vanished in the Hippodrome, where Houdini had first wowed New York. The effect of the trick was heightened by the fact that everyone knew that, whatever might be happening, the elephant could not simply drop through a trapdoor into the space below the stage. The reason was that the Hippodrome stage was built over a pool which was used for water spectaculars.

So what did happen? The procedure was simple. A large "cabinet" was pushed onstage, and the elephant was led into it. The blinds were dropped. The cabinet was then turned sideways by a dozen stagehands, and two circular panels were dropped, giving the spectators a view through the cabinet. Where was the elephant? (And where was its trainer?) Various wise guys based their guesses on the facts that a) an elephant lying down is considerably flatter than an elephant standing up, and b) the floor of the cabinet was slightly raised. Others remember the cabinet as having had a square, curtained opening in front through which, when the curtain was raised, one could see through the circular opening at the back to the rear of the stage. In this version the elephant could not have been concealed by lying down, but was standing at what was (after the turn had been made) the side of the cabinet, which was wider than the uncurtained aperture. Houdini always said his cabinet for the "Vanishing Elephant" was eight feet square; in fact it was larger than this, and he gave the wrong size to put audiences off the scent. At any rate, the cabinet, which had been wheeled on by a mere three or four assistants, needed the round dozen to wheel it off. None of this mattered. What mattered were the headlines. These were only increased by the fact that the original elephant, Fannie, hired from Ringling's Circus, proved stage-shy. Nothing would induce her to enter the theatre. (The suspicion was that Ringling was not entirely surprised to hear this.) So another elephant, Lucy, had to be found to replace her.

Vanishing elephants and melting walls were certainly sensational. But they were crude, if clever—effect, not finesse. They achieved their end, which was to draw the headlines. But in a way they underlined the gulf between what Houdini did and what more conventional magicians did. "He was a stunt man," said Walter Gibson, who wrote books for and about him, "and was so regarded in his lifetime." Stage magic was not the compulsive stuff upon which Houdini's reputation was founded. He would have to look for something else, and he knew it.

So the movies seemed like an obvious answer. Their star was in the ascendant. Their mode was melodrama. It seemed as if Houdini was made for the movies, and they for him. He began to collect helpful clippings: CHAPLIN—AND HOW HE DOES IT; AT WORK WITH CHARLIE CHAPLIN; MRS. FISKE TO THE ACTOR-IN-THE-MAKING. In

June 1918, he wrote to a friend: "I have signed to play the star part of a big serial movie and twill take up all my time in six weeks, when the plot is finished. Will play Master Detective part as I believe."

The Master Detective was called Quentin Locke (presumably an allusion to the star's well-known skills). Locke was locked in combat with a criminal corporation called International Patents Inc., whose base was the castle of a wicked tycoon. The castle was built on a cliff overlooking a stretch of water whose continuity was somewhat shaky: it was sometimes the sea, sometimes a river. International Patents' main business was the suppression of new inventions which might interfere with the business of various vested interests. The models of these inventions were stored in a cellar beneath the castle, the Graveyard of Genius. The films also featured the tycoon's beautiful and terrified daughter, Eva, and a monstrous steel robot known as the Automaton. Upon this basis was constructed a thirteen-part cliffhanger. In it, Locke–Houdini is repeatedly trapped in lethal situations and as repeatedly escapes from them. He is bound with barbed wire in the path of a stream of acid; he is tied with ropes and rolled under a freight elevator which is slowly descending to crush him; he is nailed into a box and tossed into the sea, or maybe the river . . . Old obsessions also reappeared: one of Locke's escapes is from an electric chair.

The plots were ludicrous and the acting wooden. Houdini had no idea of acting. All he had ever done was be himself. This had not merely sufficed: it had earned him an international reputation. So why should it not do for the movies?

There were of course various reasons, all to do with the differences between the movies and vaudeville. Feature films, however sensational, could not be sustained by a string of escapes. They needed plot and character to hold the audience. But Houdini's plots (which he insisted upon writing himself) were nothing more than a framework for the escapes, which indeed provide the films' only moments of tension and life. The films were to be the public's big chance to see *how he did it:* using the slack in ropes that he was always able to gain because he was slightly bow-legged; untying knots with his toes; snapping the weakened links in chains . . . Unfortunately, however, they did not produce the same mesmerising effect on film as in real life.

Will Dexter, in his book *This Is Magic,* mentions a television film about Houdini in which the actor playing Houdini flaps his cloak at an elephant "and the great beast vanished. Just like that. WHOOF! And the elephant had gone." This was done by camera trickery. But Houdini himself would never have contemplated such a cheat. All his filmed magic was for real, and so were the risks he took—or at least as real as any risks he ever took.

But two things were missing in the films which were always there in a live performance. One was the possibility of a disaster. The compelling shadow of death was never present in the films. The other, however much the star might protest, was the certainty that what you were watching was the genuine article. The question was almost irrelevant, because everyone knew it *could have been* faked. So the tension of a live show was not there.

All this might have been offset by adequate plotting or characterisation. But Houdini was not a writer nor an actor. He was a magician. Not that that need have prevented him from making excellent films. George Méliès, one of the greatest of early filmmakers, was originally a magician. Many of his delightful two- and three-minute shorts are about magical illusion; and although they clearly involve camera trickery rather than prestidigitation, this is of no account. The films are enchanting in their own right. But film as a working medium held no interest for Houdini. Its only appeal was that it allowed him to reach a wider public.

Moreover, the particular format upon which he had alighted for *The Master Mystery,* and to which he stuck throughout his film career, was in important ways peculiarly unsuited to him. Houdini saw himself as a romantic hero, a cross between Tarzan and the Scarlet

Pimpernel, whose mission was to rescue fragile heroines from name-less fates by thrilling feats of derring-do. This is the fundamental storyline of all his films, and it is the basis of all the stories which he continued to produce even when there was no more need for film scenarios and which were ghosted for him by various hands (notably H. P. Lovecraft's in *Weird Tales* magazine). As far as Houdini was concerned, this was evidently *the* story from which all other stories were mere aberrations. The only variations he introduced were those of background. Sometimes his hero was a Neanderthal figure (as in *Yar the Primeval Man*), sometimes a secret policeman, some-times the frozen relic of another century *(The Man from Beyond).* But he was always fundamentally the same person.

This storyline, if it was to carry conviction, inevitably necessitated a certain amount of masterful cuddling of the heroine by Houdini. Unfortunately this was something he could not bring himself to indulge in. He had made his gesture in the direction of the opposite sex in his once-for-all pounce upon Bess twenty years earlier and had hidden thankfully behind the role of model husband ever since. But this was no help when it came to being a film star. The customers did not care whether or not film stars were faithful to their wives. They wanted to be vicariously swept away by Rudolph Valentino or, in the present instance, Quentin Locke. But Mr. Locke would be unable to oblige if Houdini could not forget his inhibitions. And he could not. He would never touch his leading lady if Bess was not right there to see that he did nothing immoral. He insisted on pay-ing her five dollars for every kiss that passed between himself and his leading ladies. Not many did; and even those were hardly worth the money. One distraught director, after a wasted morning spent vainly trying to persuade Houdini to put a bit of enthusiasm into a kiss, requested Bess to leave the lot. He said: "Whenever we get him to the point of kissing the girl he spoils the shot by glancing anxiously at you."

The Master Mystery was made by a company called B. A. Rolfe

Productions. Its appeal, even when it was made, was pretty much as kitsch. But Houdini's name was a draw. It did not do badly—in fact it made a considerable amount of money—and the new star moved a step up the ladder. Jesse Lasky, who had just joined with Zukor to form Famous Players–Lasky, signed Houdini for two films.

Interestingly, he now proposed to turn for his scenarios to Edgar Allan Poe, whose obsessions so closely mirrored his own. But although he sensed the affinity between them, that deep and genuine pairing of morbid imaginations, he was characteristically unable to recognise its nature. "His tales," Houdini commented, "contain the desired amount of mysticism, danger and opportunity for physical exertion." So much for the dark terrors of Poe's ghastly fantasies. He went on: "I am told out here in California, where I am working away at my scenarios and productions, that my act is bound to go well in the movies; so, if you hear that the Famous Players have made a small fortune during the year 1919, you will know at whose door to lay the credit for it."

In the event, Poe was spared the Houdini treatment. Houdini's first film for Lasky was called *The Grim Game,* and like *The Master Mystery,* it was written by Arthur B. Reeve and John W. Gray, with copious help from the star. In it, he broke out of a gaol cell, climbed the outside of the building to reach a dangling rope, and used it to slide to the street. He was captured after a fight and, as one might expect, taken up to the roof of the building, strapped into a straitjacket and suspended head down over the street below. (He freed himself, fell into an awning, rolled into the street under the wheels of a moving truck, grasped its underside and rode away.) Among various other heartstopping escapades, the script required him to jump from one plane to another in midair. Houdini, on a rope, was to do the jump: the cameraman would be filming from a third plane. The lower plane turned upwards: its propeller caught the upper plane. The cameraman, a true professional, kept on turning. Fortunately the two planes disengaged before they hit the ground. They crash-landed in a beanfield. No one was seriously hurt; the storyline was revised to include the crash, and the publicity featured it avidly. ("On June first 1919, the Associated Press carried from Los Angeles a story of the thrilling aeroplane accident that took place during the filming of 'The Grim Game.' . . . It's all in the picture—and lots more! The greatest thrill in the greatest thrill picture ever made!") What nobody was told was that Houdini had not been involved in the crash. His arm was in a sling at the time: he had broken his wrist falling three feet during a gaol escape. For the plane-to-plane descent they had had to use a double, Lieutenant Robert E. Kennedy. Other doubles, for even more dangerous feats, were dummies with Houdini's clothes and painted faces, seen in long-shot. Such is the deceptive world of film.

The Houdinis liked California. They rented a bungalow in Hollywood and enjoyed the unprecedented sensation of living in one place for months at a time. When Houdini was asked to name his favourite holiday spot, he nominated Hollywood. *Terror Island,* his next Lasky film, was shot on Catalina during the fall of 1919. It was the same mixture as before. Harry Kellar, Houdini's old friend and mentor, enjoyed it. He wrote, "What particularly left an impression on my mind was the fight in the submarine . . . where the water compartment was left open and the boat was being flooded . . . The scene where you rescue the girl from the safe . . . I just sat there and enjoyed it and shouted at the villain like a gallery kid. To me it was all real and I forgot I was looking at a movie."

Houdini enjoyed making films. What was more, he found that they gave a new impetus to his act. They had made him more famous than ever. (He kept all his fan letters, stuck neatly into scrapbooks together with their envelopes whose stamps record his various films' progress around the world.) And because of this new notoriety more people than ever wanted to see him perform live. His earning power in vaudeville rose to unprecedented heights. A record weekly salary of $3,750 offered by the London Palladium—the largest salary ever offered to a single entertainer—tempted him once more to Britain, where he had not performed for six years.

He sailed in December 1919, and the crowds flocked in. In financial terms the tour was his most successful ever. But despite general acclaim, his act was not what it had been, and some people were beginning to point out that the emperor seemed to be losing his clothes. Houdini had scored some of his first great successes in the English provinces; now it looked as if he might be about to lose his reputation there. The Nottingham *Football News* ran a very disappointed review of his performances there in April 1920:

> Somebody in the head office of Moss Empires owes me an apology over the Houdini visit this week. After receiving a long and fulsome screed of preliminary matter (three large type-written pages of it) which, extravagantly worded, contained the definite statement: "He will present his water-torture sensation AMONG OTHER FEATS," I felt justified in saying that the show he would give would be well worth seeing, and should not be missed by anyone. In fact I boomed of the disadvantage of the rest of the bill.
>
> No one was more astounded than I was to see on Monday night Houdini's solitary feat, which of itself lasts only three minutes, and no one has more sympathy with the candid remarks of large numbers of the patrons after the act than I have . . . Why on earth Houdini should imagine that any audience would be entertained by hearing a long and uncalled-for account of what he has been doing during the past six years I am at a loss to understand.

Terror Island was not a success, and Lasky did not renew his contract. Undeterred, Houdini determined to go into film production himself. He formed the Officers' Mystery Pictures Corp. Its president was Houdini, and its vice-president, Hardeen. He also had a Film Development Corporation. In 1919, between *The Grim Game* and *Terror Island,* he had acquired Martinka's magic store in New York. Now he sold it again in order to have more cash to devote to movie making. He had sunk $5,000 into his movie ventures before leaving for London, and had sent a further $10,000 from Britain. He had various movie ideas. There was a serial idea about "a ring that stole five hundred motors" taken from a newspaper: "can make use of the vanishing ideas I have also disappearing motors." But he finally decided upon a story written by himself, called *The Man from Beyond*.

The Man from Beyond had, like the mammoth, been frozen in a block of ice for many years, and the film concerned his attempts, once defrosted, to come to terms with the modern world. This was the film that featured, among other thrilling stunts, the Niagara Falls rescue. Houdini boosted it to the skies. "Greatest praise ever bestowed on any production," trumpeted the full-page advertisements in the trade press. "Territory available. Unlimited exploitation opportunities."

But, like Houdini's other movies, it was a disappointment. It was not simply that they were not very good. There was also, always, the frustrating sense that they really should have been better. There was so much talent and energy in Houdini; but, in movies at any rate, it went unexpressed. "It starts out promisingly," wrote one critic of *The Man from Beyond,* "with the assumption that a man incased in a cake of ice for a hundred years may be resuscitated and brought back from the Arctic to civilisation to find his sweetheart of a century ago reincarnated as a girl of identical appearance. Many things might be done with this fantastic conception. But none of them is done in 'The Man from Beyond.' Mr Houdini's imagination seems to have run out at the inception of his idea."

What Houdini might have done with his plots, had he possessed an iota of creative imagination, is shown in the stories ghosted for him by H. P. Lovecraft, who did. *Weird Tales* for May 1924 ran a story from this team entitled "Imprisoned with the Pharaohs" where Lovecraft's embroideries add the artistry missing from all Houdini's solo ventures into the nonvaudeville world: "Far over the city toward the great Roman dome of the new museum; and beyond it over the cryptic yellow Nile that is the mother of eons and dynasties—lurked the menacing sands of the Libyan desert, undulant and iridescent and evil with older arcana . . ."

Nonetheless, and despite Houdini's ludicrous acting, *The Man from Beyond* did tolerably well, mostly on account of the Niagara Falls scene. It seemed for a while as though Houdini's movie career and his vaudeville career might keep each other going. He signed for nine weeks with the Keith Circuit at $3,000 a week for the first four theatres and $3,500 for the last five. The mixture was the one which had failed to excite the citizens of Nottingham. It opened with film of his bridge jumps, continued with talk of his adventures and the old needle-threading trick, and ended with the "Water-Torture Cell." The tour ended in January 1922. The Keiths reengaged him. "I am working very hard, drawing bigger than ever," he wrote, "but must acknowledge that the publicity I have received in motion pictures is the prime cause of the big crowds . . . Every week is like an ovation . . . Despite my enormous salary they are engaging me for five more weeks." Some of the components of his show had not seen the stage for so many years that they seemed new again. *The Boston Globe* remarked on a new sensation he was introducing: "The exchange of human beings in a locked, sealed and corded trunk."

The Man from Beyond opened in April 1920, at the Times Square Theater. To ensure attendances, Houdini made personal appearances in which he treated the patrons to a full-scale spectacular magic show, including the "Vanishing Elephant," the needles trick, a straitjacket escape, and two illusions called "Goodbye Winter" and "Welcome Summer." In "Goodbye Winter" a girl (Mrs. Houdini) wearing furs stood on the top of three stacked tables. Houdini climbed a ladder to cover her with a cloth. When he pulled it away he shouted, "Goodbye, Winter!" and the girl was gone. In "Welcome Summer" a cone-shaped wooden structure was shown empty. Houdini fired a pistol, shouted, "Welcome Summer!" and up popped the girl garlanded with flowers.

The notes for the staging of these illusions are interesting, showing the kind of minutiae that have to be taken care of in a show of this kind. "Things to look after on the new material," noted Houdini. "A run for Mrs. H. to go up into G.W."

A sure fire cloth to pull away, and a sure string or tape for Mrs. H. to take hold of so it can be released when I pull at cloth.

Strap to pull extra gag back into place.

A string or strap to place against back to poles so Mrs H. cannot go back to far. Best to have a thin piece of bent tin or hoop iron.

Belt table together.

Get new square made for bottom table, and refix the second one.

Recover all tables with black velvet.

Get long white or gold stick to wave for other two trick.

Paint bottom of run white also ladder.

Make special bottom on Comet so I can open it myself from the back, after I turn it around towards audience.

Wire or cable to pull out Mrs. H. Trapeze or swing for her to sit down on about 2 feet. try and make it pull square by having the upper ropes also have trapeze bar.

Measure cone inside, to show audience that it is just as long inside as outside, to do this turn cone sideways so that the top and bottom are away from audience.

Lay calico hopp or frame on floor to show nothing comes from under stage.

String to hold ring so it can be passed immediately to me into the box.

Fix doors with elastic so they will not swing open. doors at bottom must be practically the same.

None of this, however, could turn *The Man from Beyond* into a moneymaker—and this time it was Houdini's own money that was disappearing down the drain.

"My dear old friend," Harry Kellar had written on the occasion of the founding of the Houdini Picture Corporation, "don't be rash but weigh well what you do and if you find the enterprise a 'dead one' don't let it swamp you. Remember Mark Twain lost nearly a million in a 'dead sure proposition' which was a complete failure."

This was sound advice, and now was the moment to take it. But Houdini could not believe his film career was over. He embarked upon yet another movie. After considering two or three ideas, he fixed upon another of his own creations. This had begun life as *The Mysterious Mr. Yu* but hit the screens as *Haldane of the Secret Service*. It was the same preposterous mixture as before. Houdini boosted it with all his genius for publicity. He had thousands of small slips of paper printed with the message: "This lock is not HOUDINI-proof. He could pick it as easily as you could pick a daisy. See the Master-Man of Mystery HOUDINI in 'Haldane of the Secret Service.' A picture that will thrill you to your marrows." He had two men work an eyecatching street stunt. They were carrying identical black bags and they met on a busy street. One man shouted that the other had taken his bag. When the quarrel had drawn a good crowd, one of the bags was opened and the two men brought out a big cloth banner bearing the name of the film and the house where it was showing, and held it up for the delectation of the crowd. But in spite of all this the film flopped, definitively.

There were no more movies. It was clear, even to Houdini, that although this might be the wave of the future, he would not be riding it. Houdini the film star embodied nobody's fantasies but his own.

In 1952, a film was made about Houdini's life starring Tony Curtis. Its publicity included the following:

A set of amazing parallels surrounds the picture. Both Houdini and Curtis were born in New York. Their physical resemblance is staggering . . . Curtis' real name is Bernard Schwartz, while the man who owned the motion picture rights to "Houdini" is Berman

Swarttz. George Boston, Tony's magic teacher, is married to Janet Boston. Tony's wife is Janet Leigh. Houdini died 26 years ago at the age of 52. Twenty-six is half the count of a deck of cards. Fifty-two cards in a deck. Tony is 26 years old, again the count of a half-deck, and "Houdini" went before the cameras on August 26th. There are three Georges connected with the production: George Pal, the producer, George Marshall, its director, and George Boston, Tony's trainer. Finally, Tony's middle name in Hebrew is Harry.

Such logic would hardly have been out of place in Houdini's own films.

$\boxed{14}$

MERLIN'S CAVE

In his book *Miracle-Mongers and Their Methods,* Houdini divulges various recipes supposed to induce heat-resistance, for the benefit of prospective fire-eaters.

The formula set down by Albertus Magnus was probably the first ever made public: the following translation of it is from the *London Mirror:*

"Take juice of marshmallow, and white of egg, flea-bane seeds, and lime; powder them and mix juice of radish with the white of egg; mix all thoroughly and with this composition annoint your body or hand and allow it to dry and afterwards annoint it again, and after this you may boldly take up hot iron without hurt."

. . . Another early formula is given in the 1763 edition of *Hocus Pocus.* Examination of the different editions of this book in my library discloses the fact that there are no fire formulas in the second edition, 1635, which is the earliest I have (first editions are very rare and there is only one record of a sale of that edition at auction). From the fact that this formula was published during the time that Powell was appearing in England I gather that that circumstance may account for its addition to the book. It does not appear in the German or Dutch editions . . .

"Take half an ounce of samphire, dissolve it in two ounces of aquaevitae, add to it one ounce of quicksilver, one ounce of liquid storax, which is the droppings of Myrrh and hinders the camphire from firing; take also two ounces of hematitus, a red stone to be had at the druggist's, and when you buy it let them beat it to powder in their great mortar, for it is so very hard that it cannot be done in a small one; put this to the afore-mentioned composition, and when you intend to walk on the bar you must annoint your feet well therewith, and you may walk over without danger; by this you may wash your hands in boiling lead."

Houdini prefaces these disclosures by remarking, characteristically: "The yellow thread of exposure seems to be inextricably woven into all fabrics whose strength is secrecy." But he hasn't exposed very much here. These recipes never made anyone fireproof. The secrets of fire walking, fire eating and flame resistance in general lie more in the domain of "natural magic"—the imaginative use of the laws of physics. The skin does not combust the instant it is brought into contact with flame: a certain time is needed for it to reach the necessary temperature. A fire-walking experiment conducted by the psychical researcher Harry Price found that a man was burned crossing a trench of coals in six steps, but another who crossed the same trench in four steps was unharmed. (The trench temperature was 740°C.) Heat resistance is increased by the presence of a film of water, or other liquid, which has to evaporate before the heat can reach the skin. This is what makes fire eating possible (along with the fact that fire needs oxygen: if things get too hot, all you need do is close your mouth, or breathe out: CO_2 will extinguish the flame). If you wet your feet before you tread the burning coals, you will run even less risk. But don't stop to take a photo in the middle of the trench, even so.

Prosaic details, however, were not what interested Houdini in this instance. *Miracle-Mongers and Their Methods* was not a manual for aspiring magicians. It was, rather, an opportunity for Houdini to display his scholarly prowess and its trappings: his exhaustive acquaintance with magical arcana, his knowledgeability as a collector, the unparalleled extent of his library.

Of course it is not unusual for people to be interested in the history of their profession. A great many magicians, amateur and professional, collect magical memorabilia. Part of Houdini's own collection was bought by a famous magician, John Mulholland, after he died, and is now owned by another, David Copperfield. But Houdini's passion had deeper and more obsessively complex roots than the average collector's.

In October 1925, just a year before he died, Houdini gave an interview to *Popular Science* that was inaccurate even by his relaxed standards. "It may seem surprising," his interviewer observed, "that one whose chief fame has come from dexterity of hand and strength of body should possess so remarkable a passion for pursuits of the mind. Actually, though, there is nothing surprising about it; for Houdini was a scholar and teacher long before he became a magician. The son of a clergyman and educator, he was raised in a scholastic atmosphere, and almost before he was out of his knee pants, he taught modern and ancient languages in a school his father conducted in Wisconsin. 'Books were my hobby, even as a child,' he told me. 'I read about every book in Milwaukee Public Library before I was fifteen . . . Some of the books I didn't understand—but I read them just the same. I believed, you see, that my life work would be teaching, so I wanted to learn everything I could about every possible subject.' "

When people rearrange their childhood for public consumption, the result is often more interesting than any mere recital of the truth. The picture is not of reality, but of aspirations: not the childhood and family they actually had, but the one they would have wished for. Houdini here bends the facts of his past. They are distorted, but not unrecognisable. His father, Mayer Samuel Weiss, had attended

rabbinical college in Hungary, served as a rabbi for a while in Appleton, Wisconsin, and thereafter taught Hebrew without much success: he could loosely be described as "a clergyman and educator."
Naturally, then, the Weiss household possessed a rabbinical respect
for learning. Houdini, né Ehrich Weiss, did speak one modern language other than English—German, which his parents spoke at
home—and probably had a smattering of an ancient one—Hebrew.
He may have sat in on his father's classes, although the notion that
he would ever have taught them is laughable. And it is more than
likely that he frequented Milwaukee Public Library.

As with the disquisitions on fireproofing, the important agenda
here is intellectual acceptability. He is really saying: I am a scholar,
and I come from a long line of scholars. And this was, in a sense,
true. One of the most extraordinary aspects of his career was that the
first instinct of this in fact wholly uneducated vaudeville artist, as
soon as he had a free moment in the struggle to keep body and soul
together, was to write books. His first, *The Right Way to Do Wrong,*
was published in 1906 when he was thirty-two; his second, *The Unmasking of Robert-Houdin,* in 1908.

Houdini made no secret of his wistful yearning for education. A
clipping survives in his papers: "IGNORANCE—Root of all Evil—
This is the Master that Drives Human Beings Through Suffering to
Misery." After he died his one-time enemy and latter-day friend, Dr.
A. M. Wilson, editor of *The Sphinx,* described a visit to the Houdini
home: "We talked for hours, not on magic but on his yearnings for
a higher education, that he might qualify as a writer and lecturer on
the deeper things of life than magic afforded. I outlined a course of
study which he would have pursued had he lived." Houdini described to Dr. Wilson his plans for a university of magic: "Do you
know that thoughts have come into my head, that when I get back
to New York, I may start an organization for a sort of institution in
which degrees will be given to the experienced and reputable magicians . . . Am being dubbed, 'Doctor and Professor,' and 'Doctor of

Tricks' in the colleges [he was then on a lecture tour denouncing fake spirit mediums] and get scores of letters, Doctor Houdini, and would like to get your reaction to the thought." The idea of being Professor Houdini appealed to him more than any other: "The public knows me as a magician, a mystifier, and a Cinema star . . . It does not know that I possess one of the largest privately owned libraries on occult subjects in the world . . . It does not realise that I am a student."

But formal education never did come his way; and so he had to make do with what he had picked up. And in this respect, too, the *Popular Science* interview is revealing. For the mark of the autodidact is not so much what he doesn't know as what he can't bear to leave out. Education is not just about gathering facts but about learning how to organise them. Education enables you to select your books and avoid feeling that you must read every book in the library whether you understand it or not. That is simply a way of trying to engulf the magical essence of all knowledge which, for the wishful self-educator like Houdini, is embodied in the rows of books on the library shelves.

His need to possess a library of his own is therefore clear. Only so would all learning be, literally, within his grasp: his to contemplate and use whenever he wished: *his.* He collected in much the same way as he had used the public library: wholesale, indiscriminately. Bess called him a "pack-rat." She groaned whenever another crate of dusty papers was delivered to the house. Alfred Becks, Houdini's librarian for many years, devised a routine whereby the boxes would be elaborately smuggled into the house to avoid her disapproving eye. He would carry the boxes to the front stoop, leave them in the vestibule, and then run back to ring the basement bell. Meeting Bess's suspicious glance he would say, "Madam, you see my hands are perfectly empty!"

Bess, faced with an ever-growing accumulation of dusty tomes and piles of paper, saw only a never-ending, uncontrolled heaping-up of stuff. "We have 'arrived' home safe. Am having an awful time with the books I brought back. Never realized the amount, until I tried to get them into my home. Its a good thing I played my entire tour, and was too busy to look at all the bookshops," Houdini reported on a typical booty-laden return. He bought entire collections, warehouses full of dusty bales: after his death, the boxes kept on coming for months. "Some of the important things I have collected lately," he wrote in 1925. "The Strobridge Lithograph Company went out of the theatrical business and they gave me a five ton truck full of lithographs which are reposing in my cellar. I am contemplating building a country home to house my entire collection. At the great Everett Wendell sale, I was the largest individual buyer, and it was only by the great collectors of the past two decades dying that I was able to accumulate some of my marvellous treasures. The great collectors of the past—Augustin Daly, Todeburg, Brown, Dick, Cox, Wright, Evans, Bement, Vail, Broadley, Morrow. It was only by the disposing of these collections that I was able to obtain their accumulation of years . . . In Edinborough, I walked into a book shop during the war and bought the entire stock on the fourth floor of the house built in 1700 . . . They tore down an Opera House in Iowa and I have the forty year accumulation of all letters . . . I bought a number of dramatic critics' letter files. Have important collection of Mansfield letters, I should judge about sixty and about one hundred Clyde Fitch letters, over a hundred of Edwin Booth, very scarce letters of Edmund Kean, the Siddons family, an enormous lot of writing of a great tragedian who lived to be over one hundred years of age [this was Charles Macklin]."

Collecting was a process that had begun on his first trip to Europe in 1900—the first time he ever had spare cash in his pocket—and which had continued full spate ever since. Even when he was temporarily living with his brother's family in Flatbush he had continued to accumulate stuff. He advertised in *The New York Times:* "As I possess the largest collection (private or public) in the world of material regarding magic, magicians, books, scripts, spiritualistic effects, documents, steel engravings, automata, am still looking for anything that would embellish my collection of interest on the subject of magic or mysteries."

This compulsive need to accumulate *stuff* was part of Houdini's becoming a scholar like his father. (Asked "Who is your favourite author?" he replied, unexpectedly, "My dad.") But, as always when the question of ancestry was broached, things were less simple than they seemed.

Dr. Weiss had had no problems about assimilating the lore of his fathers. One of the books which he would undoubtedly have studied at the Budapest rabbinical college is called just that: *Pirkei Avoth,* the Sayings of the Fathers. This archaic Aramaic tome would have been both inaccessible to Houdini, and, like Dr. Weiss himself, irrelevant to his life. But his diligent search for new fathers, his fathers in magic, provided him with his own *Pirkei Avoth.* He spent his life collecting and chronicling an adopted heritage.

In it, he found that contentment which eluded him elsewhere. Vladimir Nabokov, as articulate about his sensations as Houdini was inarticulate about his, collected butterflies. He wrote movingly of the perfect happiness this passion afforded him: "The highest enjoyment of timelessness . . . is when I stand among rare butterflies and their food plants. This is ecstasy, and behind the ecstasy is something else . . . It is like a momentary vacuum into which rushes all that I love." I have little doubt that Nabokov here speaks for all collectors. Here, and perhaps here only, Houdini's tortured and obsessional soul found true and timeless happiness and peace.

Houdini's accumulation and study did bring with it the desired scholarly satisfaction and authority. In the summer of 1916, for instance, he developed an interest in the Booth family—Edwin Booth the actor and his brother John Wilkes Booth, the assassin of Abraham Lincoln (who interested him for both theatrical and ghoulish reasons). "Yesterday I bot a book Edwin Booth and his art by W.

Winter and shall 'study' Booth so that I shall be able to talk intelligently about our great actor," he reported. He soon felt the urge to know more but wrote: "I know that I cannot go in for Drama collection, the field is stupendous, and I have thrown away many an opportunity of obtaining material in foreign countries as I only sought magic. And now I am in America, and could not tie up the money required, for I will admit (privately) that the Press Agents have made me a rich man (on paper)." That was on 4 July. But less than a fortnight later he had succumbed to temptation: "I told Mr. Becks (Alfred Becks, who was later to take the job of cataloguing Houdini's own collection, was then cataloguing the Robert Gould Shaw collection at Harvard) that I was going in for Booth material, and he started in to tell me about the Booth collection in the Shaw World of Drama, and I felt my feet grow cold." And nine years later he was corresponding with a fellow enthusiast about Booth esoterica: "I have at least one hundred letters of Edwin Booth and one of every member of the family. I have the full account of the early marriage or the first marriage of Edwin Booth's father . . . If memory serves me right, the lady referred to as the first wife of Edwin Booth's father and her children are buried in Baltimore." Characteristically, he suggested that his correspondent might be helped in his Booth research by visiting the grave of the first Mrs. Booth. By the time he had finished, he was an expert on Booth.

Another collector's pleasure is that of context, "a relationship to objects which does not emphasize their functional, utilitarian value . . . but studies and loves them as the scene, the stage, of their fate." In this sense, his librarian Alfred Becks was, for Houdini, a collector's item in himself. Through him, it was possible to trace a direct connection back to David Garrick and Mrs. Siddons, and (by stretching things slightly) almost as far as Shakespeare. The line (as Houdini described it) ran thus: "Mrs. Siddons knew Mrs. Garrick; Mrs. Garrick knew Edmund Kean; Edmund Kean had as an admirer Couldack and at that time Mrs. Vestris was running a theatre. She was the great amorous actress of that time . . . At any rate, she married Charles Matthews, Jr., and Dion Boucicault who wrote a number of plays for them came to America right after Couldack and became one of the well-known authors . . . Mr. Becks was his private secretary for years . . . and Couldack and Becks intimate friends . . . Edmund Kean knew Cook, who was the competitor of David Garrick, Barton Booth, even coming to Quinn and Betterton. They all received their stage business from one another and from Burbage and perhaps from Shakespeare himself."

Once Houdini began discussing this kind of thing, he was oblivious to all else. He once took a cab to see a friend (Carl Brema) who made conjurers' apparatus, told it to wait for him, and only remembered he had done so when he emerged several hours later to find it still there. He and Brema had been immersed in magical discussions. Tiny slips of paper on which he noted items of interest are scattered through his letters: "Linsky in a gun accident killed wife de Y"; "Just run across the European Magazine and July first 1789 Thomas Denton was hanged in public with three other men . . . This occurred July and you will find full account of it in the European Magazine, it is a good life of Denton, states specifically that he wrote rather translated Pinetti's book." He added: "Save this Sargent [J. W. Sargent was his private secretary]. Sending it to you, as it records the only English magician ever hanged . . . The French Louis I was reprieved but Rollin had his head cut off during the reign of terror."

But the thrill of the chase far exceeded such passing serendipitous chances. The chase is the essence of all collecting, in which the desired object is located, stalked and finally, triumphantly, acquired. He had various trusted agents who would act for him at auctions. The English magical collector Harry Price bid for him on more than one occasion for items such as rare first editions which Price already possessed. On one occasion Alfred Becks brought a particular set of books to his attention. They were ones Becks himself particularly wanted, and he intended to bid for them. He returned from the auction crestfallen: he had been outbid by someone who could afford much more than he could. The mystery buyer had in fact been Houdini, who had also coveted the books. When he saw how disconsolate poor Becks was he felt very ashamed of himself, and the parcel of books lay hidden and unopened in his cellar. Some time later Becks died. Houdini was griefstricken. He visited three different florists and ordered three wreaths to be sent under assumed names to ensure that the funeral would be a fitting one. When he came home, he sat down and wept. Then he straightened up. "Now I suppose I can get those books from the cellar!" he observed.

He wrote to Harry Price extolling his collection:

My Dear Mr. Harry Price,
. . . My librian informs me that it will take more than a year to classify and arrange my library.
So I shall have to have a permanent man to fix my books. This will give you an index of the extent of my collection.
My dramatic portion is supposed to be the *greatest private* in this country. And that is saying a *great deal,* for there are quite a number of millionaire collectors. I do not claim its the most expensive, for Folger of the Standard Oil has a few millions in Shakespeares but my rare tracts, makes my library one of The libraries of the world, and when I get it arranged you will hear about it. My Garrick (I have his private diary) Kean, Kemble etc. etc. would cause you to think you stept into the British Museum that is one corner of it.

That last phrase rings slightly false. "One corner of it" is a mere afterthought. For Houdini it was necessary to believe, whatever lip-service he might pay to other people's mistaken prejudices, that his library was the best and the greatest with no exceptions at all. In this field as in all others, he "vehemently wanted to be first." But he admitted a few competitors for the sake of credibility. He classed his dramatic library as the fifth most important in the world (after Harvard, the British Museum, the Huntington, and the Folger). There was also his magic collection, the largest of its kind, and his materials concerning "psychic phenomena, witchcraft and kindred subjects," also the largest of its kind.

If Houdini liked to see himself as a student, even a professor, the role which embodied the acme of his ambitions was that of author. He set out his thoughts on his literary career in a sketched obituary sent to his secretary Oscar Teale:

> His research into the files of Magical History is entirely a labor of love, and though he may not be remunerated for his labor, perhaps when the years have passed, and when he has long received his Mandate for the other world, perhaps the first authentic history of magic his Robert Houdin unmasked will actually be his monument.
>
> Like Sir Wren, to whom no monument has been erected, and who is resting in St. Pauls London, when any one asks where is his monument, they say "Look around and see them."
>
> So Houdini may have erected his own monument for at no other period of printery has any one ever delved into the real magical history, and have same published.
>
> . . . Like Alexander, (Teale was it Alexander who wept because he had no more worlds to conquer) Houdini sought for other worlds to enter.

Houdini's books, the proof of his scholarship, were little more than distillations of his collection. Even the books he wrote ostensibly based upon his own career, such as *Magical Rope-Ties and Escapes* or *The Right Way to Do Wrong* or *Houdini's Paper Magic,* turned into historical compendia; *The Unmasking of Robert-Houdin, Miracle-Mongers and Their Methods* and *A Magician Among the Spirits* were overtly such, while also (in the case of *Robert-Houdin* and *A Magician Among the Spirits*) destroying the enemy of the moment. They are all profusely illustrated from his own collection.

But his books present a problem of their own. Houdini's writing style, as may be seen from his letters, was chaotic and at times barely literate. His books are hardly models of coherence. Nevertheless, it is hard to believe that they come from the same untutored hand.

This is because, on the whole, they don't. "When we speak of the writings of Houdini, we must qualify the statement," observes one commentator. "To the best of my knowledge, Houdini did very little writing himself. He always had at least one secretary, and I have been told that at times he had as many as three, all at work, on different projects. I know that Messrs. Albert Guissart, Clinton Burgess and Oscar Teale all worked on 'Elliott's Last Legacy' . . . Another secretary was Mr. John William Sargent and, in the later years, Mr. Bernard M. L. Ernst, who was Houdini's attorney, also did some writing for him. I believe he was at least partly responsible for 'A Magician Among the Spirits.' " Others, too, were involved in this factory. At the time of Houdini's death, Walter B. Gibson was preparing three volumes on simple magic which were to appear under Houdini's name. He employed ghosts, including H. P. Lovecraft, for several short stories based upon plots he provided.

His methods seem to have varied depending on his collaborator. With Lovecraft, Houdini provided the outline of the story and had the final say over the printer's proofs, while Lovecraft did all the actual writing. Oscar Teale, on the other hand, working on *A Magician Among the Spirits*—in the preparation of which he played a large part—was faced with nothing so collected as an outline. The notebook from which Houdini collated this work contains pages and pages of instances of murder induced or committed by spirit mediums for various ends, and suicides induced by them. From these, something in the nature of a connected text had to be hewn by the factory. Teale groaned: "This is a good example of the disjointed, irrational, irrelevant 'composition' or dictation by Houdini—I have never known him to dictate more than *suggestive* thought, mere fragments—followed by instruction to 'whip it into shape' and these fellows, being unfamiliar with the subject, often if not invariably confused the subject matter by erroneous statements." Even where Houdini appeared to take pains checking the truth of his allegations and obtaining permissions, he refused to allow anything so inconvenient as a refusal to spoil his effects. When the editor of the London *Times,* in a handwritten note, "present[ed] his compliments to Mr Houdini and desire[d] to inform him that he [was] unable to allow Mr. Houdini to use the name of *The Times* in connexion with his book on Spiritualism," Houdini commented: "This might have been written by the office boy! It bears no signature therefore cannot be proven by anyone."

Thus he manipulated his books into existence. But, curiously (considering his methods), there is nothing impersonal about the end result. His voice—obsessional, overbearing, unmistakable—blares out from them. This is partly because, once the material had been "whipped into shape," he made endless additions and corrections. Houdini was an editor's nightmare. The final corrections of *A Magician Among the Spirits* consist of dozens of little bits of paper, some typed, some scrawled, corrections made on the back of letters, corrections made on tour . . .

But there is also another reason: and this is that although members of his factory might grumble about his methods, they absorbed his personality to the point where their own was completely subsumed within it. The corrections to the *A Magician Among the Spirits* galleys were made by Teale; but he speaks with Houdini's voice to the extent that it is almost impossible to believe this is Teale, not Houdini, writing. The authentic aggressive, defensive tone is there: "It would take the rest of Houdini's lifetime to read *all* the books in his library. He has never made such claims. Doyle [Sir Arthur Conan Doyle, with whom Houdini was then quarrelling about spiritualism] accuses him of saying that he *has attended 10,000 séances. A statement Houdini never made.*" It is easy to imagine Houdini carrying his battles to the very margins of his galley proofs. That his secretary should feel impelled to do so on his behalf says something about the hypnotic quality of his persona.

The same quality was apparent when the question arose of credit and its apportionment. Houdini insisted upon claiming all credit for any book in which he was involved: his collaborators received little if any acknowledgement. *Elliott's Last Legacy*, mentioned above, was a case in point. Elliott was a doctor who gave up medicine to become a professional magician, and when he died his father asked Houdini to collaborate in the collating of his memoirs and tricks. The father was outraged when Houdini's name appeared as prominently as his son's on the title page. It read:

Elliott's
Last Legacy

secrets of the
KING OF ALL
KARD KINGS

. . .

By

DR. JAMES WILLIAM ELLIOTT
edited by
HOUDINI

Compiled by Clinton Burgess   *Illustrations by Oscar S. Teale*

But, for Houdini, this was merely his usual practice: Elliott's outrage would simply have surprised him.

When Henry Ridgely Evans, an old friend, was revising his *The Old and the New Magic,* Houdini contributed a good deal of information and went over the manuscript at Evans's request.

My Dear Evans, [he wrote]
It is three A.M. I have pored over the script since 7 o'clock, intending only to write a few lines, but I unpacked the script, and have reread it.
. . . I think in the preface you might thank me for my anything you wish to call it [handwritten addition: "kindness, co-ordination—or material?"], for honestly I am doing this so that the history of magic will be correct. Let OUR TIME start the acurate magic age.

And if you will send me the proofs, and I can assist you, will do so with pleasure time permitting.

I have so much material, that what you are writing does not even touch it in any way.

There are a number of places where I could let you have some programmes, that would just fit.

Think I have written enough for tonight, or morning, so will close.

. . . Well so long good morning. H. Houdini.

Next day, Houdini wrote to Evans again. He said there was so much of his material in the book that the authorship should be credited: As originally planned by Harry Houdini and Henry R. Evans Litt.D. Houdini pointed out that he was asking no money—just credit. But by this time (1917) money meant little to him (though it meant plenty to Evans, who was hard up). Credit, on the other hand, was the whole point. Credit was everything. He begrudged every morsel of it shared with someone else.

Yet Evans put up with it. His references to Houdini in the edition of *The Old and the New Magic* published after the latter's death are consistently admiring and affectionate. His friends grumbled, but they remained his friends. They had joined his cast, willingly: they accepted that the fulfilment of their allotted role, whatever that might be, was the price they had to pay. He had them in his thrall.

As the years passed, the library began to work its magic. People began to see Houdini as he dreamed of being seen. "He now appeared in his true role," commented Edmund Wilson, ". . . not precisely that of an entertainer, but of an expert on magic, equipped for his peculiar field with more intelligence, experience and learning than had perhaps ever before been brought to it. At this period, he seemed to take more pleasure in explaining how tricks were done than in astonishing people with them."

"I live in a treasure-house of mysticism and intensely interesting affairs," he wrote. Visitors to his house were shown into "a long room, rather too full of furniture, books and bric-a-brac." Here they waited before being shown up into the library; and here, unknown to them, Houdini could, if he chose, listen to everything they said. He had had the house specially wired, and enjoyed impressing his visitors with his apparent "second sight." This arrangement was satisfactory on two counts. It gave Houdini an immediate advantage over the unsuspecting visitors; and it could be used to practical effect. When psychical research circles in London were bowled over by Professor Gilbert Murray's demonstrations of kinaesthesia, in which he told people what they had been discussing in distant rooms, Houdini gleefully replicated his effects, to general consternation. (Whether Murray used a similar system is not known. It seems improbable. But far more improbable things have happened in the history of psychical research.)

The anteroom was full of souvenirs. "On a massive table stood a jewelled cup (presented to Houdini by Grand Duke Sergius of Russia), a coin-studded vase (a token of admiration from the management of the Essen Ruhr Coliseum where Houdini broke all records) and a beautiful magician's wand (a gift from the late King of Belgium) . . . In a tall case [were] a large assortment of wands that had been wielded by famous magicians. John Henry Anderson's was there, Alexander Herrmann's (and his wife Adelaide Herrmann's) and, of course, Harry Kellar's . . . On a pedestal was a strikingly lifelike head and bust of the Master Magician himself, done by Cassidy, an Irishman, to be set on Houdini's grave."

These treasures meant a lot to Houdini. "Did he feel that they linked him in some way with the original owners?" wondered one correspondent to whom he described them. He almost certainly did: owning the wands of his magical predecessors, he possessed himself of their magic. He especially treasured a writing-desk which had belonged to Edgar Allan Poe, that kindred spirit. The bust, meanwhile, towered over all these memorabilia, affirming his pre-eminence in this world. As for the next, he knew that matters regarding his own tomb, the monument that always loomed so large in his imagination, would be satisfactorily attended to. He had seen to it himself.

One visitor (who was frankly charmed) gives a graphic picture of Houdini at fifty: "Dressed, according to the season, in light trousers, with shirt open at the throat and sleeves cut off at the elbows, he evidently had been hard at work earlier that evening. He is not a large man and, as he himself will frankly tell you, not a particularly young one, but he is well built, and so full of energy and enthusiasm that it is simply impossible to ticket and pigeonhole him in terms of years. At fifty he not only looks but seems forty; after thirty-one years of marriage, his wife is still his closest friend and active partner . . . I find it difficult to translate his charm and dynamic or rather magnetic vitality into words. There is a rare delightfulness in his personality . . . In his make-up there is a dash of Puck . . . Yet nothing could be more clear-cut than the workings of Houdini's versatile mind. His fine head is well set on splendid shoulders and I noticed, as he talked, how developed were the tendons as well as the muscles of his forearms. I think it rather significant that I did not, although I particularly intended to do so, notice his hands. I have a sort of confused recollection of them but my eyes seem, oddly enough, to have been both more occupied and less observant than usual. Frequently I was too absorbed in watching what he was doing to notice details—as when he broke off the first joint of his thumb and showed it to us entirely separated from the remaining part, then calmly setting it back again where it belonged, gave his thumb a little pull and held it up once more whole . . . I could almost have sworn I heard a brittle sounding snap as he broke it off . . . 'Lady Conan Doyle nearly fainted,' he commented, 'when she first saw me do it.' "

Thus Merlin in his cave. For what was Houdini now if not a mage? He had gathered up the wisdom of the centuries, and now it was he who controlled it, ensconced in its midst, the wizard in his lair.

Magic is the search for total control. "As I do will, so mote it be," run the witchcraft spells. An adept describes the student's training in the rites of magic:

> During his process through the early grades he should be trained in emotional and mental control . . . After the individual has achieved the optimal mental, emotional and physical control over himself, which means control in function, not inhibition, it is his task to face the Dweller on the Threshold . . . [This involves] personal Agony in the Garden, Trial, Crucifixion, Descent into Hell and eventual Ascension . . . Once the process has been gone through, the individual is in a position to look everything in the face, without distortion or delusion, and to accept full realization for all that he does or has done . . . And how does he work out his destiny? By being himself—literally. By acting within the centre of his being, his essential self. Not by acting according to the dictates of his mind, his emotions or his instincts, but by using them according to his and their needs.

The allusion to the Christian Passion is evident. But what is described here is every shaman's journey. Houdini had trodden this path time after time. Now at last he had arrived, blowing his own trumpet as always, on the other side.

15

MAGICIAN AMONG THE SPIRITS

The production of ghosts—visible yet intangible—is one of the most ancient and impressive branches of magic. These illusions are produced using mirrors. The mirrors used in the earliest such deceptions were almost certainly concave. If a strongly lit object is placed where it will be reflected in the mirror, but in a position where it is invisible to the spectators of the illusion, an image of the object will be projected into the air of a darkened room. The image may be much strengthened if some sort of screen—for instance, a column of smoke—is provided for it. "As in all experiments with concave mirrors, the size of the aerial image is to that of the real object as their distances from the mirror, we may, by varying the distance of the object, increase or diminish the size of the image. In doing this, however, the distance of the image from the mirror is at the same time changed, so that it would quit the place most suitable for its exhibition. This defect may be removed by simultaneously changing the place both of the mirror and the object, so that the image may remain stationary, expanding itself from a luminous spot to a gigantic size, and again passing through all intermediate magnitudes, till it vanishes in a cloud of light." Such images are almost identical with those apparitions of the gods in their temples described by the ancients. They were intended to terrify, and doubtless that is just what they did. "A national system of deception, intended as an instrument of government, must have brought into requisition, not merely the scientific skill of the age, but a variety of subsidiary contrivances, calculated to astonish the beholder, to confound his judgment, to fuddle his senses, and to give a predominant influence to the peculiar imposture which it was thought desirable to establish." Thus wrote Sir David Brewster, author of a treatise on *Natural Magic,* whose intention was to demystify such tricks.

There is no record of any nineteenth-century medium using optical illusions of this kind to produce his or her effects. By then, such knowledge was no longer restricted to a few powerful people. Magic lanterns were generally available, and ghosts were frequently produced in stage shows—though these, by now, generally used the flat mirror technique perfected by Professor John Henry Pepper of the Regent Street Polytechnic and commonly known as "Pepper's Ghost."

Nevertheless, magical skill had not lost its power to inspire awe and terror when skilfully used, on or off the stage. The "spirit-rapping" craze which swept Europe and America during the nineteenth century was proof of the effects which could be produced by even the crudest practitioners; while for the truly skilful and unscrupulous, it provided possibilities of real wealth and influence.

One of the fundamental skills any medium had to cultivate was some sort of technique for escaping from rope-ties or other constraints. For the most basic test of supernatural powers was his or her ability to produce phenomena while securely "controlled." The medium would be held or tied so that no hand or foot was free and no movement was possible; then spirit hands would brush the sitters in the darkened room, ghosts would walk, objects would move, and wonder reign.

Among the earliest and most successful exponents of these techniques were the Davenport brothers, William and Ira. Among many
other refinements, they evolved the "cabinet" in which manipula-
tions might take place in decent privacy, and which was so central a
part of Houdini's own equipment. Their cabinet was fitted with a
bench on either side; into each bench two holes were drilled, a little
distance apart. The brothers would seat themselves opposite each
other, their feet squarely on the floor in front of them. "The end of
a rope was passed around the legs of one of the brothers, close up by
the knees, and tied. The rope was then wound around the legs several times, fastened at the ankles, the remaining portion carried
straight across the cabinet to the other brother's ankles, fastened,
wound about his legs and tied at the knees. A shorter piece of rope
was then tied to each of their wrists with the knots lying next to the
pulse. These ropes were threaded through the holes and the wrists
drawn down to the benches, and the ends of the ropes fastened to
the ankles." The room was then darkened; instruments played, bells
rang, objects flew about; what could this be but a display of supernatural powers? The Davenports were a sensation. Myths flourished.
Ira was supposed to have levitated across the Niagara River; to have
risen during a séance until his head went through the ceiling; and to
have escaped from prison by spiritual means.

The Davenports never claimed supernatural powers for themselves. But they allowed them to be claimed on their behalf by their
manager, a Dr. Ferguson. And they never disclosed the secret of
how they managed to produce their phenomena—not to their children; not to their assistant, the young Harry Kellar. Kellar nevertheless worked it out, and the "Davenport Rope-Tie" made his
reputation as a magician. Some people are of the opinion that all
magic as we know it today in America and Britain can be traced back
to the Davenports, through Kellar and through J. N. Maskelyne,
who as a young boy attended a Davenport show in the daytime
when the curtain fell by accident and all was unintentionally revealed. Maskelyne later became a noted exposer of mediums. But

those who wanted to believe remained unperturbed. "If you think it is all juggling," remarked Alfred Russel Wallace of Maskelyne, "point out exactly where the difference lies between it and mediumistic phenomena." Wallace had worked out the theory of evolution independently of Darwin, but believed avidly in spiritualism nonetheless. What he meant was that Maskelyne, contrary to his protestations, was a true medium. Maskelyne's assertion was of course just the opposite: that mediums are accomplished conjurers.

Years later, when Kellar had become the doyen of American magicians and the mentor of a new star, Harry Houdini, he revealed (to Houdini's surprise) that although William Davenport had died in 1877, Ira was still alive. He lived in Maysville, New York, where Houdini at once wrote to him. This was just before his tour of Australia, where he made a point of visiting and restoring William's grave.

On his return he hurried to visit Ira, who was the very type of those magical father figures Houdini always loved to cultivate. They spent a long and happy day together, during which Ira revealed the Davenports' secret. "Their method of releasing themselves was comparatively simple. While one extended his feet the other drew his in thus securing slack enough in the wrist ropes to permit working their hands out of the loops. (Note: They rubbed Vaseline into their hands and wrists to facilitate their movements.) The second brother was released by reversing the action. After the demonstrations were completed the brothers slipped their hands back into the loops from which they had drawn them, placed their feet in the original positions and were ready to be examined. When the cabinet was opened the ropes appeared as taut as when put on by the committee."

They never met again. Ira Davenport had survived many vicissitudes, but the curse of Houdini was too much for him. An appointment to meet the magician a second time had the same effect on the old showman as a similar appointment had had upon Wiljalba Frikell years before. "Curiously enough, I had made an appointment with Ira E. for July 9th, 1911, and was making ready for my trip to his home in Maysville, N.Y., when the sad news reached me of his death on the 8th." Houdini kept his secret until *A Magician Among the Spirits* was published in 1924. Until then, all he would say was: "Regarding the Davenport Brothers, I am afraid that I cannot say that all their work was accomplished by the spirits."

The Davenports travelled the world, generally to great acclaim. They were twice almost exposed: once in Liverpool, when their cabinet was smashed and a near-riot ensued, and once in Paris. They were guyed, to great acclaim, by Sir Henry Irving in Manchester. (Irving was annoyed because the Davenports were proving to be a potent rival draw.) Yet this did not prevent a great many people from continuing to believe in them. The famous explorer Sir Richard Burton wrote, "I have spent a great part of my life in oriental lands, and have seen there many magicians . . . I have read and listened to every explanation of the Davenport 'tricks' hitherto placed before the English public, and, believe me, if anything would make me take that tremendous jump 'from matter to spirit,' it is the utter and complete unreason of the reasons by which the 'manifestations' are explained."

The Davenports rode the first tremendous wave of spiritualist enthusiasm in the 1860s and 70s. After that the general craze for it died down somewhat. But there was, as might be expected, a great revival during and after World War I, which cruelly robbed so many families of sons, brothers and husbands.

Among those who turned to spiritualism at this time was Sir Arthur Conan Doyle. He had for many years been interested in psychical research, but in a comparatively detached way. Now, however, like so many others, he clutched at this last straw to comfort himself in a time of terrible loss. The war saw the deaths of his son, Kingsley, and the brother of his second wife, Jean. Jean had at first tried to discourage his enthusiasm, but after her brother's death she became as committed as he, and discovered in herself a faculty for automatic writing: a gift she shared with her children's governess, who had also lost three brothers in the war.

Houdini and Doyle met in 1919, when Houdini was playing at Brighton, not far from Doyle's home in Crowborough, Sussex. The basis of their friendship was a shared interest in spiritualism. Houdini had always been fascinated by it. He knew of course that most "spirit mediums" were fakes: he and Bess had themselves been fake mediums and in on the secrets of the trade. But part of him strongly resisted this knowledge. Despite all his inside information, he was never quite able to convince himself that there was no such thing as a true medium. As he himself wrote to Doyle early in their friendship: "During my tour in Australia, I met the man who was supposed to lay low Mrs. Piper [a famous medium, like all the others mentioned here]; I was in Berlin, Germany, at the trial of Miss Roth, the flower-medium; know the methods of the Bangs sisters, the famous Chicago mediums; was at the court when Ann Odelia Diss Debar was sentenced . . . And still I want to believe there is such a thing." Houdini's first experience of spiritualism, he said, was at the age of fifteen when his father died. He had persuaded his mother to give him the last dollar in the house to pay a medium who would communicate with the deceased. Nothing, however, had happened.

He had given up the trade himself on account of a number of coincidences (mentioned earlier) which had thoroughly unnerved him. "Was doing mind-reading with my good wife," he explained to a friend, "and among the numerous questions, one inquired 'Who killed—?' I have forgotten the name. At that time I was unable to answer, but the next day I made a detective of myself and haunted the place for three days, and eventually as I was getting shaved, the barber was telling how he had loaned a razor to the father of the girl, and from actual deduction, I believe to this day that the father dressed himself (disguised himself as a woman) went to the trysting place, beheld his daughter in the evolutations, and 'finish' . . . If any one ever possessed second sight, twas my sainted Mother and I have inherited the 'trait or ability' from Her." This uncertainty, or hope, never quite left him. In 1906 he wrote, "At one time I was almost a believer . . . I contemplate writing a book on spiritualistic methods, and how they do their tricks. I do not mean genuine spiritualists, who have no tricks, but those mediums who use their knowledge of magic to gain a living." This book would eventually be published as *A Magician Among the Spirits.*

At the time Houdini and Conan Doyle became friends, they were two of the most famous men in the world. No two people could have been more different. They were opposites in every way. But they were fascinated by each other. "In a long life which has touched every side of humanity," wrote Doyle, "Houdini is far and away the most curious and intriguing character whom I have ever encountered. I have met better men, and I have certainly met very many worse ones, but I have never met a man who had such strange contrasts in his nature, and whose actions and motives it was more difficult to foresee or to reconcile." Doyle dwelt on Houdini's immense physical courage, his cheery companionability, his devotion to his family, his impulsive charity—mixed with a curious frugality, so that "while he was giving away his earnings at a rate which alarmed his wife, he would put an indignant comment in his diary because he had been charged two shillings for the pressing of his clothes." He was at the same time repelled by Houdini's immense vanity and his mania for publicity.

Doyle was always conscious that he did not really understand Houdini. He put this down to the gulf between Houdini's "Oriental" nature (which he shared with "our own Disraeli") and Doyle's own "colder Western blood." (The Sherlock Holmes stories abound with sinister villains of foreign extraction.)

Houdini, for his part, viewed Doyle with a similar tempered enthusiasm. "He is a brilliant man a deep thinker, well versed in every respect, and comes of a gifted family . . . His home life is beautiful and Lady Doyle has told me on numerous occasions that he never loses his temper and that his nature is at all times sunshiny and sweet. His children are a hundred per cent children in every way and it is beautiful to note the affection between the father, mother and the children. He is a great reader who absorbs what he reads but he believes what he sees in print *only* if it is favorable to Spiritualism."

Houdini's interest in spiritualism had been reawakened by his mother's death. "There is no sacrifice I would not make to be able to get in communication with my mother," he wrote. "After years of research I still hope that there is a way of communicating with her from this life . . . I have made definite compacts with seven intimate friends and relatives to the effect that the one who died first would communicate with the others. All of my seven friends are dead. Up to the present time I have not received the slightest sign from any of them."

Houdini was happy to put any effort into this desperate search. But he was terribly handicapped in it. Where Conan Doyle and his fellow enthusiasts would happily classify any effect which they could not otherwise explain as supernatural communication from the Other Side, Houdini was in the unfortunate position of always being able not only to explain the effects but to duplicate them. What he hoped for may be seen from his dedication in *A Magician Among the Spirits:*

IN WORSHIPFUL HOMAGE
I
DEDICATE THIS BOOK
TO THE MEMORY OF MY SAINTED MOTHER
IF GOD
IN HIS INFINITE WISDOM
EVER SENT AN ANGEL UPON EARTH IN HUMAN FORM
IT WAS MY
MOTHER

Thus, while he dedicated to his father a book *(The Unmasking of Robert-Houdin)* about the destruction of a father figure, the book he dedicated to his mother embodied his dashed hopes that even death need not come between them.

The repeated frustration of these hopes, and his fury at the cheating he was so easily able to detect, soon turned Houdini into the scourge of false mediums. He delighted in exposing them with the maximum possible theatrical publicity. He would take part in séances disguised in false beards and spectacles, and at the crucial moment, flashing a light upon some tell-tale piece of apparatus, would tear off his costume and reveal himself as Houdini. Next day the newspapers would, naturally, be full of his exploits. Houdini had always delighted in the total destruction of anyone he saw as an enemy. And he saw all false mediums as his personal enemies in the fight to establish contact with his mother.

This fury naturally meant that the friendship between Houdini and Doyle could never be entirely easy, however much they liked each other personally and respected each other's sincerity. "Our relations are certainly curious," wrote Doyle, "and likely to become more so, for as long as you attack what I *know* from experience to be true I have no alternative but to attack you in turn. How long a private friendship can survive such an ordeal I do not know." And when, inevitably, the friendship ended, Conan Doyle could see nothing but a vindictive desire for personal publicity in Houdini's constant attacks on mediums. "There was no consideration of any sort which would restrain him if he saw his way to an advertisement. Even when he laid flowers upon the graves of the dead it was in the prearranged presence of local photographers. It was this desire to play a constant public part which had a great deal to do with his constant campaign against Spiritualism."

Of course this was partly true. Once again Houdini had found that the public appeasement of his personal furies was the surest route to the heroic notoriety he craved. Once again he was pitting himself against all comers. Edmund Wilson noted that "Houdini says that he has never yet been duped, that he has been able to guess all the tricks that he has ever seen, but that he lives in constant terror of being outwitted by a telepathist or a medium—in which case his dogmatic denials would be made to look ridiculous. And this has given him a certain edge and excitement as of a man engaged in a critical fight: where he once challenged the world to tie him up, he now challenges it to convince him of the supernatural."

Part of this "edge and excitement" resulted from Houdini's ambivalence towards spiritualism. The magnetism of his escape acts lay, for both his audience and himself, in the alluring possibility of failure. He was never quite sure whether he really wanted to go on with life—whether he would not in the end prefer to die. This was what he had to prove to himself anew every day before the public. The excitement was as much a function of his own uncertainty as of theirs. Similarly with spiritualism: the driving fury arose not because he wanted to prove it was all false, but because he so much wanted to believe it might be true. He wrote to Doyle: "I am willing to believe, if I can find a medium who, as you suggest, will not resort to 'manipulation' when the Power does not 'arrive' . . . Dean Harry Kellar, who lives in retirement in California, at one time had a standing challenge to all mediums (1876 to 1899), and even he will not come right out and say that all of it is humbug. And I think he knows *more* about the mysteries of magic than anyone living." This truly expressed Houdini's state of mind. He terribly wanted to be convinced. That he could not be, was his tragedy.

There was, on the other hand, no difficulty about convincing Doyle of anything that smacked of the supernatural. His gullibility seemed limitless. Its most notorious manifestation was the episode described in his *The Coming of the Fairies*. This book is about two schoolgirls from Cottingley in Yorkshire who cut out drawings of fairies, set them in a woodland glade, and photographed the resulting scene. The fairy photographs came to the attention of a Miss Scatcherd, a well-known "sensitive"; and she in turn told Doyle of them. He delegated a friend to look into the matter for him since he was just about to leave for Australia. The girls took more photographs. The friend was convinced. Doyle, on his return, was overcome. He knew, of course, that photographs could be faked. But he could not believe that two little girls could have hatched such a plot and seen it through as these two little girls had done. As far as Doyle was concerned, the Cottingley fairies lived.

You might say: if he could believe that, he could believe anything. Indeed, in this sense Conan Doyle himself was as much a mystery as any of his literary creations. How was it possible that the creator of Sherlock Holmes should turn out to be such a quintessential Dr. Watson?

It was as if the person who produced those masterpieces of literary deduction was quite separate from Houdini's new acquaintance. No one knew more than the author of the Holmes stories about how mystifying things may seem before they are explained, and how simple after. "I am afraid that I rather give myself away when I explain," remarks Holmes on one occasion. "Results without causes are much more impressive." And the formula of the stories is based upon exactly this principle. They invariably begin with some mystifying circumstance, or series of circumstances, which are by the end of the story explained in a simple and logical manner. One hardly dare ask what Holmes would have made of the Cottingley fairies, or of a man who could write (on the conditions of life after death): "The usual information is that any nutrition is of a very light and delicate order, corresponding to the delicate etheric body which requires it. Then there [is] the question of marriage, and the old proposition of the much-married man and which wife he should have. As there is no sexual relation as we understand it, this problem is not very complex and is naturally decided by soul affinity."

But this combination of, on the one hand, outstanding analytic power and, on the other, apparently boundless credulity regarding spiritualism, was by no means peculiar to Doyle. The history of psy-

chical research is crowded with comparable figures—eminent sa-
vants who happily lent their names to palpable hoaxes of the crudest
nature. The celebrated physicists Sir William Crookes, Sir Oliver
Lodge, Sir William Barrett, Lord Rayleigh; the naturalist Alfred
Russel Wallace; the French biologist and Nobel laureate Charles Richet; the vitalist philosopher Hans Driesch; psychologists such as
William McDougall and William James—these are just a few of the
more famous supporters of the spiritualist hypothesis. Parapsy-
chology today can cite similar names. At least one Nobel laureate in
physics believes that Uri Geller has supernatural powers.

Why should these people have been—why should they still be—
so reluctant to believe that they were, and are, seeing conjuring
tricks?

Perhaps the answer may lie in the particular cast of mind required
of a physical scientist. The preponderance of physicists and engi-
neers over psychologists among believers in psi is marked. The physicist's world (in contrast to that of the psychologist) is composed of
more or less immutable laws governing inanimate objects. The essence of physical science—as of Sherlock Holmes's technique—is
close and accurate observation followed by deduction. The scientist
has learned how to look; the best scientists are those who know what
to look for and how to draw the right conclusions from what they
see. In the very best scientists, these conclusions are often daring
and original. The hypothesis of spiritualism is no stranger than many
received scientific hypotheses. So the natural scientist who has
become convinced of the paranormal hypothesis may well be more
confident in his conclusions than the layman. He is accustomed to
being right in what he takes to be comparable circumstances. Similarly, Conan Doyle, that veteran of the deductive art, felt that, who-
ever was likely to be deceived, he was not. "In a fair light I saw my
dead mother as clearly as ever I saw her in life. I am a cool observer
and don't make mistakes." While for Houdini, as for many others,
the fact that people like Doyle could be convinced was a large factor

in their own willingness to believe. "It is only by knowing that Analytical Minds are going in for it, that I am treating this matter seriously," he wrote Doyle early in their acquaintance.

But there is one big difference between the phenomena generally observed by scientists in the course of their work and the phenomena of spiritualism. Scientific phenomena may be deceptive, but this is not on account of a will to deceive. Albert Einstein, who propounded the most daring theory of all, said: "The Lord God is subtle, but malicious he is not." But false mediums, unlike God, certainly are, in this sense, malicious. The process, as in any display of illusions, is one of dissimulation and misdirection. The vital thing is to control the audience without its being aware of that control. The scientist, confident of his trained powers of observation and experimentation, draws his conclusions. Because he has not seen what he thought he saw, those conclusions are incorrect. He is applying the laws of physical observation to a different world in which everything is designed to make the laws of physics seemingly stand on their head. So the physicist, metaphorically, stands on his head, confidence unimpaired. This was Conan Doyle's position.

Like Alfred Russel Wallace with J. N. Maskelyne, Conan Doyle was faced, in Houdini, with a conjurer who was able to replicate the feats of the mediums. His response, like Wallace's, was not to disbelieve in the mediums, but to attribute supernatural powers to the conjurer. "My dear chap," he wrote, "why go round the world seeking a demonstration of the occult when you are giving one all the time? Mrs. Guppy [a well-known and hugely fat medium who allegedly travelled by telekinesis from Highbury to Bloomsbury] could dematerialize, and so could many folk in Holy Writ, and I do honestly believe that you can also."

Houdini, of course, vehemently denied this. He repeated, and went on repeating, that everything he did was done by natural means. But he had a problem. He could not prove this without revealing his secrets. Thus, when Hewat Mackenzie, the president of the London College of Psychic Science, asserted in his book *Spirit Intercourse* that Houdini escaped from the Water-Torture Cell by dematerialisation, the magician was stymied. Mackenzie wrote: "The body was completely dematerialized within this tank within one and a half minutes, while the author stood immediately over it. Without disturbing any of the locks, Houdini was transferred from the tank direct to the back of the stage in a dematerialized state. He was there materialized, and returned to the stage front dripping with water and attired in the blue jersey suit in which he entered the tank . . . Dematerialization is performed by methods similar in operation to those in which the psycho-plastic essence is drawn from the medium. The body of the medium may be reduced to half its ordinary weight in the materializing séance room, but in the case of dematerialization the essence continues to be drawn until the whole physical body vanishes, and the substance composing it is held in suspension within the atmosphere, much in the same way as moisture is held by evaporation. While in this state Houdini was transferred from the stage to the retiring-room behind, and there almost instantaneously materialized."

What could be said or done to counter this short of demonstrating exactly how the Water-Torture Cell worked? Doyle himself recognised this dilemma and drew the conclusion which was, to him, inevitable: "It is said, 'How absurd for Doyle to attribute possible psychic powers to a man who himself denies them!' Is it not perfectly evident that if he did not deny them his occupation would have been gone forever? What would his brother magicians have to say to a man who admitted that half his tricks were done by what they would regard as illicit powers? It would be *exit* Houdini."

Part of Houdini's difficulty when he protested that he was in no way a magical personage was that, in symbolic terms, that was exactly what he *was*. All his power lay in his embodiment of the idea that lay at the very root of spiritualism: immortality.

Carl Jung, who defended the idea of a life after death, wrote:

". . . beyond [the intellect] there is a thinking in primordial images—in symbols that are older than historical man; which have been ingrained in him from earliest times, and, eternally living, outlasting all generations, still make up the groundwork of the human psyche. It is possible to live the fullest life only when we are in harmony with these symbols; wisdom is a return to them. It is a question neither of belief nor knowledge, but of the agreement of our thinking with the primordial images of the unconscious. They are the source of all our conscious thoughts, and one of these primordial images is the idea of life after death." Houdini, in his (literally) death-defying stunts, brought this "primordial image" to the level of conscious experience, both for himself and on behalf of his audience.

That was real magic. Descending to the trivia that constituted the everyday currency of most mediums—disembodied voices speaking through trumpets, unexplained noises, small tables rising from the ground, Ouija boards—he was forced to confront the fundamental dilemma of spiritualism: the contrast between the enormous emotional and intellectual issues at stake and the poverty of their expression in mediumistic drawing-rooms. If he, who had repeatedly dared the entry to the underworld, had not been able to contact his mother, how was it possible that some "trumpet-medium" should dare pretend to do so? And yet—what other means offered? *That* was the source of his fury.

This terrible, disproportionate triviality has always been one of the problems with spiritualism. The psychologist William James was particularly bothered by what he called "this particularly crass and low type of supernatural phenomena." James and Houdini may perhaps be said to have approached the question from opposite poles. Both spent their lives arriving at the same conclusion: that the question of life after death was the most important question of all. Houdini arrived at it instinctively; James, intellectually and emotionally. "All argument is against it," said Dr. Johnson, "but all belief is for it." Houdini, approaching the question as, so to speak, the embodiment of belief—but without argument—found spiritualism emotionally impossible and exploded in indignation. James, feeling the same way, tried to reconcile himself by intellectual means. When T. H. Huxley said, "Better live a crossing-sweeper, than die and be made to talk twaddle by a 'medium' hired at a guinea a Seance," James riposted: "The odd point is that so few of those who talk in this way realize that they and the spiritists are using the same major premise and differing only in the minor. The major premise is: 'Any spirit-revelation must be romantic.' The minor of the spiritist is: 'This is romantic'; that of the Huxleyan is 'This is dingy twaddle'—whence their opposite conclusions!"

The friendship of the Doyles and the Houdinis developed apace. The families lunched together at Crowborough; Houdini sent tickets for his Palladium show. Receiving a batch of stamps from all round the world—probably from fan-mail following *The Man from Beyond*—he sent them on to Lady Doyle, who collected stamps. Doyle wrote that he had been "planting seeds in the West—Bristol, Bath, Swindon, and now back in London. I go to the famous spirit photographer Hope to-day." Spirit photographers specialised in producing photographs of ghosts. The ghost Doyle was hoping for was that of his son Kingsley, who had appeared previously on a photograph.

Meanwhile, Houdini was investigating a very famous medium. She was known as Eva C., and had begun her career fifteen years earlier in Algiers, where she had been the means by which Charles Richet, the eminent biologist, proved that spirits were warm, had hair and exhaled carbon dioxide. At that time she had been called Marthe Béraud; but there had been a scandal and Marthe had disappeared, to reemerge as Eva. Since 1911 she had been under the protection of Mme Juliette Bisson, the wife of a well-known Parisian playwright. With Mme Bisson, Eva had gone through a series of tests with a German sexologist named Schrenck-Notzing, who was a friend of Richet's. In the course of these tests she had developed a technique for producing a substance known as ectoplasm, which took many curious and revolting forms. She was still producing it in 1920 when Houdini took part in some of her séances.

> Well, we had success at the seance last night, as far as productions were concerned [he told Conan Doyle], but I am not prepared to say that they were supernormal.
>
> I assure you I did not control the medium, so the suggestions were not mine. They made Mlle. Eva drink a cup of coffee and eat some cake (I presume to fill her up with some food stuff) and after she had been sewn into the tights, and a net over her face, she "manifested."
>
> 1st. Some frothlike substance, inside of net. It was about 5 inches long; she said it was "elevating," but none of us four watchers saw it "elevate."
>
> Committee, Messrs. Feilding, Baggally, Dingwall and myself.
>
> 2nd. A white plaster-looking affair over her right eye.
>
> 3rd. Something that looked like a small face, say 4 inches in circumference. Was terra-cotta coloured, and Dingwall, who held her hands, had the best look at the "object."
>
> 4th. Some substance, frothlike, "exuding from her nose." Baggally and Feilding say it protruded from her nose, but Dingwall and I are positive that it was inside of net and was not extending from her nose; I had the best view from two different places. I deliberately took advantage to see just what it was.
>
> It was a surprise effect indeed!
>
> 5th. Medium asked permission to remove something in her mouth; showed her hands empty, and took out what appeared to be a rubberish substance, which she disengaged and showed us plainly; we held the electric torch; all saw it plainly, when presto! it vanished.
>
> The seance started at 7.30 and lasted until midnight.

Such was the bizarre world of spiritualism in its more "scientific" form (as Mme Bisson expressed it). Houdini was convinced that Eva had "vanished" the rubbery substance by sleight-of-handing it into her mouth while pretending to have it between her fingers—the same move he used in his old Hindoo needle trick. He attended various other séances with Eva during his time in England but, much to Doyle's disappointment, remained unconvinced.

Soon after this, in the summer of 1920, Houdini returned to the United States. He wrote from there that his house had been "all fixed up" and cordially invited the Doyles to "make [it] your home when you visit New York City." Doyle tactfully deflected this invitation: "You will understand that I have to be semi-public for my job's sake." Despite his conviction that Houdini had magic powers, he worried about his new friend's safety. "All good wishes to you, my dear Houdini. Do drop these dangerous stunts," he urged him; and, again, "Our best remembrances to your wife and self. For God's sake be careful in these fearsome feats of yours. Surely you could retire now."

Conan Doyle was preparing a lecture tour of America in which he would spread the spiritualist word. Jean and their three children were to accompany him. They arrived in New York in the spring of 1922. Sir Arthur's first lecture took place in Carnegie Hall before a packed house. There followed a crowded couple of weeks in New York, then in April a short rest on the Jersey shore before the family set off on its tour across America. May saw them back in New York, where they visited the Houdinis. On 10 May Houdini noted in his day-book: "To-day at 11 o'clock Sir Arthur and Lady Doyle came up to 278, for a visit. Sir Arthur was very anxious to see my collection of books and became very much interested. I went all over the house and got together all my rare tracts, and he seemed very much surprised at my collection of literature on Spiritualism." Doyle, however, was disappointed to see that Houdini's collection was "very short of positive books." A fortnight later Doyle attended, at Houdini's invitation, the annual banquet of the Society of American Magicians. He had at first been reluctant to do so, feeling that magicians and spiritualists were ranged in opposite camps and that his views would be attacked. But Houdini persuaded him that nothing was further from his mind, and in the event it was Sir Arthur who amazed the magicians by showing them the dinosaur footage from the film which had recently been made of his novel *The Lost World*.

The friendship between the two families was by now so warm that, when the Doyles went to Atlantic City for a short holiday in June, they invited the Houdinis to join them there. "The children would teach you to swim! and the change would do you good." Houdini replied, "Mrs. Houdini joins me in thanking you for the invitation to come to Atlantic City, and if you will be there next Saturday or Sunday, Mrs. Houdini and I would like to spend the weekend with you . . . Most important of all, if the kiddies want to teach me to swim I will be there, and in return will show them how to do one or two things that will make it very interesting."

The afternoon of June 17 was to be a momentous one. It began innocently enough: "As Sir Arthur, Mrs. Houdini and I were sitting on the sand skylarking with the children Sir Arthur excused himself saying that he was going to have his usual afternoon nap. He left us but returned in a short time and said 'Houdini, if agreeable, Lady Doyle will give you a special seance, as she has a feeling that she might have a message coming through. At any rate, she is willing to try.' "

That, at any rate, was Houdini's account of how the affair began. In *Our American Adventure* Doyle says, "It was sudden inspiration of mine to ask him up to our room and see if we could get any evidence or consolation for him," while in his *On the Edge of the Unknown*, which was written after Houdini's death, he ascribes the whole thing to Houdini: "The method in which Houdini tried to explain away, minimize and contort our attempt at consolation, which was given *entirely at his own urgent request* and against my wife's desire, has left a deplorable shadow in my mind."

It seems, all in all, most probable that the suggestion did originate with the Doyles. Doyle's view at this time was expressed in a note to an American medium, Ada Besinnet (later exposed by Houdini): "Mr Houdini is deeply interested and quite sympathetic but has never had a chance of getting good evidence . . . He deserves more than has come to him, for he is a patient and sympathetic observer." What the Doyles now felt was that they might be able to provide this evidence themselves.

Houdini goes on to explain how Bess cued him as to what all this was probably about, using the system of signs they had evolved for their "second sight" act twenty years before. "In that manner Mrs. Houdini told me that on the night previous she had gone into detail with Lady Doyle about the great love I bear for my Mother. She related to her a number of instances, such as, my returning home from long trips, sometimes as far away as Australia, and spending months with my Mother and wearing only the clothes that she had given me because I thought it would please her and give her some happiness . . . I walked with Sir Arthur to the Doyles' suite. Sir Arthur drew down the shades so as to exclude the bright light. We three, Lady Doyle, Sir Arthur and I, sat around the table on which were a number of pencils and a writing pad, placing our hands on the surface of the table.

"Sir Arthur started the seance with a devout prayer. I had made up my mind that I would be as religious as it was within my power to be and not at any time did I scoff at the ceremony. I excluded all earthly thoughts and gave my whole soul to the seance."

Conan Doyle takes up the tale: "It was a singular scene, my wife with her hand flying wildly, beating the table while she scribbled at a furious rate, I sitting opposite and tearing sheet after sheet from the block as it was filled up, and tossing each across to Houdini, while he sat silent, looking grimmer and paler every moment."

The first question Jean Doyle asked of the spirit which had taken hold of her so energetically was, "Do you believe in God?" Her hand beat the table three times: affirmative. She said, "Then I will make the sign of the Cross." She marked a cross on the edge of the pad on which she was writing. Then she asked who was there, and whether it was Houdini's mother. Her hand struck the table three times once more. Then she began to write:

> Oh, my darling, thank God, thank God, at last I'm through—I've tried, oh so often—now I am happy. Why, of course, I want to talk to my boy—my own beloved boy—Friends, thank you, with all my heart for this.
>
> You have answered the cry of my heart—and of his—God bless him—a thousand fold, for all his life for me—never had a mother such a son—tell him not to grieve, soon he'll get all the evidence he is anxious for—Yes, we know—tell him, I want him to try to write in his own home. It will be far better so.
>
> I will work with him—he is so, so dear to me—I am preparing so sweet a home for him which one day in God's good time he will come to—it is one of my great joys preparing it for our future—
>
> I am so happy in this life—it is so full and joyous—my only shadow has been that my beloved one hasn't known how often I have been with him all the while—here away from my heart's darling—combining my work thus in this life of mine.
>
> It is so different over here, so much larger and bigger and more beautiful—so lofty—all sweetness around one—nothing that hurts and we see our beloved ones on earth—that is such a joy and comfort to us—Tell him I love him more than ever—the years only increase it—and his goodness fills my soul with gladness and thankfulness. Oh, just this, it *is* me. I want him only to know that—that—I have bridged the gulf—that is what I wanted, oh, so much—Now I can rest in peace—How soon—

At this point, Doyle requested Houdini to ask some question that would prove to him that his mother really was with them. "Lady Doyle did not seem to think that the spirit would answer direct questions, and I purposely evaded asking anything which might embarrass the medium, as I wanted to help all I could, so I thought of the question proposed by Sir Arthur, 'Can my mother read my mind?' in this way answering any question of which I might think."

The spirit resumed:

I *always* read my beloved son's mind—his dear mind—there is so much I want to say to him—but—I am almost overwhelmed by this joy of talking to him once more—it is almost too much to get through—the joy of it—thank you, thank you, friend, with all my heart for what you have done for me this day—God bless you too, Sir Arthur, for what you are doing for us—for us over here—who so need to get in touch with our beloved ones on the earth plane—

If only the world knew this great truth—how different—life would be for men and women—Go on, let nothing stop you—great will be your reward hereafter—Good-bye—I brought you, Sir Arthur, and my darling son together—I felt you as the one man who might help us to pierce the veil—and I was right—Bless him, bless him, bless him, I say from the depths of my soul—he fills my heart and later we shall be together—oh, so happy—a happiness awaits him that he has never dreamed of—tell him I am with him—just tell him that I'll soon make him know how close I am all the while—his eyes will soon be opened—Good-bye again—God's blessing on you all—

When Jean had finally stopped writing, Houdini asked about trying the automatic writing in his own home. He took up a pencil to see what would happen, and wrote, apparently without volition, the name "Powell."

Now it so happened that both Doyle and Houdini had close friends of this name, who were on their minds at this particular time. Houdini's old friend, F. E. Powell, was in some trouble. His wife had been paralysed by a stroke and could no longer work with him; he was wondering whether he should engage a young woman as his assistant. The Houdinis had recently had an argument about this. Mrs. Houdini maintained that it would be unfair of Powell to engage a girl; Houdini, on the other hand, could see no reason why he should not do so. This was what Houdini asserted he had in mind when he wrote "Powell." But Sir Arthur could not accept this explanation; for an old spiritualist ally of his, also named Powell, had died only the previous week. He jumped up and said, "The Spirits have directed you in writing the name of my dear fighting partner in

Spiritualism, Dr. Ellis Powell, who has just died in England. I am the person he is most likely to signal to, and here is his name coming through your hands. Truly Saul is among the Prophets."

When Houdini got home he found a letter from his Powell awaiting him, which he sent on to Conan Doyle with the comment "I judge it was just one of those coincidences." But Doyle could not accept this. Three days later he wrote: "My dear Houdini—No, the Powell explanation won't do. Not only is he the one man who would wish to get me, but in the evening, Mrs. M., the lady medium, got 'there is a man here. He wants to say that he is sorry he had to speak so abruptly this afternoon.' "

This incident, as one might expect, simply confirmed each of the men more strongly in his original attitude. Doyle was happily convinced that the spirit of Houdini's mother had indeed spoken through Jean Doyle and that he had made his friend a wonderful gift for which Houdini was duly grateful. "I see you sometime," he wrote, "as your true experiences accumulate, giving a wonderful lecture, 'Phenomenal Spiritualism—True and False.' In which, giving an account of your adventures with Fakes you will also give an account of those which bear inspection. It would be a very great draw . . . I may say your mother again came back with words of passionate love through Mrs. Metcalfe of Brooklyn last night." His view of the incident remained that "It was a long and very moving message and bore every internal sign of being genuine. There is no question at all in my mind that Houdini was greatly shaken at the time and for some days afterwards. His objections were all afterthoughts in order to save the situation."

"I was *willing* to believe, even wanted to believe," Houdini noted. "It was weird to me and with a beating heart I waited, hoping that I might feel once more the presence of my beloved Mother . . . I especially wanted to speak to my Mother, because that day, *June 17,* . . . was her birthday." This was just one of the many personal facts she had failed to mention. Indeed, the message had been couched in terms of the widest generality: there was nothing particular to Houdini in it at all. But Doyle was not persuaded. "What are birthdays on the other side?" he wanted to know. "It is the death day which is the real birthday." Houdini could still not convince himself that this was the real thing. In the margin of the letter he noted: "Message written by Lady Doyle claiming the spirit of my dear mother had control of her hand—my sainted mother could not write English and spoke broken English." And how was it possible that his mother, an orthodox Jewess, should have begun her outpourings with the sign of the cross? No wonder he looked shaken. This appeal to the very deepest of his emotions, the hopes it raised, the dashing of those hopes, the consciousness that he could say nothing without mortally offending a good friend—how could all this fail to unsettle him?

Relations between the two families remained cordial for the few days remaining to the Doyles in America. On their last night, June 22, which was the Houdinis' wedding anniversary, they all went to see Raymond Hitchcock's *Pinwheel Revue* at the Carroll Theater. The evening was a great success in a somewhat unexpected way, for Hitchcock, recognising who was in the audience, insisted upon inviting Houdini onto the stage to perform one of his tricks. He agreed, and performed the needle trick to wild applause; after which the rest of the show was scrapped and the orchestra struck up the closing number. The Doyles were duly impressed by this unique example of an artist "not only stopping but curtailing a show in which he was not programmed to have a part." They sailed next day; a telegram from Houdini wishing them bon voyage and hoping they would soon return was placed in Sir Arthur's hands as he stepped onto the gangway.

No more passed between them concerning the séance until November, when Houdini published an article in the New York *Sun* violently attacking spiritualism and mentioning his experience with the Doyles. This naturally infuriated Doyle. "I feel rather sore about it," he wrote. ". . . When you say that you have had no evidence of survival, you say what I cannot reconcile with what I saw with my own eyes. I know by many examples the purity of my wife's mediumship, and I saw what you got and what the effect was upon you at the time . . . However, I don't propose to discuss the subject any more with you, for I consider that you have had your proofs and that the responsibility of accepting or rejecting is with you."

Regretfully, Houdini replied: "You write that you are very 'sore.' I trust it is not with me, because you, having been truthful and manly all your life, naturally must admire the same traits in other human beings." He rehearsed all the reasons why he could not accept the letter as a true communication from his mother, and the Powell explanation, and ended, "I trust my clearing up the seance from my point of view is satisfactory, and that you do not harbour any ill feeling, because I hold both Lady Doyle and yourself in the highest esteem. I know you treat this as a religion, but personally I cannot do so, for, up to the present time, and with all my experiences, I have never seen or heard anything that could really convert me."

They continued to correspond for a while. But the friendship was irremediably undermined. What had happened was too personal, on both sides, ever to be forgotten or laid aside. Houdini continued to attack false mediums (which effectively meant all mediums) with renewed fury; the Doyles watched from afar in increasing anger and perplexity.

"You are to me a perpetual mystery," Doyle had written early in their acquaintance. "But no doubt you are to many. You do (and say) things that are beyond me. As an example of the latter, you said that Ira Davenport did his phenomena by normal means. But if he did (which I really don't believe) then he is manifestly not only a liar but a blasphemer, as he went round with Mr Ferguson, a clergyman, and mixed it all up with religion. And yet you are photographed as a friend with one whom, under those circumstances, one would not touch with a muck-rake. Now how can one reconcile that? It interests me as a problem."

During the years of gradual estrangement which inevitably followed the fatal séance, Houdini mercilessly attacked Doyle's credulity in his lectures while the good-hearted Doyle followed his erstwhile friend's career more in sorrow than in anger. Like Houdini, his views remained unaltered. Considering the mystery after Houdini had died, he reconciled his difficulties by reverting once more to the Davenports. "If it be true that the Davenports were real mediums (and let the inquirer really read their record before he denies it), and if Houdini produced exactly similar results, which have in each case been inexplicable to their contemporaries, then is it conceivable that they were produced in entirely different ways? If Ira Davenport was a medium, then there is a strong prima facie case that Houdini was a medium too."

16

MARGERY

The fiasco of the Jean Doyle séance and the collapse of his friendship with Sir Arthur resulted in a stepping-up of Houdini's campaign against fraudulent mediums. The most continual and unbroken disappointment was never going to kill his desperate desire to be "united in happiness" with his mother. But it could and did embitter him, and he expressed this bitterness in the increasing intensity of his campaign against fraud.

He employed two investigators full-time—Julia Sawyer, a niece of Bess's, and a Miss Rose Mackenberg. He even went so far as to buy a spiritualist church in Worcester, Mass., and the title of Reverend that went with it, where he installed Miss Mackenberg under the name of the Reverend F(rances) Raud. This somewhat crude exploit gained the headlines he craved. Others demanded more skill. It took all his powers, for example, to find out how one particularly baffling slatewriter worked his tricks. (Slatewriters produced spirit messages written on slates which had been shown to be blank and to which they could have had no apparent access.) "When he did the slate-writing at this sitting I felt someone's presence and, sure enough, when he took the slates away there was an almost imperceptible hesitation. In this fraction of a second the slates were switched through a *trap in the panel* behind me. I had a mirror on a rubber elastic fastened to my vest and as I took my seat I pulled the elastic so I could sit on it. I managed to secure the mirror and keep it palmed in my hand, and with it saw the panel slide open, the arm extended with the duplicate slates, and the exchange made."

In 1924 the House of Representatives of the District of Columbia set up a judiciary committee to discuss whether fortune-telling should be banned in Washington. During the 1920s as during the 1980s, prophets of the paranormal held sway at the White House. It was well known that Mrs. Coolidge, the president's wife, frequently attended séances, and many of the senators were in regular contact with mediums.

Of course Houdini insisted on appearing before the judiciary committee. And of course the mediums tried to discredit him. Naturally Houdini's appearance made the headlines; and naturally the mediums all suggested that his crusade was conducted, and he was now appearing, solely to gain publicity.

Perish the thought! However, he could point out that he certainly wasn't making any money out of it. In the interests of his crusade, he explained, "I positively spend between $40,000 and $50,000 every year. I brought my staff up here. They are under salary; they are under expenses." He then performed a couple of tricks popular with spiritualists and explained how they were done.

One of these was the most fundamental spiritualist trick of all. It is known as "fishing." Its most famous recent exponent was the late Mrs. Doris Stokes. Out of the blue Houdini asked, "Is there anybody here by the name of Mrs. Florence Kahn?" Of course, there was.

HOUDINI: My spirit guide tells me—George Washington is my spirit guide—he tells me in a picture. I see a lady in a ferryboat in a big, wide stream. Where is there a lady, please? Have you ever been in a ferryboat in a great broad beautiful stream? Is that right? Have I ever spoken to you, Mrs. Kahn?

MRS. KAHN: Never.

HOUDINI: Did you get a most important letter four days ago that you decided not to answer? Yes or no?

MRS. KAHN: Sixty-eight of them.

HOUDINI: This is a very particular one from a very dear old friend, yes or no?

MRS. KAHN: Yes . . .

HOUDINI: Then, the message. I am just doing the inspirational stuff for you, and I now will give you evidence of my wonderful power. This is addressed to Florence P. Kahn: "Good work. You are going to find that Julius P.'s efforts were appreciated. (Signed) Benjamin Franklin" . . . [Laughter and applause]

Houdini went on to explain how he did it:

HOUDINI: First of all when I came in, I can guess and pick out and say, "Clara is present" and make a guess. If I hit it, all right. If I did not hit it I say Thelma or Mary, and it fits some one. Then I inquire, "Who is that lady?" I heard Mrs. Kahn say, "I would like to get a message." Didn't you say that, Mrs. Kahn?

MRS. KAHN: Yes.

HOUDINI: I heard you. And you were back of me and I did not turn around. I was purposely impolite and I hereby apologize for my apparent impoliteness. I found out about you and was able to give you a life history, and I simply exchanged, deducted, and made guesses; and that is all there is to it.

Manoeuvres such as this seem so childishly simple when they are explained that it is hard to believe anyone can be taken in by them. But they *are* taken in: partly because they want to be and partly because, well-performed by an experienced practitioner, the effect can be unnerving in the extreme. As tricks, however, they are commonplace.

But Houdini was soon to meet a medium who was his worthy adversary.

Conan Doyle's American tours had been accompanied by enormous publicity. In December 1922, the publisher of the *Scientific American*, Orson Munn, decided to cash in on this. He announced that the magazine would award $2,500 to the first person producing a genuine spirit photograph and $2,500 to the first person producing genuine phenomena in the séance room. The genuineness or otherwise of entries would be judged by a committee consisting of the Harvard psychologist Dr. William McDougall; Hereward Carrington, a well-known psychical researcher; Dr. Daniel Frost Comstock, the developer of Technicolor; Dr. Walter Franklin Prince, a minister and psychologist; and Houdini. Conan Doyle was much annoyed by Houdini's inclusion. "My dear Houdini," he wrote (from the heights of his own impartiality),

> I see that you are on the *Scientific American* Committee, but how can it be called an Impartial Committee when you have committed yourself to such statements as that some Spiritualists pass away before they realize how they have been deluded, etc.? You have every right to hold such an opinion, but you can't sit on an Impartial Committee afterwards. It becomes biased at once. What I wanted was five good clear-headed men.

The kind of person Conan Doyle had in mind was the journalist and mathematician Malcolm Bird, an associate editor of the magazine. Early in 1923 Bird had visited Britain and spent some time with Conan Doyle investigating various mediums. They returned to the United States together in April 1923. Although they had found no one who seemed to qualify for the award, Bird reported on his return that he was "convinced that these phenomena do occur without fraud. I distinctly saw phosphorescent lights, heard trumpet voices and witnessed the movement of material objects under circumstances which satisfied me personally that there was no fraud."

He added: "Don't assume for a moment that this means I am endorsing spiritualism." Bird then took up the secretaryship of the committee. Conan Doyle, just before he left New York for a nationwide tour, recommended a friend of his to the committee's attention. Her name was Mina Crandon, a young Canadian woman (she was then twenty-six) married to a wealthy and fashionable Boston surgeon, Dr. LeRoi Goddard Crandon.

It was Dr. Crandon who had become interested in spiritualism first. He had read a book called *The Psychic Structures of the Goligher Circle,* published in 1919 by a Dr. W. J. Crawford. Dr. Crawford was a Belfast engineer who had become convinced that various members of a local family, the Golighers, were moving objects by means of supernaturally produced structures he called *teleplasm.* Photographs taken of this teleplasm reveal it to be something very like a rod draped in a net curtain. However, Dr. Crandon was much excited by Dr. Crawford's book, and showed it to his wife. They visited a medium who assured them that Mina possessed strong mediumistic powers. They tried some séances at home, using a table built exactly to Crawford's specifications, and to Dr. Crandon's delight it not only moved but seemed almost to dance across the room on two legs. Soon afterwards they took off on a tour of Europe during which they visited all the most august names in psychical research, including Professor Richet (who had discovered Eva C.) and Conan Doyle. All these people were much impressed by Mina's powers.

The *Scientific American* committee had been meeting with little success. Nobody of any real interest had turned up. Mr. Munn was therefore prevailed upon to increase the award to $5,000 to see if this would bring forward someone more serious. It was now, in November 1923, that Dr. Crandon contacted the magazine. He was not interested in the money, nor was Mrs. Crandon prepared to go to New York to be investigated. But if the committee would conduct its investigations in Boston, Mina (who for mediumistic purposes called herself Margery) was prepared to cooperate with them. As several of them anyway lived nearby, this was no problem.

Malcolm Bird paid the first visit. Margery's psychic abilities had progressed. She was now able to make bugle calls without a bugle and rattle a nonexistent chain. There were flashes of light in the dark. She could stop the clock just by concentrating upon it; she produced a two-dollar bill and a live pigeon. She had also developed a spirit alter ego: when she went into trance it was her brother Walter who spoke through her. Walter had been killed when still a young man some years previously: he had been crushed by a train. Speaking through Margery's lips he had a gruff voice, a penchant for repartee and an outstandingly profane vocabulary. He also had a notably cool head. Once, when Dr. Comstock brought an intricate mechanical device to a séance with a request that Walter operate it, he asked, "How long did it take you to make that thing, Comstock?"

"About three days, Walter."

"Well, if you expect me to work it in three minutes you're mistaken," Walter replied. "I have to experiment and work out things in my sphere just as you do in yours, and I may have to try it forty times before I can do it. If you think I'm here just to wander around the room making demonstrations, you're damn mistaken. I have to work hard and gather force for you people here, and light dissipates it just as water interferes with your activities." Thus Walter ensured that the séance conditions suited him. As to the provenance of his voice, Dr. Comstock said: "One time I placed one hand over Mrs. Crandon's mouth and nose, and the other over Dr. Crandon's mouth and nose, and pressed hard, so hard that I must have hurt them. And Walter's voice—a hoarse whisper—came as clearly as it did before."

Bird was much impressed. He recommended Margery to the committee, which paid her a number of visits. In the July 1924 issue of *Scientific American* he published an article describing the investigations and hinting that the prize was as good as won.

Houdini, although he was nominally on the committee, had known nothing about Margery. The first he heard of the affair was when he received a letter from Bird: "As you will observe when you get your July *Scientific American,* we are engaged in the investigation of another case of mediumship. Our original idea was not to bother you with it unless, and until, it got to a stage where there seemed serious prospects that it was either genuine or a type of fraud which our other committeemen could deal with . . . Mr. Munn feels that the case has taken a turn that makes it desirable for us to discuss it with you."

Houdini was beside himself. It was clear from Bird's article that the committee was on the point of giving Margery the award. How could they have gone so far without him? He rushed to New York and confronted Munn and Bird. It was essential that he and Munn go to Boston at once. The Crandons were happy to offer hospitality to any visiting members of the committee, but Houdini was adamant that neither he nor Munn should accept this offer. It would put them at a disadvantage vis-à-vis Margery. They booked into the Copley-Plaza Hotel, but accepted the Crandons' invitation to dine.

It was clear from the start that Houdini's relations with the Crandons were going to be tense. Houdini thought that they had been trying to keep him away from the investigation. This only made him feel the more combative. Despite his protestations, it clearly never entered his mind that Margery could be anything more than a clever trickster. She had duped the scientists, as clever mediums always had duped scientists—but she would not dupe him. "The truth is," observed Edmund Wilson, ". . . that in a committee of scientists of which Houdini is a member it is Houdini who is the scientist. Doctors, psychologists and physicists are no better qualified to check up on spiritualistic phenomena than lawyers, artists or clergymen."

Houdini's suspicions that the Crandons had been trying to keep him away were not without substance. In May Dr. Crandon had got hold of an advance copy of *A Magician Among the Spirits.* He reported to Conan Doyle, to whom he wrote weekly, that Houdini was "not in any way held back by ability or intent to tell the truth." He was disgusted at the way Houdini had used Doyle's private letters as evidence of his credulity. Walter, who was able to express Margery's real feelings when Mina might have felt constrained, had burst out against Houdini several times—more than once in verse. And if Houdini was determined to "get" Margery, his sentiments were cordially reciprocated. Crandon told Doyle that they planned to "crucify" Houdini and so prove Margery "the most extraordinary mediumship in modern history." On the morning of 23 July, the day of Margery's first séance with Houdini, the tension was palpable. Crandon told Doyle that Margery was "vomiting merrily" at the prospect of the evening's activities and "general nastiness."

The evening produced its fair share of phenomena. Houdini was sitting on Margery's left, "controlling" her left hand and left foot (i.e., he kept hold of them, or kept in contact with them, ensuring that she could not use them to produce any effects). Bird was on her right. The other members of the committee were all present. The séance was conducted for the most part in darkness. Margery, apparently fully controlled, rang a bell situated in a box on the floor; Walter threw a megaphone which landed at Houdini's feet, as requested; a heavy cabinet was tilted over. Next day (24 July) there was another séance, this time at Dr. Comstock's hotel. Houdini, once again, had charge of Margery's left side. The bell-box that evening was on the table; it mysteriously fell to the floor, and, later, the table itself tilted over.

That evening, back at their hotel, Houdini wrote Munn a letter. His emotion is evident in his syntax, which is more than usually contorted:

Dear Mr. Munn,
Please, if I may, allow me to see the exposed article before it is published, as all of the other articles were not written so as to properly place the real thing before the public.

Mr. Bird in your presence, said he believed the medium was fifty per cent genuine, when this evening there was no chance of anything she pretended to have been accomplished by "Walter," but was so done by herself. In fact she is *one hundred per cent trickster or fraud* judging by the first seance I attended, after forty or more were given . . .

I have been unfairly treated in this case being only called in when according to Mr. Bird's personal statement and in print made, to the effect that the medium, Mrs. Crandon, was fifty per cent genuine . . . facts such that could not have been written by a competent investigator, and I would like a personally written statement from all those who were present on the Committee, to check their findings.

To Harry Price, Houdini wrote: "There is no doubt in my mind, whatsoever, that this lady who has been 'fooling' the scientists for months resorted to some of the slickest methods I have ever known and honestly it has taken my thirty years of experience to detect her in her various moves."

Later, Houdini revealed just how he had detected what Margery was up to. Before the first séance he had begun his precautions early:

All that day I had worn a silk rubber bandage around [his right] leg just below the knee. By night the part of the leg below the bandage had become swollen and painfully tender, thus giving me a much keener sense of feeling and making it easier to notice the slightest sliding of Mrs. Crandon's ankle or flexing of her muscles. She wore silk stockings and during the seance had her skirts pulled up well above her knees . . .

On the evening in question the bell-box was placed between my feet with my right foot between it and Mrs. Crandon's left foot. As the seance progressed I could distinctly feel her ankle slowly and spasmodically sliding as it pressed against mine while she gained space to raise her foot off the floor and touch the top of the box. To the ordinary sense of touch the contact would seem the same while this was being done. At times she would say:

"Just press hard against my ankle so you can see that my ankle is there," and as she pressed I could feel her gain another half inch.

When she had finally maneuvered her foot around to a point where she could get at the top of the box the bell ringing began and *I positively felt* the tendons of her leg flex and tighten as she repeatedly touched the ringing apparatus. There is no question in my mind about it. *She did this.* Then, when the ringing was over, I plainly *felt her leg slide back* into its original position with her foot on the floor beside mine.

The trick with the megaphone was Margery's masterpiece.

During the second intermission "Walter" asked for an illuminated plaque to be placed on the lid of the box which held the bell and Bird went to get it. This left the right hand and foot of the medium free. ["When Bird left the circle it was *pitch dark*," Houdini wrote Bess that same evening.] Bird had difficulty in finding the plaque and while he was searching "Walter" suddenly called for "control."

Mrs. Crandon placed her right hand in mine and gave me to understand that I had both her hands. Bird was requested to stand in the doorway, but without any warning, before he could obey, the cabinet was thrown over backwards violently. *The medium then gave me her right foot also,* saying:

"You have now both hands and both feet."

Then "Walter" called out:

"The megaphone is in the air. Have Houdini tell me where to throw it."

"Towards me," I replied, and in an instant it fell at my feet.

The way she did these two tricks is as follows: when Bird left the room it freed her right foot and hand. With her right hand she tilted the corner of the cabinet enough to get her free foot under it, then picking up the megaphone she placed it on her head, dunce-cap fashion. Then she threw the cabinet over with her right foot. Then she simply jerked her head, causing the megaphone to fall at my feet. Of course with the megaphone on her head it was easy and simple for her to ask me or anyone else to hold both of her feet and also her hands, and still she could snap the megaphone off her head in any direction requested. This is the *slickest* ruse I have ever detected, and it has converted all skeptics.

Houdini had not yet finished with Margery. He now had his assistant Jim Collins construct a box which would contain her. It was shaped like a fall-front bureau and its effect was something like a pillory. Margery sat on a chair inside; the lid was closed, leaving only her head and arms sticking out, and the box was locked. Margery was now challenged to produce her usual phenomena. Malcolm Bird was no longer present at the séances: Houdini had objected that he was betraying the committee's secret deliberations to the Crandons.

The first box séance was to take place on 25 August 1924. The Crandons and their supporters did not welcome the innovation, since it was their contention that Margery produced her phenomena by means of a pseudopod, or supernormal limb, which emanated from between her legs. Dr. Crandon announced: "The psychic does not refuse to sit in the cage made by Houdini for the committee; but she makes the reservation that she knows no precedent in psychic research where a medium has been so enclosed: and she believes that a closed cage gives little or no regard for the theory and experience of the psychic structure or mediumism."

On the first evening, however, the box proved useless. It was broken open, possibly by the psychic structure. Somehow the bell was rung: it was contended that Margery was using her head. Next day the locks were strengthened and the contest resumed.

The activities of 26 August began with Malcolm Bird bursting in and demanding to know why he was being excluded. Houdini confronted him with accusations of betrayal. Bird at first blustered, then resigned from the committee and flounced out. The séance began.

According to Houdini, he suspected from the start that Margery had something concealed inside the box and repeatedly warned Dr. Prince *"not to let go of her right hand until after the seance was over and the cabinet-box unlocked."* She offered to be physically searched, but this was too much for Houdini. He declined, saying, "No, never mind, let it go, I am not a physician." "Walter" then said: "Houdini, you are very clever indeed, but it won't work. I suppose it was an accident those things were left in the cabinet?" Houdini asked what was left in the cabinet? "Pure accident, was it?

You were not here, but your assistant was," said Walter, and stated that a ruler would be found in the cabinet-box under a pillow at the medium's feet, "and virtually accused me of putting it there to throw suspicion on his sister winding up with a violent outburst in which he exclaimed: 'Houdini, you goddamned sonofabitch, get the hell out of here and never come back. If you don't, I will!' "

"This just expressed Mrs. Crandon's feelings towards me," says Houdini.

The séance proceeded: nothing happened. Houdini wrote Bess that night: "As I asked permission to have the red light turned on as soon as the bell rang as I knew she cried out take the gimmick back with the cabinet, if she used a foot rule—so she gave a complete blank séance." He added: " 'Walter' begged my pardon for calling me names and wanted it crost out of the record but it remains as is." At the end, the box was opened and, as Walter had predicted, a ruler—in fact, a folding two-foot rule—was found, with which Margery could have rung her bell.

Who planted the ruler? Houdini said it was the Crandons. The Crandons said it was Houdini, who wanted to make sure Margery would be discredited. After Houdini's death, Jim Collins is supposed to have confessed to the deed. In that case Houdini would have known about the ruler (which would be why he drew Dr. Prince's attention so repeatedly to the possibility of some such thing) but could truthfully deny having planted it himself. This seems distinctly possible. He had never been bothered by scruples when it came to showing up the unscrupulous behaviour of hated opponents.

Houdini was appearing at Keith's Theater in Boston to coincide with his investigations there. He reports an exchange between himself and Margery, who evidently thought that he was going to denounce her from the stage there during the part of his show devoted to fraudulent mediums. (His regular show at this time began with a lecture on this topic, going on to some "small magic" and finishing with the perennial "Water-Torture Cell.") She said, "If you mis-represent me from the stage at Keith's some of my friends will come up and give you a good beating."

"I am not going to misrepresent you," Houdini replied, "they are not coming on the stage and I am not going to get a beating."

"Then it is your wits against mine," she said . . .

"Yes, certainly, that is just what it is," Houdini told her.

She repeatedly told Houdini of her boy twelve years old and said that she would not want him to grow up and read that his mother was a fraud, to which Houdini replied: "Then don't be a fraud."

If ever two people were destined to hate each other, it was Margery and Houdini. It was inevitable given what they were each trying to do—Margery to play her role, Houdini to destroy it and her. Margery's feelings were expressed through Walter, who took to predicting that Houdini would be dead in "a year or less." Houdini scornfully dismissed this: "In the last 10 years my death has been predicted dozens of times, and if the spiritualists(?) guess often enough some time they will guess correctly." Nevertheless, he was deeply unsettled by Margery. For she embodied everything that made him feel most miserable and uncomfortable.

Everyone agrees that she was a beautiful and very sexy woman who had no compunction about displaying her highly desirable body. For séances during the hot summer weather she liked to wear a kimono with nothing underneath. This served two purposes. It facilitated the production of "pseudopods," which tended to ema-nate from her vagina. But it also distracted members of the commit-tee—which by now was considerably enlarged.

Mediums had rarely hesitated to use their sexual charms wherever this seemed appropriate. Eusapia Palladino, who had convinced (among others) William James, had (Houdini reported "on good authority") "[thrown] her legs into the laps of her male sitters! . . . She placed her head upon the shoulders of men sitters, and

. . . she did various other things calculated to confuse and muddle men." Margery, too, relied on being able to dazzle her sitters; and she usually succeeded. Malcolm Bird was undoubtedly in love with her (he later wrote a whole book about her). So was Hereward Carrington. And so was Eric Dingwall, a psychical researcher from England who now came over to Boston to see what was going on.

Dingwall seems principally to have interested himself in the more pornographic aspects of Margery's mediumship. Indeed, pornography was a prime interest of his. He was for some years keeper of the closed shelves in the British Museum Library; and Houdini had previously met him when they were both investigating Eva C., whose manifestations were also decidedly louche.

His relations with the prudish and puritanical Houdini on this occasion were strained from the outset. Houdini made strenuous attempts to contact Dingwall while he was in Boston and find out whose side he was on—for in this affair there could be no more pretence of impartiality: you were either on Margery's side or Houdini's. But Dingwall was not to be pinned down. "A statement which I heard, and which he did not deny, was that the London Psychic Research sent him over especially to investigate Mrs. Crandon," Houdini told Harry Price. "But not having spoken to him, I cannot say he makes the statement but he allows people to believe they are bearing the expenses . . . Since he has been over here he states she has ectoplastic arms which exude from her body and ring the bells. What do you think of this? . . . *I would appreciate anything you could tell me about what Dingwall knows about ectoplasm, if there is anything to be told.*"

It may be remembered that the original creator of ectoplasm was Eva C. Eva's ectoplasmic productions took many curious and horrid forms, but they did not resemble Margery's, which were large, floppy, handlike exudations of some meaty substance (possibly lungs) appearing from beneath her kimono. If they were not paranormal (Dingwall speculated in a report on the sittings) then they were presumably secreted in her vagina.

These pseudopods fascinated Dingwall, who took copious photographs of them for the *Proceedings of the Society for Psychical Research* and described at great length the séances at which they were produced. In the end, reluctantly, he conceded that he was not convinced, but it took time for him to arrive at this conclusion. While the séances were going on he wrote to Eva's promoter and investigator, Schrenck-Notzing: "It is the most beautiful case of teleplasm and telekinesis with which I am acquainted. One is able to handle the teleplasm freely. The materialized hands are connected by an umbilical cord to the medium; they seize upon objects and displace them . . . The control is irreproachable." He described "A cold, clammy, dark brown or grayish ectoplasmic substance that exuded from the medium's mouth and head and slowly extended to ring bells and flip papers on the floor from a nearby table." But a few months later he had concluded that "normal" production was far the most likely explanation. "By the way," Houdini queried of Harry Price, "is there any truth in the report that Dingwall was observed making ectoplasmic hands out of liver and lights. I presume for experimental purposes."

Things came to a head between Houdini and Dingwall—and indeed between Houdini and Margery—in January 1925. The previous month, Dr. William McDougall, the Harvard psychologist who was also on the Margery committee, had publicly accused Houdini of adopting an unfair and prejudiced attitude towards Mrs. Crandon. Houdini riposted by wagering $5,000 that he could reproduce every one of Margery's supposedly supernatural effects by pure trickery. At the beginning of January he presented an evening exposé where he did just that. Among other things, "with the aid of the Spirit slates I produced a photograph of Mrs. Crandon's brother 'Walter' who was killed and of all the miracles in the world—I ran across the photograph of the boy as he was crushed between the engine and the tender of the train, and which was taken one minute before he died. Can you imagine the sensation she would have created had she come across this photograph first—planted them and then have 'Walter' tell her where his last photograph could be found?" Dingwall was present at this lecture and took Margery's part. He demanded to see a trick bell-box Houdini had had constructed which rang "at command." Houdini, very much in control, turned the audience against him much as he had done with Jess Willard some years before.

> "Will you let me see that box," the voice shouted out in a challenging tone. Just as I was reaching over to hand the person the box I was thunder-struck to see that the *person* was Eric Dingwall.
>
> I said "Well, Dingwall, you here and challenging me when you know that any secret I have in Spiritualism is yours simply for the asking? You ought to be ashamed of yourself . . ."
>
> I turned to the audience, told them that he had been sent here specially by the Psychic Research Association of England, and here he was sneaking in to see me work, when he was a member of two of the Organizations to which I belong and said, "Dingwall, this is not cricket." . . . He was crestfallen, he flushed and when they yelled for him to stand up so that they could see him he said, "Kindly address your remarks to the lecturer," and sank into his seat.

The exposé finally did the trick. The committee, with the exception of Hereward Carrington, announced that it agreed with Houdini. Margery did not qualify for the *Scientific American* award.

All this stuff—flying megaphones, spirit hands carved out of liver and lights, bells being rung by mysterious agencies—now seems so ludicrous that it is hard to see how it can have been taken seriously at the time. Just how seriously it was taken, however, may be judged from the thousands of words and acres of newspaper space devoted to the Margery affair by such grave journals as the Boston *Transcript, The New York Times* and the Boston *Herald*. There were not merely headlines but enormous articles, accusations, rebuttals, justifications, discussions, Houdini's denunciations of fraud, Dr. Crandon's outrage at the slur on his wife's good name, Professor McDougall's arrival at a verdict adverse to Margery, the *Scientific American*'s withdrawal of its award, the announcement of another award by another Harvard professor, Dr. Morton Prince, Houdini's offer of $5,000 if Margery could prove herself genuine . . .

Houdini claimed the moral high ground. He had exposed a fraud and saved the *Scientific American* from making a fool of itself. Dr. Crandon, not to be outdone, took refuge in respectability. He presented his wife and himself as a decent couple of exalted intellectual and social standing who had exposed themselves to a publicity-seeking trickster purely in the interests of the higher truth. Conan Doyle supported him in weary outrage and invited Margery to England.

Margery declined Conan Doyle's invitation. MARGERY FEARS FOG MAY BLOCK LONDON SEANCES, reported *The New York Times*. MEDIUM WHO FAILED TO WIN $2,500 PRIZE NOT SURE DAMP AIR WILL AGREE WITH "WALTER" HER CONTROL.

One of the most interesting aspects of the Margery mediumship is the role played in the affair by Dr. Crandon.

That he was his wife's accomplice as well as her impresario seems beyond doubt. Dingwall observed that hand control of Margery by her husband "must be regarded as non-existent." Even the spiritualist *Banner of Light* pointed out that "In the absence of Dr. Crandon there has been a dearth of phenomena."

Dr. Crandon's sincerity, the genuineness of his beliefs, impressed everyone who met him. But if he was helping to produce the phenomena, how was it possible that he could *also* believe in their supernormal nature? And if he knew what was going on, how could he have imagined that he would not be found out?

The last question, at least, seems clearly answered by his undisguised fury at Houdini's presence. The part of him that did acknowledge what was going on also knew exactly what would happen once Houdini arrived (as, of course, did Margery and "Walter").

One of Houdini's main crimes, in Dr. Crandon's eyes, was perhaps that he forced this suppressed knowledge—as it might be, a sleight-of-mind—into Dr. Crandon's consciousness.

In a sense, "Margery" was entirely her husband's creation. It was he who was interested in the occult, he who induced her to try her hand at mediumship—for which she proved to have a hitherto un-suspected talent. Looked at in this way, they appear as almost a cliché spiritualist couple. The besotted older man and the beautiful young medium appear frequently in spiritualist annals. One thinks, for example, of Sir William Crookes, who fell comprehensively for young Florrie Cook and her "spirit" alter ego, Katie King (while professing to be a detached observer, he wrote hymns of love to Katie and conducted an altogether more material relationship with Florrie).

In such circumstances, the girl's motivation is usually clear. Put crudely, this is a poor girl's chance of respectability and a decent life. Once the man has succumbed, he lays himself open in every possible way. If he will not co-operate willingly, then he can be forced to do so. Annie Eva Fay, another of William Crookes's young protégées, took him to court alleging "more than gallantry on his part towards her" when it seemed that she might be losing her influence over him.

Mina Crandon had not needed to resort to blackmail of this sort. She had previously been married to a grocer, Earl P. Rand. They had met in church, and had married in 1909. He was just starting up the grocery business, so that they "did not live luxuriously." But they enjoyed making themselves financially independent, and were con-tented with their life and their little boy, Allan. Then, in the summer of 1917, Mina needed an operation. It was performed by Dr. Cran-don. He was then still married to his second wife, although he had filed for divorce.

In November 1917 the grocer and his wife had their first quarrel. Their relations after that were strained, and they separated on

Christmas Day, Mina going to her mother's home, Earl staying with the business. On 18 January 1918, Mina filed for divorce on grounds of cruel and abusive treatment. During this period, Earl said, he felt "dazed." He decided not to contest the divorce for the sake of Allan, who was then five years old. It was granted in March: Mina received custody of Allan and $7 a week alimony. Shortly after the decree nisi became final Mina married Dr. Crandon, who had meantime finalised his own divorce. Allan lived with them: in the doctor's Lime Street house he was known as "John." The Crandons, at the time of the "Margery" séances, still bought their groceries from Earl Rand—for what mixture of motives may be conjectured. He had not seen Mina since the divorce, but assured journalists that while she had been his wife "she never had any spiritualistic powers. She took lessons on the cornet . . . she tried the cello and she could play a few pieces on the piano, but I never knew her to be able to talk to ghosts."

From Mina's point of view, the attractions of the wealthy Brahmin Dr. Crandon were obvious. He might be thirty years older than she was, but he could offer her a life such as Mrs. Earl P. Rand could never dream of. If he wanted her to be a medium, she would be a medium. She approached the job with her customary charm, intelligence and thoroughness. He, meanwhile, saw and did not see what was going on. He had friends at Harvard. The department of psychology, founded by William James, had long-standing connections with psychical research. William McDougall held the chair there largely on account of his interest in it. Margery gave her séances before eminent men experienced in the field. She convinced them. Why not go for the *Scientific American* prize? Houdini, the potential fly in the ointment, was busy elsewhere. Why not present him with a fait accompli? Unfortunately for them, Houdini was not to be fobbed off; and not only could he see through Margery, but he was uniquely impervious to her charms. Rather, he was revolted by their display. That was Margery's bad luck.

Mina, of course, was irretrievably stuck with Margery once she had made her appearance. Her marriage probably depended increasingly upon Dr. Crandon's collusion, acknowledged or unacknowledged, in the séances. And she must have got a good deal of fun out of it all. She could express herself through Walter as she never could through the mouth of the respectable Mrs. Crandon. She could bamboozle respectable professors. She could flirt with all the men.

"It is the belief of all the committee," reported Hudson Hoagland, writing in the *Atlantic Monthly* after the event, "that Dr. Crandon is sincere in his belief in Walter as a supernormal reality—as the returned spirit, in fact, of his dead brother-in-law . . . Walter seems to most of us to be a delightful and wholly dramatic impersonation—witty, tactful, obliging, entertaining, full of wonders and tricks, swaggering with confidence, joking with the most boisterous joker, and then in a moment all sympathy and wisdom, ready with advice and counsel. Of course, with the reality of a supernormal Walter established, it becomes a rather easy matter for the medium and sympathetic attendants to help him consciously at times as one would help any friend to demonstrate important truths, although this is not in the spirit of the scientific method."

After his destruction of Margery, Houdini continued his crusade against false mediums with redoubled vigour. When he was in London he had wanted to replicate the exploit of the famous D. D. Home, who had (according to detailed reports) flown out of one third-storey window and in at another. These windows were reputedly eighty-five feet above the ground. *"Tall stories,"* Houdini remarked then of Home's witnesses, "appear to have been a specialty of these remarkably observant gentlemen."

Tall stories in all their guises were his concern now. He exposed "trumpet mediums" in Denver and New York, revealing himself at the crucial moment with a triumphant cry to the consternation of all concerned. He employed his intrepid lady secretaries to uncover fraud where he might be recognised. He was especially interested in spirit photographers, always having been a dab hand with a camera himself.

In a sense, this had become another field for his collector's instinct. He was a connoisseur of fake mediums. "Have run across 2 very fine 'trick' mediums. *Best ever,*" he crowed to Harry Price. And after another exposure: "Last night pandemonium rained supreme."

He had intended to leave all his books on spiritualism to the American Society for Psychical Research. But when they elected Malcolm Bird to be a research officer for them, he cancelled the bequest. The Margery grudge, of all grudges, was not one to be abandoned merely at death.

17

ℐNSIDE THE COFFIN

The only member of the *Scientific American* committee who continued to endorse Margery's claim to mediumship was Hereward Carrington. Carrington was an enterprising figure. He made his living as an author and showman, specialising in subjects related to conjuring and mediumship. He had for a time been the manager of Eusapia Palladino, the leg-waving Neapolitan medium who convinced many of the world's most distinguished scientists, from the Italian criminologist Cesare Lombroso and the French biologist Charles Richet in 1893 to the American psychologist William James just before his death in 1909, that she possessed supernatural powers. In November 1909, Carrington brought Eusapia to Harvard at the invitation of James's successor, Hugo Muensterberg: on that occasion she was comprehensively exposed.

Eusapia faded away, but Carrington carried on regardless. Now, in 1926, he was promoting a supposedly Egyptian dervish and fakir called Rahman Bey. The choice of nationality was a shrewd one. The East had always been the home of magic and mystery. Houdini's needle trick—"presented to me in the White Silences of the Ganges by an old Hindu priest"—was Indian for no other reason. But the East is a big place: Far, Near or Middle might all be equally apposite for presentation purposes. It happened that at this time the Middle East carried the greatest magical charge. A passion for all things Egyptian was sweeping the world. In 1922 Sir Howard Carter and his team had unearthed the lost tomb of Tutankhamen with the immortal question and answer: "What do you see?" "Wonderful things!"—and had ever since been falling like flies, victims of the fatal and inexplicable Mummy's Curse. The ancient magic of the Pharaohs had evidently lost none of its potency.

Rahman Bey purveyed mystical and possibly supernatural powers of mind over matter. In May 1926, he opened at the Selwyn Theater on Broadway. He began with a selection of familiar yogic tricks—thrusting a steel pin through his cheek, sticking a thin knife into his neck, pushing skewers through the skin of his chest. He lay on a bed of nails (placed very close together so that they didn't stick into him), increased the pulse rate in one wrist while decreasing it in the other, lay on two swords while a stone slab was hammered to bits on his midriff. Carrington provided a running commentary from the side of the stage. For the climax of his act the fakir threw himself into a trance and was buried in a coffin under a mound of sand. For ten minutes Carrington lectured the audience on living burials and sus-pended animation. Then Rahman Bey was disinterred, brought himself out of trance, and was applauded wildly.

All this belonged to the realm of "Natural Magic"—the use of material properties to produce apparently wonderful effects. Most of it was regular dime-show stuff. But it might have been designed specifically to infuriate Houdini. Firstly it was produced by his bête noire Carrington. Houdini and Carrington were old enemies. Car-rington, a supporter of Mrs. Crandon, had denounced Houdini over the Margery affair and accused him of having "No Standing as a Psychist" and of being a "pure publicist." In retaliation, Houdini leaked the *Scientific American* article which would have awarded Margery the prize, had he not turned up in the nick of time, put his spoke in the wheel and had Orson Munn stop the presses. When Dr. E. E. Free, the magazine's editor, protested at this unauthorised behaviour, Houdini's reply revealed his target: "I have never at any time asked that the 'Margery' case be reopened," he wrote. "What I have suggested, however, is that 'Dr.' Carrington's actions in the 'Margery' incident, should be investigated . . . I regret to note, nevertheless, that both you and Mr. O. D. Munn think my opinion concerning the fitness of 'Dr.' Carrington 'is entirely beside the point.' Since this is your estimate of the matter, I think I may, in all modesty, contravert it."

As though Carrington's presence was not in itself enough to turn Rahman Bey into a focus for Houdini's outrage, his act did what, for Houdini, was the most unforgivable thing of all. It infused a succession of simple tricks with a whiff of the supposed supernatural. More: Rahman Bey, with his coffin trick, was trespassing directly on Houdini's territory. He was both usurping the panoply of death and performing supposedly impossible feats of physical endurance. He even (in July) had himself thrown into the Hudson River in his coffin. This was a failure—the alarm bell with which the coffin was fitted went off, apparently inadvertently, almost as soon as he had hit the water. But in a swimming pool a little later he stayed under water, in his coffin, for a full hour. After that Carrington challenged Houdini, who had been loud in his criticisms of the "Egyptian Miracle Man," to duplicate this feat—if he could.

Houdini lost no time about it. He ordered a galvanized-iron box six-foot-six long, twenty-two inches wide and twenty-two inches high. It was fitted with both an alarm bell and a telephone. Then, in his basement workshop, he prepared to test out his theories and Rahman Bey's claims.

The Egyptian (who turned out to be more of an Italian) claimed, or Carrington claimed on his behalf, that his survival in the coffin was due to his assumption of a trance state in which both respiration and circulation stopped. But there was no proof of this, and Houdini did not believe it. Much of his own act was based upon controlled breathing. And although he had never tried what Rahman Bey was now doing—his act, on the contrary, having hitherto been based upon the principle that he would stay in the box for as *short* a time as possible—he suspected that the secret here, too, lay in breath control rather than suspended animation.

Houdini made three tests in his new coffin, two in private, one in public. He wrote them all up in a report which he then submitted to the U.S. Department of Mines: he hoped his experiences might prove useful to miners or sailors caught in an accident. For the first two tests, he recorded, he had 24,428 cubic inches of air in the box; for the third, 34,398 cubic inches.

For the first test, Houdini's coffin was not submerged, and he remained in the box for one hour, ten minutes. He reported: "Was comfortable which leaves me to believe that some air must have seeped through, though very little, it helped. I started to perspire after being in about forty-five minutes, and was completely saturated with perspiration, but at no time was I in agony. I scarcely moved. With my years of training, I can remain apparently motionless without an effort. I kept my eyes open for fear I would go to sleep."

The second test took place under water at noon on 4 August. The coffin had been strengthened and tested until it was airtight. When Houdini was inside, it was placed in a large box and lowered under water. "This time I was comfortable—somewhat cold," he reported. "There was plenty of moisture on the inside—I should judge that about an inch and a half water on the top of the coffin . . . Was much more comfortable than at the first test as far as my body was concerned. Started to draw long breaths after about fifty minutes. There was always an irritability there and thought it was simply temperament on my part . . . I gave the signal to let me out at seventy minutes and believe it took three minutes to unscrew the thirty-two bolts and screws on the coffin. There was no suffering."

The third test took place in public next day, 5 August 1926, in the swimming pool of the Hotel Shelton. Before he was submerged, Houdini made a little tension-raising speech. "If I die," he said, "it will be the will of God and my own foolishness." He added, "I am going to prove the copybook maxims are wrong when they say a man can live but three minutes without air, and I am not going to pretend to be in a cataleptic state either." (Of course he did not mention that the coffin was full of air, 34,398 cubic inches of it, to be precise.) The area round the swimming pool was filled with spectators from the press, including Hereward Carrington. They watched as it was submerged, and held under water by several men standing on top of it. Then the counting began.

"As a matter of fact I was not comfortable at all," reported Houdini, "and attribute it to the warmth of the place and the mechanical means of drawing air into the pool . . . It was warm in the coffin before the two round plates were screwed on . . . At no time can I say I was as comfortable as during the other tests. The first day, the anxiety of an accident retarded me somewhat, but as you know I trained for many years as an escape artist . . . In this test I had to breathe heavily after about fifty minutes and was not sure of staying under. I hung along over an hour and thought I would do at least ten minutes more. By this time I commenced to pant, that is draw rather long slow breaths. As I remembered in the first two tests, the temperature was less at my feet than at my head, I slid towards the foot of the box . . . When the coffin was out of the water, there was a relief all over my body . . . I counted my respirations and averaged seventeen. When I dictated this I still had that metallic taste in my stomach and mouth. Felt rather weak in the knees . . .

"When my assistant phoned me to say that I had been in there for one hour and twelve minutes, I was going to stay in three more minutes, but watching my lungs rise and fall thought I could stand the strain for another fifteen minutes . . . In ordinary circumstances I can remain under water two minutes without any trouble. When I was a boy 16–18 I could do four minutes in a bath tub where there was not much pressure.

"Am having a coffin made with a glass top and as soon as it is ready will let you know."

In fact the new coffin was not glass-topped but bronze. It was a magnificent thing. Having worsted Rahman Bey, Houdini had decided to co-opt his crowd-puller and take it on tour with him that autumn. It would be a welcome novelty. He also co-opted Rahman Bey's adoptive nationality. The poster he had printed to advertise his new act was as Egyptian as could be, with the Sphinx lowering over a painted sarcophagus containing Houdini. "Buried Alive!" it proclaimed. "Egyptian Fakirs Outdone—the Greatest Necromancer of the Age—Perhaps of all times."

In 1926 Houdini was fifty-two. He was in perfect health. Conan Doyle, who was a doctor as well as a writer, said: "I suppose at that time Houdini was, from an insurance point of view, so far as bodily health goes, the best life of his age in America. He was in constant training and he used neither alcohol nor tobacco." This opinion was echoed by his insurer, who ended one letter, "Would there were many more like you."

But the fact remained that he was getting older. He was about to embark on another gruelling tour. How much longer could he go on with this life? He showed no more sign of stopping than he ever had done. From the moment of his first great success he had been assuring correspondents that, on the completion of his next contract, he was going to retire. But he had never done so. Now that the moment might seem to be approaching, he made no such pretences. "We all have our hobbies," he wrote at this time, "and it is natural that each year I have an inclination to return to my first love— vaudeville—because it was Mr. Albee, of the B. F. Keith Circuit, who gave me an opportunity to make my name known throughout the civilized world as an entertainer. While others go to Palm Beach in the winter for a vacation, I go into vaudeville. I get paid for it, a very good salary, but I don't have to do it."

He might be impervious to age: Bess was not. She was by now drinking heavily. Her makeup was applied ever more thickly and luxuriantly: a gaudy face which did not disguise the sad middle-aged lady beneath. There is a certain charm in Houdini's dismissal of her worries. "Stop thinking that at 48½ years you are old—tush-tush— and a couple of *fiddle-de-dees*. We have our best mature years before us," he told her, adding: "I have a list of men and women at home who only started to think and act after *three* score years had flitted by."

Things started to go wrong in October. While they were playing the Opera House in Providence, Rhode Island, Bess was taken ill. Ptomaine poisoning was diagnosed: she needed rest and constant care. A nurse, Sophie Rosenblatt, was engaged for her, and one of the girls in the show took her place onstage as Houdini's partner in "Goodbye Winter, Welcome Summer" and the rest of the show. On the Friday evening, 8 October, Bess had a high fever and Harry sat up with her all night. The fever went down Saturday morning; he snatched a few hours' sleep between the matinée and the evening performance. They were due to open in Albany on Monday. After the Saturday night show, Harry saw Bess and the troupe off to Albany, and himself took the last train to New York, where he had an appointment with his lawyer, Bernard Ernst. They were to discuss how the many libel suits instigated against him by outraged spiritualists ought to be handled, and some other matters. When he arrived, the Ernsts were not at home: Houdini snatched a little sleep on the living-room sofa. Then they arrived, and Houdini retired with Ernst to the study. He phoned Albany: Bess was still ill. He went down to Martinka's to pick up some pieces of apparatus he needed for the show, then phoned Albany again. Miss Rosenblatt assured him she would stay with Bess through the night.

Houdini took the early morning train to Albany, and when he arrived, found Bess a little better. He slept briefly, and then it was time for the opening performance.

The first act went well. The second act began as usual with the needles trick; then it was time for the Water-Torture Cell. He changed into a bathing suit and sat down to have himself closed into the mahogany stocks. Then the metal frame which held the stocks in place was passed over him. After that he was ready to be hoisted into place; but this did not go smoothly. The hoist jerked suddenly, he heard a snap and felt a sharp pain in his ankle. He signalled to be lowered again, and found he was unable to stand. Jim Collins asked if there was a doctor in the house. There was, and he diagnosed a broken ankle. The diagnosis was confirmed that night in hospital, where the ankle was bandaged and splinted. Back at the hotel he constructed a leg brace which would get him through the next days in Albany and then Schenectady. After that it was on to Montreal where, on 18 October, he opened at the Princess Theater.

A doctor examined his ankle and told him to keep off his feet, in which case the bone would knit. Houdini did not take this advice. On Tuesday morning he lectured to the police, and in the afternoon he was due to fulfil a long-standing engagement at McGill University, where he would lecture about spirit fraud and the various mediums he had exposed. After the lecture he sat while faculty members and students came to talk to him. One young man had made a sketch of him: Houdini admired it and invited him backstage to make a proper portrait later in the week.

The young man, whose name was Samuel J. Smilovitch, or Smiley, kept the appointment that Friday, 22 October. He and a friend, Jack Price, met Houdini in the Princess Theater lobby at eleven in the morning. Houdini arrived with Bess, Sophie Rosenblatt the nurse, and a young woman called Julia Sawyer, Bess's niece, who had been acting as his secretary. They all went through to the dressing room. A few minutes later there was a knock on the door, and

Julia showed in another young man, a first-year McGill student called Whitehead.

Jack Price told what happened next:

Houdini was facing us and lying down on a couch at the time reading some mail, his right side nearest us. This first-year student engaged Houdini more or less continually in a conversation whilst my friend Mr. Smilovitch continued to sketch Houdini. This student was the first to raise the question of Houdini's strength. My friend and I were not so much interested in his strength as we were in his mental acuteness, his skill, his beliefs and his personal experiences. Houdini stated that he had extraordinary muscles in his forearms, in his shoulders and in his back, and he asked all of us present to feel them, which we did.

The first-year McGill student asked Houdini whether it was true that punches in the stomach did not hurt him. Houdini remarked rather unenthusiastically that his stomach could resist much, though he did not speak of it in superlative terms. Thereupon he gave Houdini some very hammer-like blows below the belt, first securing Houdini's permission to strike him. Houdini was reclining at the time with his right side nearest Whitehead, and the said student was more or less bending over him. These blows fell on that part of the stomach to the right of the navel, and were struck on the side nearest to us, which was in fact Houdini's right side; I do not remember exactly how many blows were struck. I am certain, however, of at least four very hard and severe body blows, because at the end of the second or third blow I verbally protested against this sudden onslaught on the part of this first-year student, using the words, "Hey there. You must be crazy, what are you doing?" or words to that effect, but Whitehead continued striking Houdini with all his strength.

Houdini stopped him suddenly in the midst of a punch, with a gesture that he had had enough. At the time Whitehead was striking Houdini, the latter looked as though he was in extreme pain and winced as each blow was struck.

Houdini immediately after stated that he had had no opportunity to prepare himself against the blows, as he did not think that Whitehead would strike him as suddenly as he did and with such force, but that he would have been in a better position to prepare for the blows if he had risen from his couch for this purpose, but the injury to his foot prevented him from getting about rapidly.

At first the blows seemed to have had no ill effect. But by mid-afternoon Houdini was aware of a nagging ache and tenderness in his stomach, and by the evening both his ankle and his stomach were giving him great pain. However, as usual the show went on. Houdini was Superman, the death and resurrection hero. Such a figure is not deterred by trifling discomforts such as a broken ankle or a stomachache. So, in his dressing room between the acts, he sat on the couch and doggedly dictated letters to old collaborators about a projected new collection of mathematical problems and tricks. On one, to Will Goldston, he scrawled, "Broke a bone in my left leg." He did not mention the stomachache.

All that night he suffered terrible pain in his stomach. At about two A.M. he told Bess he thought he had a cramp or a strained muscle. She massaged him and he said he felt better. When she awoke next morning she found a note:

> *Champagne* coquette
> I'll be at theatre about 12.00—
> H H
> Fall Guy

Bess wrote on this note: "This is the last letter my darling wrote to me. We had a Champagne party in his room, Julia the nurse and I, and made him pay the bill."

Houdini closed in Montreal that Saturday, 23 October, and was due to open in Detroit the following day for a two-week run. On the train he was no longer able to conceal his suffering. Bess, distraught, and barely recovered from her own illness, telegraphed ahead to the show's Detroit advance man instructing him to get the best doctor in Detroit ready to examine Houdini before the opening.

The train was late—too late for them to check in at the hotel before leaving for the theatre. The doctor was waiting, meanwhile, in the hotel lobby. Finally the advance man, waiting with the doctor, thought to telephone the theatre. The doctor rushed round and examined Houdini on the dressing-room floor, there being nowhere else he could lie down. He diagnosed acute appendicitis and said an ambulance should be called at once to take Houdini to hospital. Bess did not hear this, and Houdini did not tell her. Nor did the theatre manager, who was present during the examination. He had his own worries. The house was sold out and queues were still waiting outside the theatre. He said, "We have a $15,000 advance sale. What are we going to do?" to which Houdini replied, "I'll do this show if it's my last."

He was by now running a temperature of 104°. Several times during the show he nearly collapsed. The *Detroit News* described him as being "a little late, a little hoarse and more than a little tired." Spectators reported he was nervous, missing his cues, and hurrying the show along. Between the first and second acts he was taken to his dressing room and ice packs were placed upon him, and the same thing was done between the second and third acts. He did the "little magic" with silks and coins, the card sleights, the lecture exposing fraudulent mediums, the questions and challenges from the audience. Just before the third act he turned around to his chief assistant and said, "Drop the curtain, Collins, I can't go any further." He returned to his dressing room, changed his clothes, and still would not go to hospital.

The impulse to suicide, which was such a fundamental part of his makeup, had hitherto always been thwarted by the reflex which compelled him to save himself each time. But now it had found an ally stronger than any reflex: Houdini's cult of bodily imperviousness, which denied his own mortality. This became the instrument by which his death, so often sought, was finally to be achieved.

Back at the hotel, Bess threw a tantrum—her weapon of last resort. The hotel physician was called. He summoned a surgeon who arrived at three A.M. and said Houdini must be rushed to hospital at once: his condition was critical. Houdini still demurred. He insisted on calling his personal physician, Dr. William Stone, in New York. Stone talked to the doctors in the hotel room. Then he spoke to Houdini again. Houdini gave in. He was taken to Grace Hospital, where his gangrenous appendix was removed that afternoon. Dr. Kennedy, the surgeon who performed the operation, said: "We found that his appendix was a great long affair which started in the right lower pelvis where it normally should, extended across the mid-line and lay in his left pelvis, exactly where the blow had been struck. Reconsidering the history afterwards, we concluded that his appendix had ruptured some place near St. Thomas, Ontario, and that he had carried on the entire performance the same evening at the Garrick Theatre with a ruptured appendix spreading peritonitis."

Now, at last, no effort or expense was spared. A specialist in postoperative technique was called from a nearby hospital. The family was summoned, all except Leopold, the errant brother, whom Houdini had still not forgiven for the fact that he, Ehrich, had not been present at his mother's death.

"As I entered the lobby, Dr. Kennedy, the doctor who had performed the operation, was just coming out of the operating room," Theo recalled. "I asked him, 'How is he?' Dr. Kennedy . . . said, 'He will never get well.' . . . He said he might live twenty-four hours at the most. Houdini was powerfully built and fooled the doctor. Monday, Tuesday, Wednesday and Thursday went by and the doctor came to me and said 'We must perform another operation on Houdini as the bowels have become paralyzed.' . . . All Houdini said was, 'You are the doctor. Go ahead.' . . . During all the hours of agony Houdini never thought he was dying—never gave that a thought. All he talked about was having to lay off work for six or seven weeks and keep his assistants out of work that long. After the second operation [he] seemed to get stronger. In fact on Friday he was stronger still, but on Saturday afternoon Dr. Kennedy came and told me that it was a matter of a few hours . . . Sunday at eleven o'clock Dr. Kennedy came out of the sick-room and I could see tears streaming from his eyes. He did not say a word to me but I went in and sat alongside of Houdini's bed. Houdini reached over and took my hand in his and said, 'Dash, I'm getting tired and I can't fight any more.' "

He died in Bess's arms at one twenty-six that afternoon. The Detroit *Free Press* reported: "He . . . closed his eyes for all time with the name of Robert Ingersoll on his lips." Ingersoll was a writer and lecturer on agnosticism who had been one of Houdini's heroes all his life. "It was a beautiful sunny day," Theo remembered, "and when the doctor said 'He is gone' the heavens clouded over and it poured rain like I have never seen it pour before."

It was 31 October, Halloween. He was fifty-two years old.

All the properties for the show had been crated up and shipped to New York when Houdini was taken to hospital. But Jim Collins was notified by the Detroit Transfer Co. on the Friday that one crate had been left behind accidentally. This, when investigated, turned out to be the box containing the bronze casket which had been the chief prop for the Rahman Bey exposure. Houdini's attorney, telephoning from New York, disclosed that one of the first provisions of the will was a desire to be buried in this casket in the event of death. So fate and Houdini remained in cahoots until the end.

The body in its casket was taken by train to New York. Houdini had left meticulous instructions regarding the conduct of his funeral. It was held at the huge Elks Lodge Ballroom on West Forty-third Street. Two rabbis officiated: the crowd was two thousand strong.

All his life Houdini had been a joiner. He liked belonging to clubs, societies and lodges. Perhaps they enhanced that sense of rootedness he was always looking for. All of them took part in his funeral. A cedarwood wand was broken in half over the coffin to a funeral chant by members of the Society of American Magicians, of which he had for so long been president. There were tributes from the National Vaudeville Artists, the Jewish Theatrical Guild, and rites by the St. Cecile Masonic Lodge, the Mount Zion Congregation and the Elks. The cortège taking the body to Machpelah Cemetery was twenty-five cars long. The honorary pallbearers included E. F. Albee, Martin Beck, Marcus Loew, Lee Shubert, Charles Dillingham, Adolph S. Ochs, Adolph Zukor and many others. As the coffin was lowered one pallbearer whispered to another (the impresario Florenz Ziegfeld), "Suppose he isn't in it!"

Theo, Nat and Gladys were there, but not Leopold. Houdini's assistants, James Collins, James Vickery, Frank Williamson, John Arden, Beppo Vitorelli and Elliott Sandford, lowered the coffin into its place by the side of his mother. As he had requested, his head rested on a black bag containing her letters to him.

A year later, as Jewish custom requires, the bust which had been waiting for so long in his living room was set in its appointed place atop the enormous tomb. Beneath it, under a plaque recording his presidency of the Society of American Magicians from 1912 until 1926, enormous letters read simply HOUDINI.

Mystery continued to surround him. Even the circumstances of his death were (and remain) slightly mysterious. Indeed, Robert Lund, a magic collector who worked for many years in Detroit and took a particular interest in the details of the death, found no fewer than seven different versions of how it occurred:

> And there you have the true story of Houdini's death. How he died
> in the arms of Larry Lewis and Beatrice Houdini in Boston and
> Chicago while suspended upside down in a glass tank on the stage
> of the Oriental Theatre while performing on the bottom of the river

locked in a casket and suffering from a ruptured appendix and hardening of the arteries, the same afternoon, within twenty-four hours, or five days later. Truth will out.

What really happened is in a sense clear: he died of peritonitis brought on by a ruptured appendix. But how did that appendix rupture in the first place?

The assumption (not unnaturally) was that the blows to the stomach were the precipitating factor. But the consensus is that this is medically impossible. Bernard Meyer conducted a computerised search of the medical literature and talked to a number of experienced surgeons, and could find not a single instance of acute appendicitis being caused by physical injury. Such a trauma can rupture the large intestine, and in fact this was the initial diagnosis of Dr. Charles Kennedy, the surgeon who examined Houdini in his hotel room and later operated on him. But what he found was a ruptured appendix. He said, "It is the only case of traumatic appendicitis I have ever seen in my lifetime, but the logic of the thing seemed to indicate that Mr. Houdini died of appendicitis, the direct result of the injury."

What seems most likely is that Houdini was already suffering from appendicitis before the famous incident, and that this either aggravated it or prevented him from realising that his condition was something more than a mere bruise until it was too late. It will be remembered that Jack Price had noticed that "at the time Whitehead was hitting Houdini, the latter looked as though he was in extreme pain and winced as each blow was struck." And after Houdini's death, Professor William Tait, who introduced him at the McGill lecture, remarked how precipitately he had sat down at its conclusion, as though he were in some pain. Tait concluded at the time that this was due to the pain from his ankle, but it might have been abdominal; the fracture was by then eight days old. This possibility is borne out by a letter written by one Gertrude Hills to the

New York *Sun* some time later. Ms. Hills described how, during the summer, Houdini had agreed to take part in a charity fund-raising show. "He was delighted to be of assistance and promised to perform his 'straitjacket' act and to try to beat his own record in escaping. In attempting to do so he hurt himself so badly that for a number of days he suffered pain in his side. Closely following upon this injury he had an attack of what was diagnosed as 'ptomaine poisoning.' From this he really never seemed to recover. When he left on his tour he told me that the effects of the injury and 'poisoning' were still evident."

Meanwhile, reports from clairvoyants who claimed to have predicted Houdini's death and to have witnessed signs and portents began to flood in. A Mr. Gysel reported that at ten fifty-eight on the evening of 24 October 1926, a photograph of Houdini which he had framed and hung on the wall "fell to the ground, breaking the glass. I now know that Houdini will die."

Mr. Gysel's experience would have come as no surprise to Houdini's spiritualist adversaries, for (as he himself had noted) they had been predicting his death for years, and one day they would inevitably get it right. In 1924 "Walter" had given him "a year or less." Then the Crandons had foretold the event for 25 December 1925. Conan Doyle recorded that "In my own home circle I had the message some months before his death, 'Houdini is doomed, doomed, doomed!' " On 13 October, a medium called Mrs. Wood wrote a letter to the novelist Fulton Oursler: "Three years ago the spirit of Dr. Hyslop said, 'The waters are black for Houdini,' and he foretold that disaster would befall him while performing before an audience in a theatre. Dr. Hyslop now says that the injury is more serious than has been reported, and that Houdini's days as a magician are over."

Houdini himself had apparently had his own premonitions of the coming event. Among his clippings is one from 1919 recording the collapse, onstage at Detroit, of a comedian named Sidney Drew.

Drew had been taken ill in St. Louis, but had continued to play, against all advice, until in Detroit he could go no further . . .

A friend and fellow magician, Joe Dunninger, reported that one morning in October Houdini called him in New York with a request to come at once with his car to West 113th Street as he was in a hurry and had to move some stuff. When the car was loaded he said, "Drive through the park, Joe."

> When we got to the exit on Central Park West around 72nd Street he grabbed my arm; in a hollow, tragic voice he said, "Go back, Joe!"
> "Go back where?"
> "Go back to the house, Joe."
> "Why—did you forget something?"
> "Don't ask questions, Joe. Just turn around and go back."
> I drove back to the house. By this time it was raining even harder, if that was possible, but Houdini ignored it; he got out of the car, took off the straw hat, and stood looking up at the dark house with rain streaming down his face. Then he got back in the car saying nothing. When we again approached the western exit of the park his shoulders began to shake. He was crying. Finally he said, "I've seen my house for the last time, Joe. I'll never see my house again." As far as I know he never did.

Nevertheless, it seems clear from Theo's account that, even in the agonies of appendicitis, Houdini had no morbid presentiments. Fulton Oursler, who shared Houdini's interest in spiritualism (but was more inclined to believe), noted: "I had written to Houdini in care of the Garrick Theater in Detroit, and when he arrived there on Sunday [after Montreal and the fatal blow] he found my letter waiting for him. In his dressing room he typed me a note in which he stated that he hoped to go to Toledo and have a seance with Ada Bessinet. Here . . . is evidence that he had no real suspicion his days were numbered. A few hours afterwards he was stricken and taken to the hospital from which he never emerged alive." And as late as 30

October—the day before his death—he wrote to a friend: "Box offices here are S.R.O. which certainly makes me sunny and quite happy. Except that I feel none too well at the moment, but suppose I will get over this waviness in no time."

Houdini thus proved that, as he always insisted (but never really believed), he was not clairvoyant.

┌─────┐
│ **18** │
└─────┘

$\mathcal{H}$OUDINI LIVES!

 On Halloween 1992 I attended a séance. It was held at the Holiday Inn, Rochester, N.Y., an improbable venue for the supernatural. There were nine participants besides myself and the medium. We were trying, on the anniversary of his death, to raise Houdini. "If it is possible for anyone to get through after death," he always asserted, "that person will be me."

The eleven of us sat around a table on a kind of dais. Apart from a surviving niece, the medium and myself, the participants were male, mostly middle-aged or elderly, dressed in tuxedos: a family gathering, a group of uncles. Everyone knew each other well. They had met on countless Houdini-related occasions in the past. Several were noted collectors of Houdiniana, for which there is an avid and ever-growing market. Around us clustered a bevy of press photographers and television crews. The body of the room was filled with wives, friends and spectators. In the middle of the table were a bust of Houdini, a pair of his handcuffs and an envelope containing the message he promised to send Conan Doyle, should he ever return. The message has never yet been transmitted. Would it be received today? Would the spirit of Houdini accept us as satisfactory Doyle substitutes?

Most of the participants seemed to assume that this or any other manifestation was unlikely. Still, at the appointed hour—one in the afternoon, twenty-six minutes before the moment of death—we all joined hands and shut our eyes. The medium told us to relax. As my chair was very close to the edge of the dais, the fear of falling over backwards made this hard for me. But I did my best, although it must be said that this was not a relaxing occasion. The medium, a healthy-looking lady with very red cheeks and a black dress, intoned from time to time, "Houdini, are you there?" We kept our eyes shut. Nothing happened. After a while Mrs. Blood, Houdini's niece, announced that she had felt someone touch her. But it was a press photographer, not a spirit. This was the nearest we got to a sign.

Past séances have tried more tangible temptations. In 1978, at the American Museum of Magic in Marshall, Michigan—an altogether more conducive location—an attempt was made to lure the elusive spirit with a basket of his favourite snack, bagels and lox. But Houdini did not descend. He might have reacted more favourably to bread-and-butter custard, the recipe he contributed to *A collection of the Favorite Foods of Famous Players:* "I happen to have a weakness for sweets, and this one you will not find in any other cookbook."

The Houdini séances did not start out in such lighthearted fashion.

After her husband died, Bess found herself even more at a loss than most widows. Since the age of eighteen she had lived inside Houdini's closed world. Every member of this tiny circle had his or her particular role, from which no deviation was tolerated. All these roles were strictly relative to Houdini, planets to his sun. So his death presented all his close associates with problems of identity and occupation. What were they to do next? They had never really lived their own lives—they had simply been bit players in Houdini's.

For Theo Hardeen, the answer was straightforward. He had always been his brother's copy—*"Houdini der zweite."* Now the original was gone, he was free at last to "come into his own." This turned out to mean that he remained his brother's copy. That was all he knew: it was too late for him to redesign himself as himself. He inherited all Houdini's illusions and apparatus (though he could never use the Water-Torture Cell, as he was much too big for it). He also took over Jim Collins. Together they finished Houdini's uncompleted tour, and started on further tours of their own. Eventually he became, as his brother had been for so many years, president of the Society of American Magicians.

From time to time, Theo tried to contact his brother. He did not really believe he would succeed. After the death of their brother Bill in 1925, "We . . . agreed that . . . the first Sunday we were to go to Houdini's office at midnight and wait to see whether we would get any sign from Bill . . . We did as arranged . . . and, as expected, nothing happened. It was also agreed that if nothing should happen on Sunday night, then we were to go out to the cemetery and sit at Bill's grave, midnight on Wednesday, this we did, and again nothing happened except that we got wringing wet as it was pouring with rain.

"It was then that Houdini turned to me and said, 'We will keep the same code between you and me. Whichever one of us passes away first, if the other one should ever receive a message from any medium and it does not contain any of the ten words of our compact, he will know that the message must be a fake.' This is ten years ago," Hardeen added, "and up to the present time, I have not had as much as a peep from Houdini."

For Hardeen, this was just one part of a crowded life. He had his family, he had his work. But for Bess, the emptiness was complete. She had not only lived through her husband: more than most wives, she had lived *with* him. They had been partners in a very real sense. When his safe was opened after his death, a bundle of photographic negatives was found. He bequeathed them to "My beloved wife Beatrice Houdini and the only one who has actually helped me in my work." Their life together had not been perfect. But it had never been dull. And, however intolerable his huge ego may have been, he had never made any secret of the fact that he depended upon her utterly. He had once been asked his idea of perfect pleasure. He replied, "Sitting in a comfortable chair in my library and hearing Mrs. Houdini call up the stairs 'Young man, your lunch is ready.'" As an image of married life after thirty years, this has much to commend it.

Of course, this life had been distinctly lopsided: his, not hers. That was a fact that all the declarations of undying devotion could not negate. "Dear Mrs. Houdini," ran a typical missive in that voluminous, one-sided domestic correspondence. "Professor Brainien, Astronomer of Columbia College, has been invited for luncheon, for 12.30 on Tuesday next, provided you OK same. If quite all right, get in touch with Houdini himself, in person, notifying him of what's what. If you refuse I will have a hell of a time squaring him, because the invitation has already been given and accepted." The letter was signed "Your fond Husband, Houdini," and there was a postscript: "It has been so long since I have written you a letter, so hope this is the proper way to address a loving wife." And a terrible poem about nightingales was cut out and stuck on the end. But the meat of the communication was clear. The professor was coming and that was that. This might sound like a request, but it was purely informative.

Bess's increasing reliance on the bottle indicates that she did not find this life easy. She put up a certain resistance. There were the tantrums, the disapproval he dreaded, the grumbles in the dressing room. But in the end life went on—*his* life: and hers followed in its wake.

Now not only was he not there, but there was nothing to do. She could hardly go on tour with Hardeen. And there was never any prospect of her carrying on the act as Adelaide Herrmann had done with such success on the death of her husband Alexander "The Great" Herrmann. It was not that kind of act; she could never be anything but a secondary participant.

Nor was she rich. Houdini had earned enormous amounts of money, but he had spent it as fast as he earned it. The motion-picture ventures had swallowed up oceans of dollars, and were in chaos. Prints of Houdini's films had been widely distributed with no records to show who had them: anyone might exhibit them, and nobody would be any the wiser. Boxes of books he had bought kept arriving for months after his death, and had to be paid for. The terms of Houdini's will provided for a trust fund to be set up; but when B.M.L. Ernst, his lawyer and old friend, showed the prospective trustees the accounts relating to the estate, they declined to take on the position as there was no fund with which to set up any trust. Bess advanced money out of her own funds (all the real estate was in her name) to pay administration expenses, debts and inheritance taxes. She might have sold the library to pay for all this, but preferred to donate it, as Houdini had wished, to the Library of Congress in Washington—such as was left after friends and collectors had possessed themselves of many of the choicer items. Ernst never charged her for all the work his own firm did on behalf of the estate: "Because of my long and close personal friendship with Houdini, such services were rendered even though there were no funds to pay for them."

Bess was not left penniless, however. For years Houdini had spent substantial sums on life insurance policies. These (as his publicity liked to announce) provided for double indemnity in the event of accidental death. One of the insurance companies, New York Life Insurance, conducted a special investigation to ascertain what had really happened in Montreal and Detroit. After getting signed statements from all concerned, they accepted that the blow to the stomach had been the precipitating factor. When they agreed to pay the double indemnity, all the other companies followed suit. Mr. Ernst estimated that Bess would receive half a million dollars in insurance payments. She would have to pay heavy inheritance taxes, but even so, there would be enough to live on comfortably for the rest of her life.

But what was she to do with it?

She sold the house on West 113th Street to Rose Bonanno, whose father had for years looked after it when the Houdinis were away. As time went on and the locality got rougher, Rose's connections with the famous (or infamous) Bonanno family stood her in good stead. She lived in the basement, along with trunkfuls of neatly piled photographs, and did nothing to dispel the legend of Houdini's secrets. She would never open the padlocked attic because "Mrs. Houdini wouldn't like it." And there were all Houdini's mahogany bookcases, with their extra-deep ceilings and bases. What was hidden in those? Rose didn't know, or wasn't telling; and after her death, it was too late to find out. The collectors moved in *en masse* and everything movable disappeared.

Bess moved to Payson Avenue in another part of the city. There, for a while, she lapsed into drink and misery. A glimpse into her sad life at this time is given by a diary she began to keep in 1927. On its cover she wrote: "One of the few happy days." She had spent it visiting cemeteries—"How peaceful. Home early, only one drink."

Clearly life could not go on like this. For a while she tried a few desultory occupations. She opened a tearoom in Manhattan, in a building later torn down to make room for the Rockefeller Center. She thought of taking a vaudeville act on the road, in which a man was to be frozen into a block of ice from which he would make his escape (a stunt from *The Man from Beyond*). But the freezing and subsequent melting processes took too long, and the act never got past the tryout stage.

Most of her life, however, was still spent in the company of her husband. She commissioned and helped with the preparation of his biography, which appeared in 1928. And she spent a good deal of time trying to contact him. Every Sunday at the hour of his death she shut herself in her room opposite his photograph and waited for a sign. There was a standing offer of $10,000 for any medium who could produce the secret message Houdini had arranged to send her, and of which he had reminded her on his deathbed. No one did; and towards the end of 1928 the offer was withdrawn.

But it was clear that any medium who could come up with the message would put him or herself in the way of a good deal more than $10,000. The publicity alone would be worth ten times that.

It was, therefore, hardly surprising that a possible medium did eventually present himself. This was the Reverend Arthur Ford, who was at this time pastor of the First Spiritualist Church of Manhattan. He had recently distinguished himself by challenging the famous magician Howard Thurston to a debate at Carnegie Hall—a debate which Ford won. Thurston had been continuing the magical tradition of exposing fake mediums, but Ford was able to produce some effects which Thurston could not explain. Rumour now had it that he was planning a lecture tour with Bess. He meanwhile did his very best to get in touch with Houdini. On 8 February 1928, he claimed to have done so, or at any rate to have contacted old Mrs. Weiss, which was the next best thing. While in trance, she had apparently transmitted, via Ford's control, the word "Forgive"—the last word she had ever spoken. "Capitalize that," the old lady was quoted as having instructed through Ford's "control," "and put it in quotation marks. His wife knew the word, and no one else in all the world knew it. Ask her if the word which I tried to get back all these years was not 'Forgive.' " It will in fact be recalled that Mrs. Weiss's last word, whatever it may have been, was spoken to Hardeen, not Houdini or Bess, so that she can hardly have been the only person who knew it. But maybe Mrs. Weiss's spirit was carried away by the emotion of contact.

All this came to the attention of one of the reporters for a notorious scandal sheet, the New York *Graphic*. She was called Rea Jaure. Jaure was interested in Bess Houdini for her own reasons.

These, predictably, were to do with Houdini's supposed love life. In the 1928 Kellock biography, which was very much Bess's view of things, the picture given of her relations with her husband was an idyllic one (though not without its wholly unintended bizarreries). But there were those who were ready to hint that this was not the way things had been at all. One of these was a pretty redhead named Daisy White.

Daisy White had been a magician's assistant, and had later become a popular member of Martinka's staff. She, like all the close-knit magic community, knew about Houdini's terror when faced with flirtatious ladies. So, as a joke, she had sent him some steamy love letters. He never replied. But he kept them, together with various other such letters that he received from time to time. Inevitably, Bess found them after his death. The story was that she gave a tea party for the various ladies concerned, at which nothing was said, but which ended with each, as a farewell present, being given a packet which proved to contain her letters. It would be nice to believe this. Bess's feelings when she discovered the letters must have been mixed, although, knowing her husband as she did, she cannot have believed he ever did more than read them.

In the end, Bess and Daisy White became good friends. But this was not before Rea Jaure had done her worst.

Rea Jaure met Daisy White one lucky day, and forthwith decided to approach Mrs. Houdini for the *real* story—the story that had not been told in the biography. In December 1928, she managed to get Bess to agree to a series for the *Graphic,* to be written by Jaure and signed by Bess. It was to be called *The Life and Loves of Houdini.* There was also a question of some letters supposed to have been written to Bess by Charles Chapin, a former New York newspaper editor serving a life sentence for murder in Sing Sing, whom the Houdinis had befriended: the linking of his name with Mrs.

Houdini's might provide a sensational story. But before any of this could be put into effect, Bess became ill and went to hospital.

This should have presented no problem. After all, it was not Bess who was writing the pieces. But Jaure wanted a picture of Mrs. Houdini to go with them, and when the hospital staff would not allow anyone in to visit her, got one of the *Graphic*'s photographers to smuggle himself in disguised as a doctor. However, when he got to the ward, his magnesium flash set a Christmas tree on fire. In the ensuing uproar, Bess let it be known that the series was off and that she never wanted anything to do with the *Graphic* again.

Rea Jaure was furious, and determined to have her revenge. On 8 January 1929, the *Graphic* ran a report of a séance which Arthur Ford had held at Bess's sickbed. This was the culmination of a number of séances—eight separate sittings, beginning on 8 November 1928—at each of which one word of the message from Houdini to his wife was received by Arthur Ford's "control." The first word was "Rosabelle"—the word, said Ford, which was going to unlock the rest. Two weeks later a second word—"now"—was added; and on 18 December "look"—the sixth word in the code, said Ford—was transmitted by a lady believed to be Houdini's mother. The next word to be added was "now." Then came "Rosabelle" once more, together with "answer," "pray" and "tell." Finally, on the evening of 5 January 1929, came the final séance at which the entire message was to be transmitted. The sitters were an associate editor of the *Scientific American,* John Stafford, and his wife Dorothy, Francis R. Fast, Mrs. Helen E. Morris, and of course Arthur Ford. All except Ford were strangers to Mrs. Houdini. Ford was in deep trance. His control said, "A man who says he is Harry Houdini, but whose real name was Ehrich Weiss is here, and wishes to send to his wife, Beatrice Houdini, the ten-word code, which he agreed to do if it were possible for him to communicate. He says you are to take this message to her, and, upon acceptance of it, he wishes her to follow out the plan they agreed upon before his passing. This is the code: 'Rosabelle answer tell pray answer look tell answer answer tell!' "

The message was duly carried to Bess by John Stafford and Francis Fast. She had by now returned home, though she was still not very well. She read the letter, then dropped it and said, "It is right." Then, "Did he say 'Rosabelle'?" Then, "My God!" Another séance was then arranged at Bess's house for the second day following, 8 January, when all would be elucidated.

At this decisive séance, Rea Jaure was present, along with three of Ford's group and, of course, Bess. Ford went into trance: the voice of his control came through. "This man is coming now, the same one who came the other night. He tells me to say, 'Hello, Bess, sweetheart,' and he wants to repeat the message and finish it for you. The code . . . is one that you used to use in one of your secret mind-reading acts." The ten words were repeated; Mrs. Houdini confirmed that they were correct. "He smiles and says 'Thank you,' now I can go on," said the control. "He tells you to take off your wedding ring and tell them what 'Rosabelle' means."

Bess drew her left hand from under the cover and took off the ring. Holding it in front of her she sang softly:

> Rosabelle, sweet Rosabelle,
> I love you more than I can tell;
> O'er me you cast a spell,
> I love you! My Rosabelle!

It was the song the Floral Sisters had been singing on Coney Island on the night when they had first met the Houdini Brothers.

The séance continued. Houdini, through Ford's control, explained the code governing the next nine words of the message: "The second word in our code was 'answer.' 'B' is the second letter of the alphabet, so 'answer' spells 'B.' The next word in the code is 'tell,' and the fifth letter of the alphabet is 'E.' The twelfth letter of the alphabet is 'L' and to make up twelve we have to use the first and second words of the code."

The code he was referring to was the one (described in Chapter 6) used by Harry and Bess in their mind-reading act many years before. The nine words which had been "transmitted" spelt: "believe."

"The message I want to send back to my wife is, 'Rosabelle, believe!'" "Is that right?" the control asked, and Bess replied, with great feeling, "Yes." She was reported as adding: "Later when I get well I shall open the vault in your presence and prove it."

The next day she signed a message which was witnessed by three independent persons: "Regardless of any statement made to the contrary, I wish to declare that the message, in its entirety, and in the agreed upon sequence, given to me by Arthur Ford, is the correct message pre-arranged between Mr. Houdini and myself. Beatrice Houdini." The St. Louis *Post-Dispatch* commented:

"It is too bad we are deprived of the comment of the earthly Houdini on this extraordinary occurrence."

The *Graphic* reported the 8 January séance in appropriately sensational style. But on 10 January, Rea Jaure produced an even greater sensation. It was headlined HOUDINI HOAX EXPOSED!—" 'Seance' Prearranged by 'Medium' and Widow"—and it alleged that it was Beatrice herself who had given the code to Ford. Rea Jaure recounted how she had lured Ford to her apartment where, overheard by two witnesses hidden in a convenient steamer trunk, he admitted the hoax, declaring that he and Bess were indeed planning a tour. He would finance it; "Mrs. Houdini supplied the code as her part of the bargain."

This of course caused an uproar, as it was intended to do. Bess indignantly denied having passed him the code. She wrote to Walter Winchell, who was also at that time on the *Graphic:* "I am writing you this personally because I wish to tell you emphatically that I was no party to any fraud . . . When the real message, THE message that Houdini and I had agreed upon, came to me, and I accepted it as the truth, I was greeted by jeers? Why? Those who denounced the entire thing as a fraud claim that I had given Mr. Arthur Ford the message. If Mr. Ford said this I brand him as a liar. Mr. Ford has stoutly denied saying this ugly thing, and knowing the reporter as well as I do I prefer to believe Mr. Ford . . . However, when anyone accuses me of GIVING the words that my husband and I labored so long to convince ourselves of the truth of communication, then I will fight and fight until the breath leaves my body."

But how else would he know it? Joseph Dunninger, entering the fray, pointed out some possibilities. The code, he reminded everyone, had been printed in the Kellock biography only the previous year. As for "Rosabelle, Believe"—Mrs. Houdini had not been alone with her husband when he had murmured it to her. The nurse, Sophie Rosenblatt, had also been in the room; she might have mentioned it to someone, and it might have reached Arthur Ford's ears. Another possibility raised, once again, the spectre of Daisy White. A fish peddler who had a girlfriend who was a friend of Miss White's declared that Daisy White had learned the secret message from Houdini before he died. The New York *Telegram* ran this story: it ended, "Little Daisy White at Ford's apartment admitted knowing the fish-peddler slightly but denied everything else!"

Poor Bess relapsed into illness, muddle and despair. Ford was using a copy of her signed statement in some advertisements. "I wish to say that I did sign that letter," she wrote Ernst. ". . . I did not say that I believed that the message came through spiritual aid or that I believed in spiritualism. I did say the words I heard were the words I expected to hear, etc. . . . I had a copy of the original letter I wrote to him somewhere but I am too ill to look for it and I really don't care. I never said I believed the letter came from Houdini. I never said I believed in spiritualism and I still say the same. I don't care what Sir Arthur Conan Doyle or Will Goldston say or do. I don't and never did believe the message genuine nor did I believe in spiritualism. I will write you clearly later if you will just give me a chance to get well. I don't care what you do to or about Mr. Ford."

Shortly afterwards, Arthur Ford was expelled from the United Spiritualist League of New York. He denied Jaure's story, and shortly afterwards was reinstated "on the ground of insufficient proof." He continued to maintain that the message was authentic. "Until the message was proved false, he would consider the Houdini matter closed."

Bess thrashed about for some years in this unsatisfactory world of spirit mediums and disappointed hopes. "There was a period when I was ill—really mentally ill as well as physically," she told an interviewer some years later. "I wanted so intensely to hear from Harry that spiritualists were able to prey on my mind and make me believe they really had heard from him." She was only finally disillusioned when he gave her, via a medium, some bad business advice: "I asked him about signing certain papers—I did what he was supposed to have advised and it was all wrong. Harry wouldn't have done that."

She was finally rescued by another denizen of that world of carny shows and freak stages where she and Houdini had always felt at home. His name was Edward Saint; he had once been a living statue, and had done a little magic.

His was not altogether a chance appearance. Bess's friends were worried by her vulnerability. So they introduced her to Eddy Saint, and suggested that he might act as her manager. In fact (although Bess never realised this), his duties were more those of a watchdog. A genuine affection soon arose between them, and eventually they shared a small Spanish-style bungalow in Hollywood. She had enjoyed living there with Houdini during his film-making period, and it is clear that she enjoyed living there with Eddy Saint. Everyone found him a charming, amiable and dignified figure. "Mrs. Houdini," recalled the magician John Booth who visited them at this period, "was a white-haired, gracious and lively little lady of complete naturalness. Edward Saint was an immaculately dressed elderly man of refined manners whose most noticeable characteristic was a goatee with waxed mustache pointed and turned up at the ends." They enjoyed playing practical jokes on some of their visitors. When Booth first telephoned for an appointment, "a male voice answered the phone. There was an unusually long delay while Mrs. Houdini gaily answered. We talked for several minutes." That was the day before his visit. During it, "We were sitting in the small living room talking when the spooky voices began. I was absent-mindedly gazing up at an heroic sized portrait photograph of Houdini, on the wall opposite, when I became aware of other voices in the room. They were coming from an indeterminate source. My friends had stopped talking. We listened. It was as though radio voices had suddenly begun to penetrate the air around us . . . I noticed the trace of smiles in the expression of Mrs. Houdini and Mr. Saint. Then I recognized my own voice. I was chatting with a woman. When had this happened?" It was a recording of his conversation with Bess the previous day. She had delayed answering until the machine was set up. She was making a collection of recordings of her conversations with famous magicians. None of them knew they were being recorded, so all spoke quite spontaneously. She must have got the idea from Houdini, who had regularly eavesdropped on his visitors. But the effect was quite different, the flavour Bess's, not Houdini's. With him, it had been a question of power; with Bess and Eddy Saint, the whole thing was a gentle joke.

It was not until Bess left for California that she began to free herself from Houdini's spell. Not that life with Eddy Saint was life without Houdini. Much of their time was taken up with Bess's unique position as Houdini's widow. "We spent the morning engrossed in talk about the late showman, going over mementoes of a lifetime. I suspected that Mrs. Houdini had been through this routine a thousand times since his death. I also felt that both she and Saint had assumed a duty to keep alive his memory wherever possible in the world outside," remarked John Booth.

It was Eddy Saint who was with Bess for what was billed as the Final Houdini Séance. This took place on top of a skyscraper in Hollywood on 31 October 1936, the tenth anniversary of the magician's death. Coverage of this event, which was broadcast live to a waiting world, was enormous. Saint's scrapbook of clippings concerning it is three feet by two, six inches thick, and can barely be lifted. Every page is thick with clippings. One picture of Bess and Saint appeared in seventy different publications. "Over 300 invited guests formed the outer circle, while 13 scientists, occultologists, newspapermen, world famous magicians, spiritual leaders, boyhood friends of Houdini, joined Madame Houdini in the Inner Circle," intoned the commentator. "Bathed in the weird glow of ruby light, trained observers and spirit mediums joined under controlled conditions to evoke the shade of the late mystifier."

Saint—referred to in this account as "Dr. Saint," perhaps because of his distinguished and doctorly appearance, immaculately bearded and moustached—took charge of the proceedings. They were heralded by the playing of Elgar's "Pomp and Circumstance" march, which Houdini had used as his entry music during the latter years of his life (it would boom out and he would come bounding onto the stage, tearing off his false sleeves above the elbow and crying, "Hi, everyone, I'm Harry Houdini!" in that lightly accented Central European voice of his). He noted that "Every facility has been provided tonight, that might aid in opening a pathway to the spirit world. Here in the Inner Circle, reposes a 'Medium's Trumpet,' a pair of slates with chalk, a writing tablet and pencil, a small bell, and in the center reposes a huge pair of silver handcuffs on a silk cushion. Facing the Inner Circle stands the famous 'Houdini Shrine,' with its doors ajar."

Eddy Saint talked on. Everyone waited. "Houdini! Are you here?" he cried. "Are you here, Houdini? Please manifest yourself in any way possible . . . We have waited, Houdini, oh, so long! Never have you been able to present the evidence you promised. And now—this, the night of nights. The world is listening, Harry . . . Levitate the table! Move it! Lift the table! Move it or rap it! *Spell out a code, Harry!* Please! Ring the bell! Let its tinkle be heard around the world!"

But all was in vain. Nothing happened. Finally Dr. Saint said to Mrs. Houdini, "Mrs. Houdini, the zero hour has passed. The ten years are up. Have you reached a decision?" She replied, "Yes. Houdini did not come through. My last hope is gone. I do not believe that Houdini can come back to me—or to anyone . . . The Houdini Shrine has burned for ten years. I now, reverently—turn out the light. It is finished. Good Night, Harry!"

But of course she was wrong. It wasn't finished at all.

Discussing this book at a dinner party, my neighbour expressed surprise that it was to be a biography. "You mean he really existed?" she said.

This, it seems to me, is an extraordinary confirmation of Houdini's ascent to the level of myth. He embodied it: now he has become it. It was not that my neighbour had never heard of Houdini. Far from it. How could she have failed to do so? His name is constantly in the newspapers. While he was alive, his publicity frequently mentioned the fact that he had become a verb. "To houdinize" was listed in Funk and Wagnall's Dictionary, meaning, to escape from an apparently impossible situation. I have never heard it used. Even so, this was a legitimate source of pride: it is not given to many of us to become a part of speech. And Houdini's name is constantly invoked to symbolise the slippery skills needed or displayed by sportsmen or politicians. It was used in this way twice in one paper last Sunday—both times with reference to politics. The week before that, it described the feat of a football team—LUTON TOWN HOUDINIS SNATCH VICTORY. He may not be a verb, but he has undoubtedly become a metaphor.

Moreover, he appears in countless works of reference. Robert Lund of the American Museum of Magic in Marshall, Michigan, has made a collection of reference books—dictionaries, encyclopedias, etc.—in which Houdini's name appears. His rule is that none of them must cost more than one dollar. He reckons to possess several hundred of these books. How many would there be had he not imposed the one-dollar rule? This notoriety does not please Lund, who is no fan of Houdini's. "Houdini's name gets bigger and bigger—but several others who were as big a draw in his lifetime are unheard of now," he grumbles.

But the myth refuses to fade. The Library of Congress lists thirteen children's books about Houdini, four of them published within the past three years. The rare books room of the library holds one of his early scrapbooks. The librarian says it is their most-requested item. Parents and children come in together to look at it. He has at least one notorious soi-disant descendant: Frank Gilmore, father of the mass murderer Gary Gilmore, was the son of a circus medium and always averred he was Houdini's bastard son. So the Handcuff King maintains his grip upon the world's imagination.

Part of the reason is of course that Houdini epitomised an aspect of the human condition. This is in itself a mythic attribute. But it was not his only mythic attribute. Perhaps as important was the timing and manner of his death.

Jack Flosso, talking about this, said, "The timing was a very important thing. Had he lived on— Imagine it! Here's a man selling virility, with flabby flesh and varicose veins."

He was right. In life, as onstage, timing is important. Would Marilyn still be Marilyn if she had sunk, like Elizabeth Taylor, into fat, alcoholism, and husbands of ever-decreasing stature? Big stars die young. The statistics prove it. *Variety* magazine reports that "the average American lifespan is 71.9 years, the average star dies at age 58.7. The normal American woman dies at age 75.8, while female stars die at the age of 54.3."

"Death defines life," says the Mexican poet Octavio Paz. "Our deaths illuminate our lives . . . Each of us dies the death he is looking for, the death he has made for himself . . . If we do not die as we lived, it is because the life we lived was not really ours; it did not belong to us, just as the bad death that kills us does not belong to us."

This is especially true of those symbolic figures who, through their early deaths, achieve an immortality quite disproportionate to their lives. From the days of the ritual king killed every year in the Attic grove, the human imagination has fed upon these untimely deaths. In some cases, as with Jesus, the death becomes an icon in itself. In others—JFK, John Lennon—the death defines the life by framing it at its peak. So they achieve the immortality that speaks to us, Kennedy forever unsullied by Vietnam, Lennon shrouded in mysterious glamour. Superstars are bathed in media-inspired love. Martyrdom, added to that love, resulting from it, ensures a continuing cult.

This is the kind of death Houdini achieved. It was poetic, appropriate to the life he had led. It was not the prosaic details of either his life or his death (the arrays of keys and miniature jacks, peritonitis) that mattered. What mattered was the effect they achieved. The important things were the appropriate framing (the impregnable box, the fatal blow), the suspense (the spellbound audience, the refusal to succumb), the right equipment (the Water-Torture Cell, the bronze coffin). And the aura of magic: Houdini's secrets; the plethora of stories surrounding his death. He mystifies us to the end and beyond.

This is a biography. Biography ends in death. But this is Houdini's biography; and Houdini, who defied death so many times while he lived, finally defeated it—after he had died.

Notes

List of abbreviations used:

HH:	Harry Houdini
ACD:	Sir Arthur Conan Doyle
BRTC:	Billy Rose Theater Collection, New York Public Library
HC:	Houdini Collection, Library of Congress
HPL:	Harry Price Library, University of London
HTC:	Harvard Theater Collection, Harvard University
McMYC:	McManus-Young Collection, Library of Congress
MKC:	Messmore Kendall Collection, Harry Ransom Humanities Research Center (HRHRC), University of Texas at Austin
RLC:	Robert Lund Collection, Marshall, Michigan (private)
SRC:	Sidney Radner Collection, Appleton, Wisconsin

1: The Manacled Diver

3 "Houdini . . . arrived at the dock gates . . .": Aberdeen *Daily Free Press,* 1 July 1909.

5 "I expect . . .": Liverpool *Daily Post,* 8–13 December 1908.

5 List of fifteen different preferred types of cuff: McMYC.

2: Rabbits from a Hat

8 "all magicians are shy . . .": *Strand Magazine,* January 1919.

10 "Father insulted by Prince Erik . . .": facsimile in *Houdini Birth Research Committee's Report:* from the Stanley Palm Collection, Brooklyn, New York.

12 "You must remember . . .": facsimile in *Houdini Birth Research Committee's Report.*

12 The rumour about Samuel Weiss being Houdini's stepfather was brought to my attention by Charles Reynolds, and it is mentioned in the book he wrote with Doug Henning, *Houdini: His Legend and His Magic,* p. 24. He attributed it to J. G. Frazee.

13 "Re the Birthdays . . .": facsimile in *Houdini Birth Research Committee's Report.*

3: Metamorphosis

14 As with most illusions, the secrets of the "Substitution Trunk" are simple. They rely on the fact that people will look for what they expect to see. Because the lid of the trunk opens upwards, the assumption will be that ties must be loosened if it is to be opened again; but the exit from the trunk is effected via an inward-opening panel in the side, worked by a secret lock. Likewise with the bag: because it was entered from the top, all the audience's attention is concentrated on the original ties and seals. But the exit is made through the bottom: the original occupant carries a small razor and makes a neat slit, or cuts a seam. And when the substitute occupant is discovered, he of course makes his final exit from the top of the bag (after the knots have been untied, seals broken, etc.) and remains standing on the slit at the bottom. Finally, as to the speed which is essential for the effective execution of this trick—the expectation is that the occupant of the trunk will not start preparations for the escape until the screen conceals the apparatus. On the contrary: by that time, he will already be out of the bag. The rest is practice, and presentation.

15 "Polish . . . is becoming . . .": Eva Hoffman, *Lost in Translation,* London, 1989, pp. 120–2.

15 "My mother . . .": note in Houdini's annotated copy of *A Magician Among the Spirits,* p. 157, Hoblitzelle Theater Arts Library, HRHRC.

16 The one extant recording is in the possession of Mr. Jay Marshall, of Chicago.

16 "Who that has seen Appleton . . .": *Appleton Crescent,* 14 February 1874.

16 "My parents spent . . .": HH to Edna Ferber, 1 November 1914, SRC, Appleton.

17 "I actually dreampt . . .": facsimile in Walter B. Gibson, *The Original Houdini Scrapbook.*

17 "It may interest you to know . . .": HH to Dr. Waitt, 8 September 1907, HTC.

20 "twenty-eight years . . .": Milbourne Christopher, *Houdini: The Untold Story,* p. 18.

20 "Such hardships . . .": ibid., p. 10.

20 "I did not like it . . .": HH to Augustus Rapp, 24 December 1912, SRC.

21 "darling mother . . .": note, MKC.

21 "I am going . . .": from a scrapbook, McMYC.

22 "We lived there . . .": Christopher (1969), p. 13.

22 "Shake me! I'm magic!": this story is told in Christopher (1969), pp. 13–14.

23 "Compars is the real name . . .": letter, MKC.

23 The fact that Compars performed for President Lincoln appears in a letter from Houdini to Dr. A. M. Wilson, HC.

23 "My dear old Dad and Compars . . .": letter to F. E. Powell, 30 December 1916.

23 "You know how a fresh kid is . . .": *Haldeman-Julius Monthly,* October 1925.

24 "a circus coming to the town . . .": Houdini souvenir programme.

25 "I really believed . . .": quoted in Bernard C. Meyer, *Houdini: A Mind in Chains,* p. 11.

25 "Thus, to any young man . . .": Houdini, "Confessions of a Jail-breaker," 1918.

26 "One day the son . . .": *Photoplay,* June 1920.

27 "I want to be first . . .": Sydney *Daily Telegraph,* 16 April 1910.

28 Mrs. Williams "held forth in a house . . .": Joseph Rinn, *Searchlight on Psychical Research,* p. 69.

28 "My interest in conjuring . . .": Houdini, *The Unmasking of Robert-Houdin,* p. 7.

4: Aaron's Rod

31 "And Moses and Aaron . . .": Exodus 7:10–12.

31 For an extended discussion of Moses' secret magical texts, see Paul Kurtz, *The Transcendental Temptation,* pp. 179ff.

32 "all the people . . .": Exodus 20:20.

32 And it came to pass . . .": Exodus 33:9–11.

33 "All the folk in our circle . . .": Isaac Babel, "Awakening," *Collected Stories,* London, 1961 (Penguin Edition), p. 267.

33 "I register tomorrow . . .": William L. Gresham, *Houdini: The Man Who Walked Through Walls,* p. 201.

35 "It may exist . . .": HH to Dr. Waitt, 8 September 1902, HTC.

35 "I don't want anything to do with your cause . . .": Philip French, *The Movie Moguls,* pp. 111–12.

5: Two Ladies

39 The secret of Houdini's version of sawing a woman in half, as with many such tricks, lies in the platform, which is hollow. The hinged bottom of the box tips the original woman down into it; the "twins" have crept out from inside it under cover of the open doors and lid and concealed themselves behind it before these are shut. The girls are of course dressed exactly like the original woman. From Walter B. Gibson, *Houdini's Escapes and Magic,* pp. 214 ff.

40 "One day I was hired . . .": *Photoplay,* June 1920.

40 Mrs. Houdini's own recollections appear in Harold Kellock, *Houdini: The Life Story,* p. 44.

41 "properly married . . .": ibid., p. 46.

41 "The brothers Houdini . . .": ibid., p. 55.

41 "Risey . . .": quoted in William L. Gresham, *Houdini: The Man Who Walked Through Walls,* pp. 25–26. The clipping is in an early scrapbook, SRC.

42 The holy water story is according to Bernard C. Meyer, *Houdini: A Mind in Chains,* p. 55.

43 "I was perhaps fortunate . . .": Kellock, p. 47.

43 "My dear girl . . .": MKC.

44 "[Mrs. Weiss's] instant acceptance . . .": Kellock, pp. 47–48.

44 "We were romantically in love . . .": ibid., p. 46.

44 "still a Honeymoon . . .": letter, MKC.

45 "Adorable . . .": MKC.

46 "Within a few days . . .": Kellock, p. 51.

47 "Houdini asked his brother . . .": ibid., pp. 52–53.

48 "He said the show . . .": ibid., pp. 80–81.

48 "To be delivered . . .": ibid., pp. 81–82.

49 "My own entire family . . .": ibid., p. 51.

49 "I was paralyzed . . .": ibid., p. 54.

50 The theory that Bess was simply a more suitable stage partner than Dash is given by Will Goldston in *Sensational Tales of Mystery Men*, p. 115.

50 "What the hell . . .": Kellock, p. 60.

50 "It was pleasant . . .": ibid., p. 52.

51 "Bess had a brain storm," etc.: quoted in Meyer, p. 56.

51 "Listen to him! . . .": personal communication from James Randi.

51 "Houdini created a dream child . . .": interview with Bess, Philadelphia *Evening Bulletin*, 9 January 1933. This fantasising was not confined to Houdini. There is an interview, given in 1911, in which Bess refers to a daughter, aged 17, whose trousseau she is preparing (*Ohio State Journal*, 6 December 1911). I am indebted to Ronald Hilgert for this reference.

52 Bess's X ray theory appears in *Houdini's Strange Tales*, ed. Patrick Culliton and T. L. Williams, Los Angeles 1992, p. 5.

52 "your husband until . . .": HH to Bess, September 1926, MKC.

52 "a girlish woman . . .": "The Marvelous Adventures of Houdini," quoted in Meyer, p. 57.

52 "I'm afraid I'm not much of a ladies' man . . .": Kellock, p. 293.

53 "I have uncanny feelings . . .": letter to Quincy Kilby, 5 September 1915, MKC.

53 "stopped sharply in the doorway . . .": Kellock, pp. 295–56.

54 "Houdini: Step this way . . .": "Fortune Telling" Hearings 1924.

55 "Mrs. Houdini . . .": Kellock, p. 194.

6: Freaks

56 "I have often sat . . .": New York *Tribune*, 1 November 1921.

58 "Houdini always missed it . . .": Kellock, p. 64.

59 "The pain . . .": Houdini, "Handcuff Secrets Exposed," *Conjurer's Magazine*, 1908.

59 "NOTICE TO MANAGERS . . .": Joseph F. Rinn, *Searchlight on Psychical Research*, p. 86.

60 "Your attention . . .": New York *Tribune*, 1 November 1921.

60 "when I was playing . . .": HH to Quincy Kilby, 22 June 1916, MKC.

62 "stumbled about . . .": Harold Kellock, *Houdini: The Life Story*, p. 72.

63 "The ringmaster . . .": Kellock, p. 71.

63 "In the lock-up . . .": Kellock, pp. 76–77.

66 "Even a small stake . . .": Houdini, *The Right Way to Do Wrong,* p. 80.

68 "You're a monkey . . .": Michael Freedland, *Al Jolson,* p. 40.

69 An effective technique was that known as "one ahead." Sealed messages are collected in a basket. The medium lifts one to her forehead, holds it there and "reads" it. But the message she is reading (and replying to) is one that she has made up. Then she hands the "used" message to her partner, who has opened it and conveyed its contents to her before she takes up the next. And so on.

69 "Where is my brother John? . . .": Kellock, pp. 107–9.

70 The story about the boy with the broken arm comes from Kellock, pp. 123–24.

72 "Get me to the theatre . . .": Milbourne Christopher, *Houdini: The Untold Story,* p. 35.

73 Jack Flosso told me about the book on freaks—his father, Al Flosso, was helping with the illustrations.

7: Handcuff King

74 "I started in the show business . . .": Washington *Times,* 7 January 1906.

75 "It was opened . . .": Morris N. Young, MD, "Houdini's Trunk No. 8," *Houdini Historical Center Newsletter,* vol. 2, no. 2, originally published in *M.U.M.,* December 1951.

77 "The key in this set . . .": Letter, MKC.

77 "In Berlin . . .": Walter Gibson and Morris Young, *Houdini on Magic,* New York, 1954, p. 14.

78 "for it is obvious . . .": Hereward Carrington, *The Physical Phenomena of Spiritualism,* quoted in H. R. Evans, *The Old and the New Magic,* p. 489.

78 "The primary lesson . . .": Houdini, "Handcuff Secrets Exposed," quoted in Walter B. Gibson, *Houdini's Escapes and Magic,* p. 17.

80 "While in St. Johns . . .": Houdini, "Handcuff Secrets Exposed," *Conjurer's Magazine,* 1908; reprinted *Genii,* October 1972.

82 "He lived his own drama . . .": Edmund Wilson, "A Great Magician," *New Republic,* 17 October 1928.

82 "MANACLES DO NOT HOLD HIM": Omaha *World-Herald,* 1 April 1899.

83 "The ad man put a pair . . .": Kansas City *Star,* 21 August 1899.

85 "so I trust you will . . .": HH to Dr. Waitt, 18 February 1900, HTC.

85 "I have no room . . .": quoted in Edwin Dawes, *The Great Illusionists.*

85 "Who created . . .": Milbourne Christopher, *Houdini: The Untold Story,* p. 39.

85 "Possibly we may sail . . .": HH to Dr. Waitt, 21 May 1900, HTC.

8: With One Bound He Was Free

87 "headliner" . . . "at the salary of . . .": Milbourne Christopher, *Houdini: The Untold Story,* p. 42.

88 "That is not true . . .": Harold Kellock, *Houdini: The Life Story,* p. 141.

89 "Properly presented . . .": MKC.

89 "Cirnoc is dead . . .": 13 November 1903, MKC.

90 "It appears he must have . . .": "Houdini Issues Challenge to 'Spirit' of Northcliffe," newspaper cutting c. 1925, McMYC.

90 "You can well imagine my feelings . . .": quoted in Christopher (1969), p.46.

91 "THEATRICAL NEWS . . .": HTC.

92 "because he is a *native* . . .": Christopher (1969), p. 47.

92 "COME OVER . . .": ibid.

92 Al Flosso, for instance, spoke of the rumour about Dash having killed someone to his son Jack, who told me of it.

93 "Why, you have acted . . .": quoted in Bernard C. Meyer, *Houdini: A Mind in Chains,* p. 42.

93 "Theo Hardeen . . .": ibid.

94 "I don't think . . .": HH to Dr. Waitt, HTC.

94 "My Dear Bro. Dash . . .": Bess to Hardeen, 1911, SRC.

94 "He did it by saying . . .": A. Conan Doyle, *On the Edge of the Unknown,* p. 5.

94 "When Harry passed on . . .": "My Pal Dash," by Joe Hayman, *Conjuror's Magazine,* Hardeen Memorial Issue, July 1945.

95 *"which is something . . .":* Houdini, *The Adventurous Life of a Versatile Artist,* p. 7.

95 "It would be boastful . . .": HH to Dr. Waitt, 7 January 1901, HTC.

95 "We closed . . .": HH to Dr. Waitt, 21 February 1901, HTC.

95 "To avert suspicion . . .": Houdini, "The Thrills in the Life of a Magician," *Strand Magazine*, 5 January 1919.

96 "I am not well . . .": HH to Dr. Waitt, 31 March 1901, HTC.

97 "The 'digs' . . .": *Vaudeville News*, 20 August 1920.

97 "To tell the truth . . .": HH to Dr. Waitt, May 1901, HTC.

97 "Letters starting with . . .": typed note, McMYC.

99 "stood up and cheered . . .": Blackburn *Star*, 25 October 1902. I should like to thank Frank Koval for giving me the background to this incident.

102 The third commentator is quoted in Arthur Setterington, "Houdini and the Hippodrome Handcuffs," *The Linking Ring*, October 1966.

102 The correspondent was Pat Culliton, to the author, 27 May 1992.

102 For a detailed discussion of relations between performer and audience, see Richard Sennett's *The Fall of Public Man*.

105 "It does seem strange . . .": HH to Dr. Waitt, 30 November 1901, HTC.

107 "My God, we should be ruined! . . .": Kellock, p. 164.

108 "carrying their black . . .": quoted in Christopher (1969), p. 70.

109 "On the inside . . .": Kellock, pp. 166–67.

109 "The lithograph . . .": Christopher (1969), p. 71.

109 "The superstitious court . . .": Minneapolis *Star*, 1928, McMYC.

110 "Have managed to send . . .": to Dr. Waitt, 11 August 1903, HTC.

110 "After you leave Russia . . .": Christopher (1969), p. 75.

111 "After listening . . .": quoted in Kellock, pp. 147–48.

9: The Disappearing Fathers Trick

112 "I borrowed . . .": Robert-Houdin, *Memoirs*, quoted in Jean Hugard, *Houdini's "Unmasking,"* pp. 49–53.

114 "Any unprejudiced . . .": ibid., p. 54.

115 "My interest . . .": Houdini, *The Unmasking of Robert-Houdin*, pp. 7–8.

115 "My investigations . . .": ibid., p. 8.

116 "I am the Great . . .": Hugard, pp. 13–14.

116 "At that time . . .": *Conjurer's Magazine*, first issue, 15 September 1906.

117 "I, as a representative . . .": Milbourne Christopher, *Houdini: The Untold Story,* pp. 55–56.

117 "What a great difference . . .": *Conjurer's Magazine,* 15 September 1906.

118 "Visited the grave . . .": postcard, MKC.

119 "Horace Goldin has arrived . . .": *Conjurer's Magazine,* 15 September 1906.

119 "W. T. STEAD FOOLED AGAIN . . .": ibid., 15 January 1907.

120 "The master-magician . . .": Houdini, *The Unmasking of Robert-Houdin,* pp. 318–19.

120 "Wrote until 2.30 . . .": Harold Kellock, *Houdini: The Life Story,* p. 182.

121 "Darling Kadaria . . .": 28 March 1903, MKC.

121 "your husband . . .": MKC.

122 "The rare signature . . .": MKC.

122 "My legal name . . .": to H. R. Evans, 14 December 1917, MKC.

122 "Q: What kind of magicians . . .": I am indebted to Jack Flosso for this one.

122 "The money mentioned here . . .": Walter B. Gibson, *The Original Houdini Scrapbook,* p. 178.

123 "We have decided . . .": *M.U.M.* November 1917.

123 "Old Mortality of Magic . . .": H. R. Evans, *The Old and the New Magic,* p. 495.

124 "The cemetery of a little Jewish town . . .": Isaac Babel, "The Cemetery at Kozin," *Collected Stories,* London, 1961 (Penguin Edition), p. 93.

125 "It's a bit like collecting . . .": James Hamilton, in conversation with the author.

125 "Cemeteries . . . induce the triumphant . . .": Elias Canetti, *On Crowds and Power,* p. 275.

126 "I have had an argument . . .": HH to Hardeen, 11 October 1903.

128 "It appears . . .": HH to F. E. Powell, 24 February 1919, MKC.

129 "Poor Evanion . . .": quoted in Kellock, pp. 180–181.

130 "For every conjurer . . .": *Conjurer's Magazine,* 15 April 1907.

130 "In my many conversations . . .": Gibson and Young, *Houdini on Magic,* p. xi.

130 "When a magician advertizes . . .": HH to F. E. Powell, 1919, MKC.

10: All in the Mind

132 This version of the story appeared in Houdini, "The Thrills in the Life of a Magician," *Strand Magazine,* January 1919.

133 " 'HANDCUFF KING' JUMPS . . .": quoted in William L. Gresham, *The Man Who Walked Through Walls,* p. 141.

133 "If I don't come to America . . .": quoted in Milbourne Christopher, *Houdini: The Untold Story,* p. 64.

134 "There is no possible chance . . .": HH to Dr. Waitt, 25 March 1904, HTC.

134 "Saw all that was left . . .": quoted in Bernard C. Meyer, *Houdini: A Mind in Chains,* p. 81.

135 "He is a quick nervous chap . . .": *Appleton Crescent,* 23 July 1904.

135 "Better give this . . .": Edna Ferber, *A Peculiar Treasure,* New York, 1939, pp. 114–15.

136 "Then I will return . . .": HH to Dr. Waitt, 2 June 1905, HTC.

136 "A rich man . . .": Elias Canetti, *On Crowds and Power,* p. 397.

136 The stories about Adolph Zukor and Louis B. Mayer appear in Neal Gabler, *An Empire of Their Own.*

137 "You should rather . . .": scrapbook, BRTC.

137 "The Northern District . . .": *Glasgow Herald,* 23 September 1904.

139 "In my own particular work . . .": Houdini, *The Right Way to Do Wrong,* p. 89.

140 "Disgraced, they are . . .": ibid., pp. 9, 11.

140 "Guess he didn't know . . .": quoted in Edmund Wilson, "A Great Magician," *New Republic,* 17 October 1928.

140 "A despot . . .": Canetti, p. 377.

141 "I am induced . . .": Houdini, "Light on the subject of Jail-breaking as done by my Imitators," Gibson and Young, *Houdini on Magic,* p. 3.

141 Houdini's methods for escaping from coffins are outlined in Gresham, pp. 122–23.

142 "I am strong . . .": Sydney *Daily Telegraph,* 16 April 1910.

144 "unquestionably better": Christopher (1969), p. 98.

145 "Manager Tate informs me . . .": Harold Kellock, *Houdini: The Life Story,* p. 199.

145 "Downs has retired . . .": MKC.

146 "I never do handcuffs . . .": HH to Augustus Rapp, 24 December 1912, RLC.

146 "1910 New York Can . . .", etc.: Kenneth Silverman, "More Houdini Trunks," Houdini Historical Center *Newsletter,* vol. 2, no. 2.

146 "This stunt . . .": Kellock, p. 200.

146 The explanation of how the Milk Can worked is from Gresham, pp. 151–52.

147 "His act . . .": Augustus Roterberg to HH, 20 July 1910, SRC.

147 "To ease your mind . . .": Horace Goldin to HH, 5 April 1909, MKC.

11: The Death and Resurrection Show

149 "The Death and Resurrection Show": Apologies to Rogan Taylor, the title of whose excellent book I have stolen for this chapter.

149 "February 24 . . .": quoted in Bernard C. Meyer, *Houdini: A Mind in Chains,* p. 81.

150 Notes written in 1911 on "buried alive" appear in Walter B. Gibson, *Houdini's Escapes and Magic,* p. 139.

151 "I tried out 'Buried Alive' . . .": ibid., p. 138.

151 "Despair . . .": E. A. Poe, "The Premature Burial," *Tales of Mystery and Imagination,* Everyman edition, London, 1966, p. 278.

154 "I smashed . . .": Milbourne Christopher, *Houdini: The Untold Story,* (1969), p. 112.

155 "They charge you . . .": ibid., p. 114.

156 "We, the undersigned . . .": Henning and Reynolds, *Houdini: His Legend and His Magic.*

156 "Never in any fear . . .": Harold Kellock, *Houdini: The Life Story,* p. 217.

156 "But when only . . .": Sydney *Herald,* 2 April 1910.

156 "As soon as I was aloft . . .": ibid.

156 "I have been very bisy . . .": HH to Mr. Fay, 6 May 1910, MKC.

157 "It is time . . .": Kellock, p. 218.

157 "in which I offered you . . .": MKC.

157 "I knew . . .": Houdini, "Nearly Dying for a Living."

157 "He had . . .": Doyle (1930), p. 2.

158 "I carry 40 pieces . . .": HH to Augustus Rapp, 24 December 1912, RLC.

159 "Laying off . . .": Kellock, pp. 281–82.

159 "In the first place . . .": Houdini, *Magical Rope-Ties and Escapes,* pp. 56–57.

161 "No matter what . . .": Edwin Dawes, *The Great Illusionists,* p. 183.

162 "The moment of *survival* . . .": Elias Canetti, *On Crowds and Power,* p. 227.

162 "On the one hand . . .": Robert Jay Lifton, *The Broken Connection,* p. 272.

163 "Sometimes I think . . .": Houdini, "The Thrills in the Life of a Magician," *Strand Magazine,* 5 January 1919.

163 "The list . . .": Lifton, p. 25.

164 "It all comes . . .": Doyle, pp. 2–3.

164 "The practice . . .": McMYC.

167 "No, no, . . .": Kellock, pp. 277–78.

168 The remains of shamanism have been traced by Rogan Taylor in *The Death and Resurrection Show.*

169 "organization of mythological symbols": Joseph Campbell, *Myths to Live By,* p. 97.

12: The Lady Vanishes

172 Description of how "Gone" is performed from Will Dexter, *This Is Magic,* pp. 59–60.

173 "It is his act . . .": quoted in Milbourne Christopher, *Houdini: The Untold Story,* p. 131.

174 "I am doing . . .": HH to T. Nelson Downs, 7 October 1901, MKC.

175 "Think I started . . .": Houdini's diary, quoted in Harold Kellock, *Houdini: The Life Story,* p. 229.

175 "This day Cecilia . . .": diary, Kellock, p. 235.

175 "Mother-fixated men . . .": Erich Fromm, *The Anatomy of Human Destructiveness,* p. 360.

176 For discussion of birth as causation of Houdini's neuroses, see Otto Rank's remarks in Louis Bragman, "Houdini Escapes from Reality," *Psychoanalytic Review,* 14 October 1929.

177 "in order to hear her heart . . .": Houdini, *A Magician Among the Spirits,* p. 151.

178 "Some time ago . . .": HH to Ottokar Fischer, 4 May 1909, MKC.

179 "Have no desire . . .": HH to Harry Price, October 1926, HPL.

179   "It hurts me to think . . .": HH to Hardeen, 22 November 1913, Gibson (1976).

179   "This is my new letterhead . . .": ibid.

179   "I never knew . . .": 5 July 1915, SRC.

179   "Dash, I knew . . .": HH to Hardeen, 23 September 1913, SRC.

180   "Time heals . . .": HH to Hardeen, 22 November 1913, SRC.

180   "I hope [Nat] . . .": HH to Hardeen, 19 January 1914, Gibson (1976).

181   "This is the picture . . .": Bernard C. Meyer, *Houdini: A Mind in Chains,* pp. 35–36.

181   "It is my express . . .": ibid., pp. 36–37.

182   "I was about to sail . . .": Houdini, "Confessions of a Jail-breaker," 1918.

184   "last resting places for Houdini's . . .": scrapbook, BRTC.

185   "January First . . .": HH to Bess, 1 January 1916, MKC.

187   "Monday Feb 15 . . .": MKC.

188   "Good Morning . . .": MKC.

188   "Am doing needle trick . . .": MKC.

188   "Dismal day . . .": Kellock, pp. 237–38.

189   "When you say . . .": HH to Dan Turley, 1915, MKC.

190   "almost every stunt . . .": Bragman, "Houdini Escapes from Reality."

190   "A number of times . . .": Boston *Post,* n.d., McMYC.

191   ". . . Urbane, smiling . . .": *The Sun,* Pittsburg, 6 November 1916.

192   "I don't know how long . . .": scrapbook, BRTC.

13: Film Star

193   "The idea . . .": Walter B. Gibson, *Houdini's Escapes and Magic,* pp. 126–27.

194   "It was said later . . .": Milbourne Christopher, *Houdini: The Untold Story,* p. 164.

195   "filled . . . with . . .": Neal Gabler, *An Empire of Their Own,* p. 18.

195   "Fifty-five percent . . .": ibid., p. 67.

196   "Our fur offices . . .": ibid., p. 18.

196   "that these short . . .": ibid., pp. 24–25.

197   "movies . . . now almost monopolize . . .": *M.U.M.,* December 1913.

198   "I don't like his style . . .": Bob Lund, magic collector par excel-

lence and owner of the Museum of Magic in Marshall, Michigan; to the author.

198 "My Dear Sister . . .": Harold Kellock, *Houdini: The Life Story,* pp. 258–62.

199 "Nothing is more offensive . . .": Houdini, "Handcuff Secrets Exposed," quoted in Bernard C. Meyer, *Houdini: A Mind in Chains,* p. 45.

200 "Suppose I want . . .": Houdini, "The Thrills in the Life of a Magician," *Strand Magazine,* 5 January 1919.

200 The Bernhardt story appears in Kellock, p. 264.

201 "Good heavens . . .": Houdini, *A Magician Among the Spirits,* p. xv.

201 "It is when . . .": Houdini, "The Thrills in the Life of a Magician," *Strand Magazine,* 5 January 1919.

202 "People are much more interested . . .": ibid.

203 The helpful clippings on acting are now in McMYC.

204 "I have signed . . .": HH to O. S. Teale, 17 June 1918.

205 "and the great beast . . .": Will Dexter, *This Is Magic,* p. 128.

206 "Whenever we get him . . .": Kellock, pp. 267–68.

207 "His tales . . .": Houdini, "Confessions of a Jail-breaker."

207 The aeroplane stunt is described in Christopher (1969), pp. 156–57.

208 "What particularly . . .": ibid., pp. 157–58.

209 "Somebody in the head office . . .": Nottingham *Football News,* 3 April 1920.

210 "a ring that stole . . .": note in MKC.

210 "It starts out promisingly . . .": clipping, MKC.

211 "I am working very hard . . .": Christopher (1969), p. 165.

211 "The exchange of . . .": *The Boston Globe,* 9 September 1924.

212 "Things to look after . . .": MKC.

213 "My dear old friend . . .": Harry Kellar to HH, 24 April 1918, RLC.

213 "This lock is not . . .": Christopher (1969), p. 174.

213 "A set of amazing parallels . . .": quoted in Robert Lund, "Afterword on Houdini," no. 3, *Abracadabra,* 1956.

14: Merlin's Cave

215 "The formula . . .": Houdini, *Miracle-Mongers and Their Methods,* ch. 6.

216 The firewalking experiments by Harry Price: *Two Experimental Firewalks* and *Three Experimental Firewalks,* University of London Council for Psychical Investigation, Bulletins II and IV (1936 and 1938).

217 "It may seem surprising . . .": *Popular Science,* October 1925.

218 "IGNORANCE . . .": *The Star,* n.d., HC.

218 "We talked . . .": *The Sphinx,* November 1926.

218 "Do you know . . .": HH to A. M. Wilson, 17 March 1926, McMYC.

219 "The public knows me . . .": interview by George Dilnot for Associated Press, n.d.

219 "Madam, you see . . .": Harold Kellock, *Houdini: The Life Story,* p. 282.

220 "We have 'arrived' . . .": HH to Harry Price, 1 August 1920, HPL.

220 "Some of the important things . . .": HH to Fred Black, quoted in Robert Lund, "Afterword on Houdini," no. 4.

220 "As I possess . . .": *The New York Times,* 18 June 1916.

221 "Who is your . . .": *Picture Plays Confessions Album,* in Gibson (1976), p. 170.

221 "The highest enjoyment . . .": Nabokov, *Speak, Memory* quoted in Danet and Katriel, "Books, Butterflies, Botticellis—A Life-span on Collecting," p. 1.

221 "Yesterday I bot . . .": HH to Quincy Kilby, 27 June 1916, MKC.

222 "I know that I cannot . . .": HH to Quincy Kilby, 4 July 1916.

222 "I told Mr. Becks . . .": HH to Quincy Kilby, 16 July 1916.

222 "I have at least . . .": HH to Fred Black, quoted in Lund, "Afterword on Houdini," no. 2.

222 "a relationship . . .": Walter Benjamin, quoted in Danet and Katriel, p. 5.

222 "Mrs. Siddons . . .": HH to Fred Black, 5 May 1925, RLC.

223 "Just run across . . .": 14 May 1920, MKC.

224 "My Dear Mr. Harry Price . . .": HH to Harry Price, 5 September 1920, HPL.

225 "His research . . .": HH to O. S. Teale, McMYC.

226 "When we speak . . .": *Genii,* October 1967. Preface to Manuel Weltman's *Houdini: A Definitive Bibliography.*

226 Regarding Lovecraft, see introduction to reprint of "Imprisoned with the Pharaohs," scrapbook, McMYC.

226 This notebook is in McMYC.

226 "This is a good example . . .": Teale correspondence, McMYC.

227 "present[ed] his compliments . . .": MKC.

227 The final corrections to *A Magician* . . . are in the Hoblitzelle Theater Arts Library, HRHRC.

227 "It would take . . .": galleys, McMYC.

228 "My Dear Evans . . .": HH to H. R. Evans, 14 December 1917, MKC.

229 "He now appeared . . .": Edmund Wilson, "A Great Magician," *New Republic,* 17 October 1928.

229 "I live in a treasure-house . . .": HH to Fred Black, 5 May 1925, RLC.

230 "On a massive table . . .": Marcet Haldeman-Julius; "An Interview with Harry Houdini," *Haldeman-Julius Monthly,* Girard, Kansas, October 1925.

230 "Did he feel . . .": Fred Black, quoted in Lund "Afterword on Houdini," no. 2.

231 "Dressed, according . . .": *Haldeman-Julius Monthly.*

231 Magic is the search . . .: T. M. Luhrmann, *Persuasions of the Witch's Craft,* p. 258.

232 "During his process . . .": "Knight in Fortune," quoted in Luhrmann, p. 258.

15: Magician Among the Spirits

233 "As in all experiments . . .": Sir David Brewster, *Letters on Natural Magic,* p. 65.

234 "A national system . . .": ibid.

235 "The end of a rope . . .": Houdini, *A Magician Among the Spirits,* p. 21.

236 "If you think . . .": quoted in Brandon, *The Spiritualists,* New York, Knopf, 1983, p. 168.

236 "Their method . . .": Houdini, *A Magician Among the Spirits,* pp. 21–22.

237 "Curiously enough . . .": HH to ACD, 28 March 1920.

237 "Regarding . . .": HH to ACD, quoted in Carrington and Ernst, *Houdini and Conan Doyle,* p. 87.

237 "I have spent . . .": ibid., p. 35.

238 "During my tour . . .": HH to ACD, 30 March 1920, McMYC.

238 Houdini told the story of his first experience with a medium in a lecture on spiritualism to Springfield Union YMCA, 1925, McMYC.

238 "Was doing mind-reading . . .": HH to Quincy Kilby, 5 September 1915, MKC.

239 "At one time . . .": Houdini, *The Right Way to Do Wrong,* p.6.

239 "In a long life . . .": A. Conan Doyle, *On the Edge of the Unknown,* p. 2.

239 "while he was . . .": ibid., p. 5.

239 "He is a brilliant . . .": Houdini, *A Magician Among the Spirits,* pp. 138–39.

240 "There is no sacrifice . . .": Houdini, "Ghosts That Talk—By Radio," *Popular Radio.*

241 "Our relations . . .": Houdini, *A Magician Among the Spirits,* p. 164.

241 "There was no consideration . . .": Doyle (1930), p. 5.

241 "Houdini says . . .": Edmund Wilson, "Houdini," *New Republic,* 24 June 1925.

242 "I am willing . . .": Carrington and Ernst, p. 88.

243 "I am afraid . . .": Doyle, "The Stockbroker's Clerk," from *The Memoirs of Sherlock Holmes,* London, 1893.

243 "The usual information . . .": Doyle, *Our American Adventure,* p. 16.

244 "In a fair light . . .": ACD to HH, 26 January 1922, McMYC.

245 "It is only by knowing . . .": HH to ACD, 3 April 1920, McMYC.

245 "My dear chap . . .": quoted in "The Case of Doyle versus Houdini," *The Month,* August 1930.

246 "The body . . .": J. Hewat MacKenzie, *Spirit Intercourse,* pp. 86–87.

246 "It is said . . .": Carrington and Ernst, p. 47.

247 ". . . beyond [the intellect] . . .": quoted in Robert Jay Lifton, *The Broken Connection,* p. 15.

247 "this particularly crass . . .": William James, *The Last Report,* quoted in Brandon, *The Spiritualists,* p. 230.

248 "Better live . . .": T. H. Huxley, *Life and Letters,* vol. 1, quoted in Brandon, ibid.

248 "The odd point . . .": James, *The Last Report,* quoted in Brandon, ibid.

248 "planting seeds . . .": Carrington and Ernst, p. 129.

249 "Well, we had . . .": ibid., pp. 59–60.

250 "all fixed up . . .": HH to ACD, 27 July 1920.

250 "You will understand . . .": Carrington and Ernst, pp. 132–33.

250 "To-day at 11 o'clock . . .": ibid., p. 143.

250 "very short . . .": ibid., p. 144.

251 "The children . . .": ibid., p. 159.

251 "As Sir Arthur . . .": Houdini, *A Magician Among the Spirits,* p. 150.

251 "The method . . .": Carrington and Ernst, p. 162.

252 "Mr Houdini . . .": ACD to Ada Besinnet, 3 June 1922, McMYC.

252 "In that manner . . .": Houdini, *A Magician Among the Spirits,* p. 151.

252 "It was a singular . . .": Doyle, *Our American Adventure,* quoted in Carrington and Ernst, p. 162.

253 "Oh, my darling . . .": Carrington and Ernst, pp. 165–66.

254 "I *always* . . .": Houdini's memorandum of 18 June 1922, quoted in Carrington and Ernst, p. 162.

255 "My dear Houdini . . .": Houdini, *A Magician Among the Spirits,* p. 155.

255 "I see you . . .": ACD to HH, 19 June 1922, McMYC.

255 "It was a long . . .": Doyle (1930), p. 43.

255 "I was *willing* . . .": Houdini, *A Magician Among the Spirits,* p. 152.

256 "I feel rather sore . . .": Carrington and Ernst, pp. 172–73.

257 "You are to me . . .": ACD to HH, 26 January 1922, quoted in Carrington and Ernst, p. 46.

258 "If it be true . . .": Doyle (1930), pp. 47–48.

16: Margery

259 "When he did the slatewriting . . .": notes, HC.

260 "I positively spend . . .": "Fortune Telling" Hearings, 1924, p. 70.

260 "Is there anybody here . . .": ibid., pp. 171–72.

262 "My dear Houdini . . .": quoted in Houdini, *A Magician Among the Spirits,* pp. 159–160.

262 "convinced that these . . .": New York *Tribune,* 6 April 1923.

264 "How long did . . .": Boston *Herald,* 19 December 1924.

265 "As you will observe . . .": quoted in Milbourne Christopher, *Houdini: The Untold Story,* p. 189.

265 "The truth is . . .": Wilson, "Houdini," *New Republic,* 24 June 1924.

266 "not in any way . . . ," "crucify," "the most extraordinary . . ." etc.: Meikle, Jeffrey; " 'Over There': Arthur Conan Doyle and Spiritualism," University of Texas at Austin Library *Journal,* 1974, p. 33.

266 "Dear Mr. Munn . . .": Houdini, "Houdini Exposes the Tricks Used by the Boston Medium Margery," New York, 1924, p. 11.

267 "There is no doubt . . .": HH to Harry Price, 28 September, 1924, HPL.

267 "All that day . . .": Houdini, "Houdini Exposes . . ." p. 7.

268 "During the second intermission . . .": Houdini, "Houdini Exposes . . ." pp. 7–8.

268 "When Bird left the circle . . .": HH to Bess, 24 July 1924, MKC.

269 *"not to let go . . .":* Houdini, "Houdini Exposes . . ." pp. 17–18.

270 "As I asked . . .": HH to Bess, 26 August 1924, MKC.

271 "If you misrepresent . . .": Houdini, "Houdini Exposes . . ." p. 21.

271 "In the last 10 years . . .": Boston *Herald,* 22 December 1924.

271 "[thrown] her legs . . .": handwritten correction to *A Magician Among the Spirits,* HRHRC.

272 "A statement . . .": HH to Harry Price, 8 February 1925, HPL.

273 "It is the most beautiful . . .": E. J. Dingwall to Schrenck-Notzing, *Progressive Thinker,* 18 April 1925.

273 "A cold, clammy . . .": Boston *Herald,* 1 February 1925.

273 "By the way . . .": HH to Harry Price, 4 July 1925, HPL.

273 "with the aid of the Spirit slates . . .": HH to Harry Price, 5 January 1925, HPL.

274 "Will you let me see . . .": ibid.

275 "must be regarded . . .": "A Report on a Series of Sittings with the Medium Margery," *Journal of the Society for Psychical Research,* 1926.

275 "In the absence . . .": *Banner of Light,* 30 May 1925.

276 "more than gallantry . . .": reported in *The Manufacturer and Builder,* December 1876.

277 "she never had any . . .": *Boston American,* 20 December 1924.

278 "It is the belief . . .": Hudson Hoagland, "Science and the Medium," *Atlantic Monthly,* November 1925.

278 *"Tall stories . . .":* Houdini, *A Magician Among the Spirits,* p. 48.

279 "Have run across . . .": HH to Harry Price, 20 March 1925, HPL.

279 "Last night . . .": HH to Fred Black, quoted in Lund, no. 7.

17: Inside the Coffin

281 "No Standing . . .": Boston *Herald,* 22 December 1924.

282 "I have never . . .": HH to Dr. E. E. Free, 5 March 1925.

283 "Was comfortable . . .": this and the following quotes are taken from Houdini's report on the tests written to Dr. W. J. McConnell of the U.S. Department of Mines. He liked to think that his experiences would be of some use to miners or sailors involved in an accident. The letter is in the Library of Congress.

284 "If I die . . .": Milbourne Christopher, *Houdini: The Untold Story,* p. 231.

284 "As a matter of fact . . .": letter to Dr. McConnell, U.S. Dept of Mines.

285 "I suppose . . .": A. Conan Doyle, *On the Edge of the Unknown,* p. 15.

285 "Would there were . . .": H. W. Bateson to HH, 1917, SRC.

285 "We all have our hobbies . . .": letter to editors of Cleveland newspapers denouncing Malcolm Bird, McMYC.

286 "Stop thinking . . .": HH to Bess, MKC.

288 "Houdini was facing us . . .": Doyle (1930), pp. 18–19.

289 "Broke a bone . . .": Christopher (1969), p. 243.

289 *"Champagne* coquette . . .": MKC.

290 "We have a $15,000 advance . . .": Hardeen, Lecture on Houdini to Chicago Kiwanis, 1936, McMYC.

290 The spectators' reports appear in Robert Lund, "The Final Chapter," *The Sphinx,* December 1952.

290 "Drop the curtain . . .": Hardeen lecture, 1936.

291 "We found that his appendix . . .": Lund, "The Final Chapter," *The Sphinx,* December 1957.

291 "As I entered the lobby . . .": Hardeen lecture, 1936.

292 "He . . . closed his eyes . . .": Detroit *Free Press,* 1 November 1926.

292 "It was a beautiful sunny day . . .": Hardeen lecture, 1936.

292 The story of the coffin having been left behind comes from Lund, "The Final Chapter."

293 "And there you have . . .": quoted in Edwin Dawes, *The Great Illusionists*, p. 202.

294 Bernard Meyer's findings from Bernard C. Meyer, *Houdini: A Mind in Chains*, p. 176.

294 "It is the only case . . .": Lund, "The Final Chapter."

295 "He was delighted . . .": cutting, SRC.

295 "fell to the ground . . .": Doyle (1930), p. 22.

295 The Crandons' prophecy appears in Samri Frikell (Fulton Oursler), *Ghost Stories*, cutting in scrapbook, McMYC.

295 "In my own home . . .": Doyle (1930), p. 15.

295 "Three years ago . . .": ibid., p. 17.

296 "Drive through . . .": quoted in William L. Gresham, *The Man Who Walked Through Walls*, p. 278.

296 "I had written . . .": Oursler, *Ghost Stories*.

297 "Box offices . . .": letter, RLC.

18: Houdini Lives!

299 "I happen to have . . .": Dan Waldron, "Houdini's Favourite Food," *Magicol*, November 1984, pp. 6–7.

300 "We . . . agreed . . .": Hardeen, Lecture on Houdini to Chicago Kiwanis, 1936, McMYC.

301 "My beloved wife . . .": MKC.

301 "Sitting in a comfortable chair . . .": *Picture Plays Confessions Album*, in Walter B. Gibson, *The Original Houdini Scrapbook*, p. 170.

301 "Professor Brainien . . .": 28 July 1926, MKC.

302 The chaos of the motion-picture ventures is described in a letter from B.M.L. Ernst to Hardeen, McMYC.

302 "Because of my long . . .": B.M.L. Ernst to Theodore Hardeen, Jr., 16 January 1937, in the possession of Robert Lund.

303 "Mrs. Houdini wouldn't like it": I am indebted to James Randi for this information on Rose Bonanno.

303 "One of the few . . .": diary, MKC.

304 "Capitalize that . . .": Francis Fast, *The Houdini Messages*, p. 3.

306 "A man who says . . .": a séance which Arthur Ford had held: ibid., pp. 5–9.

307 "This man is coming now . . .": ibid., pp. 9–10.

308 "The message I want to send . . .": report for U.P., New York, January 1929, scrapbook, McMYC.

308 "Regardless of any statement . . .": scrapbook, McMYC.

308 "HOUDINI HOAX EXPOSED!": William L. Gresham, *The Man Who Walked Through Walls*, p. 294.

308 "I am writing you this personally . . .": Milbourne Christopher, *Houdini: The Untold Story*, p. 237.

309 "Little Daisy White . . .": ibid., p. 258.

309 "I wish to say . . .": Gresham, p. 296.

310 "on the ground of . . .": New York *Telegram*, 25 February 1929, quoted in Christopher (1969), p. 259.

310 "There was a period . . .": Philadelphia *Evening Bulletin*, 9 January 1933.

310 "Mrs. Houdini . . . was a white-haired . . .": John Booth, "Memoirs of a Magician's Ghost," *The Linking Ring*, August 1966, p. 25.

310 "a male voice . . .": ibid.

311 "We spent the morning . . .": ibid.

312 "Over 300 invited guests . . .": *Genii*, 20, 1955, pp. 81–83.

314 Frank Gilmore's claim appears in Mikal Gilmore, "Family Album," *Granta*, "They Fuck You Up," vol. 41, 1992, p. 13.

314 "the average American lifespan . . .": *Variety*, 25 May 1992.

314 "Death defines life . . .": quoted in Robert Jay Lifton, *The Broken Connection*, p. 100.

Select Bibliography

In addition to published works, I have made use of the following specialist and manuscript collections:

McManus-Young and Houdini Collections, Library of Congress, Washington, D.C.

Messmore Kendall Collection and Hoblitzelle Theater Arts Library, Harry Ransom Humanities Research Center, University of Texas at Austin

Sidney Radner Collection, Houdini Historical Center, Appleton, Wisconsin.

Harry Price Library, University of London

Waitt Letters, Harvard Theater Collection, Harvard University

Billy Rose Theater Collection, New York Public Library

Robert Lund Collection, Marshall, Michigan (private)

Books

Arcuri, Lawrence, ed., *The Houdini Birth Research Committee's Report,* reprint with additional material (originally compiled by Milbourne Christopher, 1972).

Barnouw, Erik, *The Magician and the Cinema,* Oxford, 1981.

Bergreen, Laurence, *As Thousands Cheer: The Life of Irving Berlin,* London, 1990.

Berlin, Isaiah, *Against the Current: Essays in the History of Ideas,* London, 1979.

Brandon, Ruth, *The Spiritualists,* New York, 1983.

Brewster, Sir David, *Letters on Natural Magic,* London, 1833.

Campbell, Joseph, *The Hero with a Thousand Faces,* New York, 1949.

Campbell, Joseph, *Myths to Live By,* New York, 1972.

Cane, Melville, *The First Firefly,* New York, 1974.

Canetti, Elias, *On Crowds and Power*, tr. Carol Stewart, London, 1972.

Carrington, Hereward, and Ernst, B.M.L., *Houdini and Conan Doyle: The Story of a Strange Friendship*, London, 1933.

Christopher, Milbourne, *Houdini: The Untold Story*, New York, London, 1969.

Christopher, Milbourne, *Mediums, Mystics and the Occult*, New York, 1975.

Crandon, L.R.G., *The Margery Mediumship: Unofficial Sittings at the Laboratory of the Society for Psychical Research, London, December 6, 7 and 8, 1929*, Boston, 1930.

Dawes, Edwin, *The Great Illusionists*, Newton Abbott, 1979.

De Camp, L. Sprague, *Lovecraft, a Biography*, New York, 1975.

Dexter, Will, *This Is Magic*, London, 1958.

Doerr, H. R., *The Secrets of Houdini's Feats Explained*, Philadelphia, n.d.

Doyle, A. Conan, *On the Edge of the Unknown*, London, 1930.

Doyle, A. Conan, *Our American Adventure*, London, 1923.

Dunninger, Joseph, *Houdini's Spirit Exposés*, New York, 1928.

Evans, Henry Ridgely, *The Old and the New Magic*, Chicago, 1906.

Fast, Francis, *The Houdini Messages*, New York, 1929.

Fitzsimons, Raimund, *Death and the Magician: The Mystery of Houdini*, London, 1980.

French, Philip, *The Movie Moguls: An Informal History of the Hollywood Tycoons*, London, 1969.

Fromm, Erich, *The Anatomy of Human Destructiveness*, London, 1974.

Gabler, Neal, *An Empire of Their Own: How the Jews Invented Hollywood*, New York, 1988.

Gibson, Walter B., *Dunninger's Secrets*, Secaucus, N.J., 1974.

Gibson, Walter B., *Houdini's Escapes and Magic*, New York, 1932.

Gibson, Walter B., *Houdini's Fabulous Magic*, New York, 1961.

Gibson, Walter B., *The Original Houdini Scrapbook*, New York, 1976.

Gibson, Walter B., and Young, Morris N., eds. *Houdini on Magic*, New York, 1953.

Goldston, Will, *Sensational Tales of Mystery Men*, London, 1929.

Gresham, William L., *Houdini: The Man Who Walked Through Walls*, New York, 1959.

Grey, Margot, *Return from Death*, London, 1985.

Hammond, Paul, *Marvellous Méliès*, London, 1974.

Hardeen, Theodore, *Life and History of Hardeen,* California, 1926.

Henning, Doug, with Charles Reynolds, *Houdini: His Legend and His Magic,* New York, 1977.

"Hoffman, Professor" (Angelo Lewis), *Modern Magic,* London, 1874.

Houdini, Harry, *The Adventurous Life of a Versatile Artist,* 1906.

Houdini, Harry, *Houdini's Paper Magic,* New York, 1922.

Houdini, Harry, *A Magician Among the Spirits,* New York, 1924.

Houdini, Harry, *Magical Rope-Ties and Escapes,* London, 1920.

Houdini, Harry, *Miracle-Mongers and Their Methods,* New York, 1920.

Houdini, Harry, *The Right Way to Do Wrong: An Exposé,* Boston, 1906.

Houdini, Harry, *The Unmasking of Robert-Houdin,* London, 1909.

Huntington, Richard, and Peter Metcalf, *Celebrations of Death: The Anthropology of Mortuary Ritual,* Cambridge, Mass., 1979.

Hugard, Jean, *Houdini's "Unmasking"; Fact vs. Fiction* (With an Introduction and Supplementary Chapter by Milbourne Christopher, 1957–59), reprinted in book form, New York, 1989.

Jastrow, Joseph, *Wish and Wisdom,* New York, 1935.

Jung, C. G., "On the Psychology and Pathology of So-called Occult Phenomena," *Collected Works,* pp. 3–92, London, 1953.

Kellock, Harold, *Houdini: The Life Story (From the Recollections and Documents of Beatrice Houdini),* New York, 1928.

Koval, Frank, *The Illustrated Houdini Research Diary,* Oldham, Lancashire, 1993.

Kurtz, Paul, *The Transcendental Temptation,* Buffalo, N.Y., 1991.

Leach, Edmund, *On Culture and Communication,* Cambridge, 1976.

Lifton, Robert Jay, *The Broken Connection: On Death and the Continuity of Life,* New York, 1983.

Luhrmann, T. M., *Persuasions of the Witch's Craft,* Cambridge, Mass., 1989.

MacKenzie, J. Hewat, *Spirit Intercourse,* London, 1916.

Menninger, Karl, *Man Against Himself,* London, 1938.

Meyer, Bernard C., MD, *Houdini: A Mind in Chains: A Psychoanalytic Portrait,* New York, 1976.

Mitchell, Adrian, *Houdini: A Circus Opera,* Amsterdam, 1974–76.

Mulholland, John, *Quicker than the Eye,* Indianapolis, 1932.

Napier, A. David, *Masks, Transformations and Paradox,* California, 1989.

Oursler, Fulton (Anthony Abbott), *Behold This Dream,* New York, 1964.

Oursler, Fulton, *These Are Strange Tales,* Philadelphia, 1948.

Randi, James, and Sugar, Ber Randolph, *Houdini: His Life and Art,* New York, 1976.

Reik, Theodor, *The Temptation,* New York, 1961.

Rinn, Joseph F., *Searchlight on Psychical Research,* New York, 1950.

Robert-Houdin, Jean Eugène, *Memoirs of Robert-Houdin, King of Conjurers,* London, 1859.

Sardina, Maurice, *Where Houdini Was Wrong,* Tr. and ed. Victor Farelli, London, 1950.

Sennett, Richard, *The Fall of Public Man,* New York, 1976.

Sharpe, S. H., *Introducing Houdini versus Robert-Houdin: The Whole Truth,* Reighton, 1955.

Taylor, Rogan, *The Death and Resurrection Show,* London, 1985.

Tietze, Thomas R., *Margery,* New York, 1973.

Urbain, Jean-Didier, *L'archipel des morts,* Paris, 1980.

Weltman, Manuel, *Houdini: Escape into Legend,* Los Angeles, 1993.

Wilson, Edmund, *Classics and Commercials,* New York, 1950.

Magazine Articles and Papers

Bragman, Louis J., "Houdini Escapes from Reality," *Psychoanalytic Review,* 14:404, October 1929.

Danet, Brenda and Tamar Katriel, "Books, Butterflies, Botticellis—A Life-span on Collecting," paper for sixth international conference on Culture and Communication, Philadelphia, 1986.

Dingwall, E.J., "A Report on a Series of Sittings with the Medium Margery," *Journal of the Society for Psychical Research,* vol. XXXVI, June 1926.

"Fortune Telling," Hearings before the Subcommittee on Judiciary of the Committee on the District of Columbia House of Representatives Sixty-ninth Congress, First Session, on H.R. 8969, February 26, May 18, 20 and 21, 1924, Washington, 1924.

Frazee, William, "When Houdini Was President," *M.U.M.,* November 1953.

Houdini, Harry, "Confessions of a Jail-breaker," 1918.

Houdini, Harry, "Handcuff Secrets Exposed," *Conjurer's Magazine,* 1908.

Houdini, Harry, "Houdini Exposes the Tricks Used by the Boston Medium Margery," New York, 1924.

Houdini, Harry, "The Thrills in the Life of a Magician," *Strand Magazine*, 5 January 1919.

Lund, Robert, "Afterword on Houdini," seven articles in *Abracadabra*, 561–67, October–December 1956.

Lund, Robert, "The Final Chapter," *The Sphinx*, December 1952.

Silverman, Julian, "Shamans and Acute Schizophrenia," *American Anthropologist*, vol. 69, no.1, February 1967.

Wilson, Edmund, "A Great Magician," *New Republic*, 17 October 1928.

Wilson, Edmund, "Houdini," *New Republic*, 24 June 1925.

Young, Maurice N., "Houdini's Trunk No. 8," *M.U.M.*, December 1951.

Zolotow, Maurice, *New York Times Book Review*, 23 March 1969.

Index

ABOUT THE TYPE

This book was set in Galliard, a typeface designed by Matthew Carter for the Mergenthaler Linotype Company in 1978. Galliard is based on the sixteenth-century typefaces of Robert Granjon, which give it classic lines yet interject a contemporary look.